Evernote®

FOR

DUMMIES®

by David E. Y. Sarna
with Vanessa Richie

To my favorite Jenny ever,

Lots of love,

Vanessa Richie

WILEY

John Wiley & Sons, Inc.

Evernote® For Dummies®

Published by
John Wiley & Sons, Inc.
111 River Street
Hoboken, NJ 07030-5774
www.wiley.com

Copyright © 2012 by John Wiley & Sons, Inc., Hoboken, New Jersey

Published by John Wiley & Sons, Inc., Hoboken, New Jersey

Published simultaneously in Canada

For general information on our other products and services, please contact our Customer Care Department within the U.S. at 877-762-2974, outside the U.S. at 317-572-3993, or fax 317-572-4002.

For technical support, please visit www.wiley.com/techsupport.

Wiley publishes in a variety of print and electronic formats and by print-on-demand. Some material included with standard print versions of this book may not be included in e-books or in print-on-demand. If this book refers to media such as a CD or DVD that is not included in the version you purchased, you may download this material at http://booksupport.wiley.com. For more information about Wiley products, visit www.wiley.com.

Library of Congress Control Number is available from the Publisher upon request.

ISBN: 978-1-118-10738-6 (pbk)

ISBN 978-1-118-22410-6 (ebk); ISBN 978-1-118-23730-4 (ebk); ISBN 978-1-118-26232-0 (ebk)

Manufactured in the United States of America

10 9 8 7 6 5 4 3 2 1

WILEY

About the Authors

David E. Y. Sarna is a writer and a technologist. He has more than forty-three years of experience as a management consultant and as an executive of high-technology companies. David has invested in several start-up companies, primarily in the areas of information technology, medical devices, and hydrogen on demand.

David is the Interim CEO and a director of WoodallTech, Inc, which is commercializing the hydrogen-on-demand technology of Prof. Jerry Woodall, National Technology Medal Laureate. He has been a director of publicly traded companies specializing in computer technology and has served as chairman of audit and compensation committees, as well as in advisory position to the boards of directors of public, private, and not-for-profit organizations. He served for many years on the Advisory Board of Hudson Venture Partners. As an entrepreneur, David attracted investments from first-tier venture capital firms, and has taken two companies public on the NASDAQ through underwritten offerings. Earlier in his career he worked for Honeywell, IBM, and Price Waterhouse.

David has authored or co-authored six books, holds several patents, and has published 120 articles in professional magazines, and in such major publications as *The Washington Post* and *The Jerusalem Post*.

His books included *PC Magazine Windows Rapid Application Development* (Ziff-Davis Press, 1994, and translated into several languages), *Implementing and Developing Cloud Computing Applications* (CRC Press, 2010), *History of Greed* (Wiley, 2010), *Computer installation effectiveness reviews.* Melville, NY: FAIM Technical Products, 1978, and (with Lawrence H. Schiffman, *A Computer-aided Critical Edition of the Tosefta Sotah*, Waltham, MA: The Jewish Theological Seminary of America, 1970).

Since 1975 David has been married to Dr. Rachel C. Sarna. He has three grown children and makes his home in Teaneck, NJ.

Vanessa Richie is a Microsoft application specialist. Although she is proficient in almost everything Microsoft, she is an expert in the main Office programs, such as Word, Excel, and Outlook. Having realized at an early age that writing was a viable option as a "real" job, Vanessa has written and edited numerous technical documents over a large range of fields, but software is where she is most at her ease. She recently stepped out of the Microsoft realm to co-author *Evernote For Dummies* with David.

Dedication

This book, which helps you remember everything, is lovingly dedicated to my favorite dear aunt, Edith Maagan, who recently celebrated her 90th birthday, and who (unlike me) still has instant command and recall of all her memories.

Author's Acknowledgments

That this book has seen the light of day is due, in no small part, to Vanessa Richie, who collaborated to make this book happen when health issues impeded my progress. To her, my heartfelt thanks.

Charlotte Kughen is a great, sensitive, and thoughtful editor; this book has benefitted greatly from her efforts, as well as from the support of all of the other hardworking folks at Wiley, who labored, mostly anonymously, to make this book much better than I could by myself.

Kelly Ewing is a masterful Dummifier, and helped make this book look and feel like all the great books in the Wiley *For Dummies* series.

My literary agent Bill Gladstone and his colleagues at Waterside Productions saw the potential of this book and prodded me to get it done despite many distractions.

Phil Libin, CEO of Evernote, enthusiastically supported this project, and all of the folks at Evernote, especially Andrew Sinkov, contributed freely of their prodigious expertise in all matters Evernote — and beyond.

I would be remiss if I did not thank Dr. Fabian Bitan, Dr. Neil Lyman, and Dr. Lyle Dennis, who helped me through some difficult medical issues while this book was being written.

As always, my family has been helpful in ways small and large.

Publisher's Acknowledgments

We're proud of this book; please send us your comments at http://dummies.custhelp.com. For other comments, please contact our Customer Care Department within the U.S. at 877-762-2974, outside the U.S. at 317-572-3993, or fax 317-572-4002.

Some of the people who helped bring this book to market include the following:

Acquisitions and Editorial

Project Editor: Charlotte Kughen, The Wordsmithery LLC

Acquisitions Editor: Bob Woerner

Copy Editor: Kathy Simpson

Technical Editors: Andrew Sinkov, Seth Hitchings

Editorial Manager: Jodi Jensen

Editorial Assistant: Amanda Graham

Sr. Editorial Assistant: Cherie Case

Cover Photos:
©iStockphoto.com / Katey Jones;
©iStockphoto.com / Oliver Malms;
©iStockphoto.com / thesuperph;
©iStockphoto.com /hohos;
©iStockphoto.com / ppart;
©iStockphoto.com / Darren Falkenberg

Cartoons: Rich Tennant (www.the5thwave.com)

Composition Services

Project Coordinator: Katherine Crocker

Layout and Graphics: Melanee Habig

Proofreader: Evelyn Wellborn

Indexer: BIM Indexing & Proofreading Services

Publishing and Editorial for Technology Dummies

Richard Swadley, Vice President and Executive Group Publisher

Andy Cummings, Vice President and Publisher

Mary Bednarek, Executive Acquisitions Director

Mary C. Corder, Editorial Director

Publishing for Consumer Dummies

Kathleen Nebenhaus, Vice President and Executive Publisher

Composition Services

Debbie Stailey, Director of Composition Services

Contents at a Glance

Table of Contents

Introduction

Welcome to *Evernote For Dummies*. I asked to write it because Evernote has changed my life. My hope is that Evernote improves your life just as much.

Before I found Evernote, I was a typical messy-desk person and a pack rat. Piles were everywhere. File cabinets were overflowing. When I found something of interest, I printed it and piled it. I never had time to file it. And if I did file it, I could never remember where I'd put it. When I did remember which stack something was in, I'd have to determine how deep I needed to excavate based on the item's presumed age. Then I'd dig in. This system — if you can call it that — worked as badly as you can imagine. I never lost anything because I didn't throw things out. On the other hand, actually retrieving things was frustrating and time-consuming. Getting older didn't help any. Many times, I would initiate an Internet search to locate something I'd already found. My messy surroundings and frequent archaeological excavations made me the butt of jokes at home and in the office.

Then, in January 2010, I saw a review of Evernote, then two years old, by my fellow Brandeis alum Walt Mossberg. He described a wondrous "Digital File Cabinet You Can Bring with You Anywhere" in AllThingsD (`http://all thingsd.com`), a highly regarded website devoted to news, analysis, and opinion on technology, the Internet, and media.

Even at that point, Evernote already had 2 million downloads. (It's now been downloaded tens of millions times.) It was free to try, so I did. Evernote immediately grabbed me. It was the product I'd been dreaming about. The more I used Evernote, the more addicted I became and the more valuable it became for me.

I was hooked. Goodbye, messy desk. Hello, Evernote, with access to everything everywhere.

About This Book

Evernote For Dummies is a reference book, which means that it isn't meant to be read from front to back. Each chapter is divided into sections, each of which includes self-contained information about a specific task in Evernote.

Just as in Evernote, you don't have to remember anything in this book because you can look up what interests you in the table of contents or index and immediately find what you need to know — and nothing more.

Conventions Used in This Book

For an iconoclast and rebel like me, doing something the same way over and over can be boring (like the way Mr. Rogers always wore the same kind of sweater), but sometimes consistency can be a good thing. For one thing, it makes stuff easier to understand. In this book, those consistent elements are *conventions*. In fact, using italics to identify and define new terms is one convention in this book.

Evernote is a unique product that helps you wherever you are, and it supports almost all devices. So I cover Evernote on Windows PCs, Macs, iPhones, iPods touches, iPads, Android devices, and BlackBerry smartphones and tablets. I also cover the way it works in the Internet Explorer, Apple Safari, Mozilla Firefox, and Google Chrome web browsers.

Except where noted, I used the Chrome Browser for all screenshots.

If I ask you to type a command, that text appears in boldface, like this:

Type me.

I list menu commands in this format:

Edit⇨Copy

This example indicates that you should click the Edit menu and then choose the Copy item from the menu that appears.

When I type URLs (web addresses) within a paragraph, they look like this: http://bit.ly/EvernoteForDummies.

By the way, that website is real. It's where I try to keep this book up to date. You're also invited to check out my little corner of the web at www.hshco.com.

What You Don't Need to Read

If I talk about a device you don't use, you can just skip that information. Likewise, when I discuss how Evernote interfaces with software you aren't interested in, you can move on, if you like.

If I lapse into technical jargon when I discuss how to extend Evernote, interface with it in other companies' products, or drive it by remote control from within applications you don't use, you can just ignore me. I won't get offended, and you won't miss out on anything important.

In addition, whenever you see sidebars (little gray boxes), you can safely skip them if you're so inclined. They contain information that's nice to know but not mandatory.

Foolish Assumptions

If you're not an engineer with an advanced degree in Cognitive Engineering (there aren't many of them), you don't need to worry! Here's a reasonably complete list of what's *not* required to use this book:

- I make no assumptions about your previous knowledge of Evernote.
- I make only the most basic assumptions about your use of the Internet or any devices that Evernote supports.
- I don't assume any knowledge of the many products that Evernote works with.

So what is required? A supported device (refer to the list I mention in the "Conventions Used in This Book" section), a connection to the Internet, and a desire to clear your clutter and actually find things when you want them. Pretty simple.

How This Book Is Organized

I've divided this book into seven parts, organized by topic. The parts point out the most important aspects of Evernote. In addition, an appendix gives techies more details for developing simple add-ons for Evernote.

Part 1: Starting Evernote

In Part I, you get an overview of what Evernote is all about. I also talk about the different kinds of information that Evernote organizes for you. You find out how to get the right versions of Evernote for your devices and the kind of account that best serves your needs. You even create your first notes.

Part II: Increasing Your Reach

Part II is where the training wheels come off and you discover how to ride the Evernote bike down Main Street. You find out how to clip web content and articles; work with audio; and create notes from e-mail, tweets, scans, or supported cameras. You can also access your notes in various ways, even from a Kindle or a Nook.

Part III: Managing Information

Part III is for accomplished Evernote users. You find out how to tag, merge, and share your notes. The real fun comes when you discover all the powerful methods you can use to find and share your information. Because life's not perfect, I also cover troubleshooting for those times when you run into a jam.

Part IV: Just For You — Device-Specific Features

Evernote's *basic* look and feel are the same for all devices of the same class (desktops, smartphones, and so on). In this part, you discover the ingenious ways that Evernote takes advantage of your device's unique features.

Part V: Expanding Your Skills

Evernote supports a whole ecosystem, and in Part V, I cover the awesome things you can do by going beyond the Evernote basics, such as interfacing with social media, email, and third-party applications, special equipment such as pens, cameras, and scanners, and working with third-party notebooks.

Part VI: Adding Professional Power

Part VI shows you how to extend Evernote yourself. I introduce Evernote's open scripting capabilities, the application programming interfaces (APIs) that only a developer can love, and Evernote's Ambassador Program, which can actually get you fame if not fortune.

Part VII: The Part of Tens

No *For Dummies* book is complete without the Part of Tens. This infamous part offers tips and ideas for using Evernote at home, at school, and at work.

Icons Used in This Book

To make your experience with the book easier, I use various icons in the margins of the book to indicate particular points of interest:

Whenever I give you a hint or a tip that makes an aspect of Evernote easier to use, I mark it with this little icon. It's my way of sharing what I've figured out the hard way so that you don't have to.

This icon is a friendly reminder or a marker for something that you want to make sure that you keep in mind.

Ouch! This icon is the equivalent of an exclamation point. Warnings give you important directions to keep you from experiencing any nightmares.

Sometimes I feel obligated to give you some technical information, although it doesn't really affect how you use Evernote. I mark that stuff with this geeky fellow so that you know it's just background information.

Where to Go from Here

If you're looking for information on a specific Evernote topic, check the headings in the table of contents or skim the index. By design, this book enables you to get as much (or as little) information as you need at any particular moment. (Need to know how Evernote works with Twitter, for example? See Chapter 12.) If you want to focus on the specific ways that Evernote works with a device, jump right in to Part IV.

Occasionally, we have updates to our technology books. If this book does have technical updates, they will be posted at www.dummies.com/go/EvernoteForDummiesupdates.

About My Public Evernote Notebook

Evernote is easy and fun to use. When you use it, you'll benefit immediately. The more you use it, the more useful Evernote becomes. Use Evernote everywhere. Don't get bogged down in details; you can always tag, change titles, and merge notes later. When you come across something useful and want to find it again, store it in Evernote. You'll be glad you did.

I've created a public Evernote notebook, accessible at `http://bit.ly/EvernoteForDummies`, to keep readers up to date about Evernote and about new tips and tricks that I learn. It's my way of thanking you for purchasing a copy of this book.

Part I
Starting Evernote

In this part . . .

In Chapter 1, I introduce you to Evernote, and give you a taste of what it can do for you, such as accessing your one account from many devices, capturing information in notes, and categorizing notes. Chapter 1 also touches on how Evernote recognizes all types of images and the basics of finding and storing information.

Chapter 2 is about account management, including descriptions of the different kinds of Evernote accounts so you can decide what's best for you.

In Chapter 3, I help you create your first notes and introduce you to instructional videos, the knowledge base, and other tools you can turn to if you don't find what you need in this book.

Chapter 1

What Evernote Can Do for You

In This Chapter

▶ Using Evernote no matter where you are

▶ Saving all types of data

▶ Keeping track of your notes

*E*vernote combines four ingredients that help make it a success:

✔ It's useful for your job and your personal life.

✔ It integrates with mobile devices.

✔ It's accessible anywhere you have Internet access.

✔ It's easy to use.

That's a powerful combination.

Another reason for Evernote's success is that it recognizes a fundamental aspect of the human condition. *You* are one person. You have a life. Part of life, for many people, is devoted to work, and part is devoted to personal, leisure, and not-so-fun stuff like (ugh!) taxes and bills. Evernote becomes part of your life. All of it.

Evernote is about you and your information and interests.

Using Evernote Everywhere — One Account, Many Devices

Evernote is for couch potatoes and for those who are always on the go. It's for the geek who has one of every type of device, at least, and who pecks or taps away at them incessantly many hours a day, often using two simultaneously (guilty as charged). It's for the road warrior vying with Hillary Clinton for the "most traveled" award. Evernote is for the occasional user who's satisfied with one or two devices, as well as for everyone using some kind of device who needs to remember and find things.

That means Evernote is for nearly everyone.

At this writing, Evernote has tens of millions of users, so you're far from being alone. Evernote reports that 25 percent of users use it on a single device, 46 percent on two devices, 18 percent on three, 7 percent on four, and 4 percent on five or more (just imagine).

I've been playing with computers since I was growing up with Abraham Lincoln, more or less — or 1964, to be more exact — and I tend to think I've seen it all. Remarkably, Evernote is the first piece of software I've ever seen, much less used, that pulls off a credible balance among four contradictory attributes:

✔ It runs nearly the same way on many very different devices, each of which has its own user interface and natural ways of working.

✔ It still manages to look native on each device and takes advantage of the unique features of each, letting you use it on each device to best advantage.

✔ It keeps everything securely in one place.

✔ It lets you work locally (offline).

That's a tall order, and Evernote pulls it off with aplomb. To be honest, that benefit comes with a few trade-offs, too:

✔ There are some inconsistencies among the different versions, and a few of your favorite features on one device may not work exactly the same way — or even be implemented at all — on another.

✔ Not all devices are created equally, not all Internet browsers are created equally, and not all Evernote versions are equally polished. Not surprisingly, the most popular, hottest devices and browsers sport the best Evernote implementations, but even the weakest is completely serviceable. (I don't pull punches, and I give kudos and point out the benefits and flaws of each platform in Part IV.)

The bottom line, however, is that Evernote supports PCs and Macs; the Google Chrome, Apple Safari, Mozilla Firefox, and Internet Explorer web browsers; iPads, Android devices, and Chrome OS tablets; and iPhones and iPod touches, BlackBerry phones and tablets, Palm Pre and Pixi devices, and Windows Phone 7 smartphones, too. Whew!

Cloud computing and Evernote

When you work with Evernote from a laptop or desktop computer, or from an iPad, BlackBerry device, or Android device, you can have your cake and eat it, too. You have all the benefits of fast, local storage for your notes and the comfort that comes from knowing you always have an up-to-date backup in the cloud. You can use the backed-up version everywhere you have connectivity.

The good news is that you need one — and only one — Evernote account to access all your information from any of your devices.

Evernote has something for everyone, but it's not known to walk on water. At least, not yet!

Accessing and Securing Your Data

A complete copy of everything you've saved on Evernote's servers is kept up to date (synchronized) on each of your desktop or laptop machines (Windows and Mac). With the iPad and Android and Blackberry devices you also have the option to store files locally as well. All other devices are assumed to be connected, and you access information by retrieving it from Evernote's storage vaults.

Systems with local copies of the repository are called *thick clients,* and Evernote keeps them synchronized with the master copies stored on Evernote's servers. All other supported devices have *thin clients,* which forward requests to Evernote's servers and then receive the replies. On Blackberry and Android devices, the choice is yours whether you go with the thick client option or the thin client option. If you aren't space challenged, choose the thick client for best performance.

Capture anywhere; access everywhere

I'm an old guy (62) with a lifelong love of computers. I was an early adopter of things like personal productivity assistants (PDAs), such as the original Palm Pilot, which was first manufactured in 1996. It was a blessing, but it only became really useful once you could synchronize it with your desktop computer.

That was then.

Now, desktop computers themselves are going the way of the dodo bird and the Palm Pilot. Nielsen says that one in two Americans had a smartphone by the end of 2011. Laptops outsell desktops, and tablets (iPads and Android tablets) outsell laptops. Americans have many productivity tools; we're increasingly mobile; and we're continually buying the latest gee-whiz-bang device (at least some of us are). It's just mind-boggling for me to know that Evernote not only supports all these devices, but also captures information on any of them, keeps the information securely in a nonproprietary format, and keeps everything in sync.

Is my data safe and secure?

You may wonder how safe your data is with Evernote. After all, you own your data, and it holds all the secrets of your life. Like me, you may want to know how secure your data is from theft or unintended access by third parties with malicious intent. Is your data really safe? Is it secure?

I posed these questions to Phil Libin, Evernote's CEO. The answers come down to consideration of several factors, including these:

- ✔ The physical security of the data center
- ✔ The security of the data communications
- ✔ The trustworthiness of the Evernote team
- ✔ The processes in place at Evernote

The Evernote data center is professionally run, housed in a physically secure location with 24-hour on-site staff, with logged access control via electronic ID cards. The Evernote center uses biometrics for identification and lockout guard posts for everyone who attempts entry. Only the select Evernote personnel who are charged with operating the data center are permitted inside. All administrative communication with the servers is encrypted. All user authentication is also encrypted.

Passwords are never seen or stored on the servers. You're able to encrypt any portion of a note, and Evernote never sees or stores the additional encryption keys. Data access for Evernote premium users goes over Hypertext Transfer Protocol Secure (HTTPS), a combination of the standard Internet Hypertext Transfer Protocol with the SSL/TLS protocol, to provide encrypted communication and secure identification of a network web server. The network is protected by a series of regularly maintained routers, firewalls, load-balancers, and so on.

How safe is my data from accidental loss?

With Evernote, each user's data is stored on a logical server. Each physical server has fully redundant RAID hard drives. Each server is paired with a full-time, hot-failover mirror server into a logical *shard,* a method of horizontal partitioning in a database. All data from the data center is backed up daily and stored in a secure location remote from the data center.

All your data is also stored locally on your own device (if you're using the Windows or Mac client or an iPhone, BlackBerry smartphone, or Android device with offline notebooks enabled), which can be encrypted and/or backed up as you desire. So your data is stored in at least five physical locations (RAID drives on each server, two servers per shard, and offsite backup) plus your local computer(s). It's pretty unlikely that all your data would be lost in the event of a full or partial system failure. Evernote also says that it can add new shards quickly to scale the system.

Do I really own my own data?

You may question how safe your intellectual property is and whether your privacy is protected from intrusion by Evernote or its business partners. You don't give up any legal rights by storing your data in Evernote. In fact, only the few Evernote personnel who provide tech support to users are permitted to access account information. Evernote promises that it doesn't crawl through your data for ad targeting, recommendations, or anything like that. Unless it's ordered to do so by a court, Evernote also promises that it won't share your data with any third party without your explicit permission.

You do grant Evernote the right to access your data for the purposes of running services so that it can do backups, indexing, synchronization, and so on. Evernote provides fully documented standards-based exporting of all your data.

Am I locked in?

Trust me on this one: You're going to create one valuable collection of useful information in Evernote. Accordingly, you're right to ask, "Am I locked in?" or "What happens if . . . *(fill in the contingency you're concerned about)?*"

No. There is no data lock-in at Evernote. The Evernote folks want you to stay forever, of course, but they think that you're more likely to do so if you know that you're free to leave at any time.

Evernote lets you export all your data in several formats. The Evernote ENEX format provides a complete export of your notes using *Extensible Markup Language* (XML), a universal set of rules for encoding documents in machine-readable form. XML is understood by hundreds of applications, and you can easily move the data into other applications and services.

Capturing Information

Storing voice and music for later playback goes back to Thomas Alva Edison, who in 1877 stored "Mary Had a Little Lamb" and replayed it from a strip of tinfoil wrapped around a spinning cylinder. (A timeline giving the progress in that field is available from the Audio Engineering Society's website at www. aes.org/aeshc/docs/audio.history.timeline.html.) In addition, over the past 25 years, the field of computer graphics has become very well developed. (You can find a nice introduction to what's under the covers at http://fieggen.com/ian/graphics.htm.) It's developments like these that have made the technology behind Evernote possible.

With Evernote, you can save, or *capture,* just about anything: your ideas, things you like, things you hear, and things you see. You can save web pages or portions of them, photographs, scanned documents, and music, almost without limit. You can also set up machines (such as electronic cameras and scanners) so that the information on them (such as photos and faxes) is transferred like magic directly to Evernote, where it's stored forever (or until you erase it) and is accessible from all your devices. Perhaps by the time you read this, you'll be able to capture video, but not as we go to press.

Punchcard data-processing technology

To be useful, information has to be stored somewhere; to be found again, it has to be coded. Punchcards were first used around 1725 by Basile Bouchon and Jean-Baptiste Falcon to store information for controlling textile looms in France. Much later, Herman Hollerith took things a giant step forward. He invented the recording of data on a medium that could then be read by a machine. Previous uses of machine-readable media had been for control,

not data. Hollerith developed punchcard data-processing technology for the 1890 U.S. Census. His company later became IBM.

As amazing an advance as they were, Hollerith codes had severe limitations. For a long time, the data was limited to text — no formatting information like typeface and font, no images, no sounds, no music, no video.

Notes and research

Evernote is ideal for taking notes and for doing research.

Whenever you want to remember something, don't write it down anymore. Papers create clutter and are easily misplaced. Just make a note of it with Evernote.

I use Evernote to make raw notes, to outline, to make a bibliography, and to clip web pages or parts of them. I'm not too comfortable dictating text, although many of my fellow authors use Evernote to do that. I do voice-record interviews consensually, and Evernote is ideal for storing and rough-transcribing the conversations, too. One key advantage: All the information is in one place. Another advantage: It doesn't matter what device I used to gather the information, because I can store information from each in Evernote.

That's huge.

Notes, notebooks, and stacks

A *note* is a thing of some sort. It's the atomic unit of Evernote. A *notebook* is a collection of notes — a giant molecule. You can group notebooks into *stacks*. If you want to keep the chemistry analogy going, think of stacks as being organisms. (Part I provides the basics on working with notes and notebooks. Notebook stacks are a little more advanced and are covered in detail in Chapter 14.)

It's not necessary to get overly involved in the taxonomy, though. A lot of how you use and organize Evernote depends on how you like to work. A shopping list can be a note, for example. A collection of stuff related to shopping may be grouped in a notebook. You may have one notebook for bills and another to keep track of tax deductions. All your notebooks related to home stuff can be grouped into a stack.

If you like.

Or not.

It's up to you.

Web-page clips

When I surf the web, I find interesting things I'd like to refer to. Bookmarks just don't cut it, especially because webmasters don't need to consult you when they update their web pages. Now you see it; now you don't.

Here's a nifty solution: Clip what you want to save, and create a note. Then you can easily find it again. Even better, you can search the web-page information at the same time you search all your other interesting stuff, no matter how you collected it.

The web-clipping feature is one of the most convenient features of Evernote, allowing easy clipping of sections, images, or entire web pages. Part II provides some web-clipping basics, and Chapter 16 covers some exclusive ways to use clipping in different web browsers.

Task and to-do lists

A popular use of Evernote is to maintain task and to-do lists. Sure, lots of dedicated tools are available to do these jobs, but who needs another tool when you already have Evernote? You can not only use Evernote to prepare and update your task and to-do lists, but also use it on the web and on all your devices.

Part III contains many of the basics on synchronizing and working across the many possible platforms and devices to make your information more portable. Part VII offers ideas on how to effectively use task and to-do lists in your everyday interaction with Evernote.

Snapshots and photographs

You're not in Kansas anymore, Alice. It's not just text. Most people want to keep and find their favorite photographic memories. Once again, myriad programs and websites offer this service. Evernote, however, does them all one better — and maybe two or three better.

You can go directly from a suitably equipped scanner, digital camera, webcam, or other capturing device directly into Evernote — passing Go not required. You can save your photographs right alongside clipped pages, audio, notes, and all your other related memories. And, as you can with any note, you can access the photos from all your devices.

Part II introduces how to create notes that help you remember everything of importance to you in your world. Chapter 15 gives you a detailed look at the plethora of devices on which you can make and save notes. Part V takes you to the limit, expanding your skills to maximize your visual notes.

Photos of whiteboards and blackboards and more

Maybe you're wondering why I'm singling out whiteboards and blackboards. After all, aren't they just pictures? They are, but here's the magic part: Evernote uses its handwriting-recognition feature to try to interpret what it sees, and what it sees, it indexes automatically. So if you write "Einstein's Equation: e=mc^2", you can search for either *"Einstein's Equation"* or *"e=mc^2"* so that Evernote can find the note quickly, as well as all the others in your notebooks that contain the same reference. (This handy feature is incorporated with the other visual notes in Parts II and V.)

If it can be read, it can be searched. You can count on that.

Saving notes from whiteboard or blackboard sessions is especially useful when you've been working collaboratively and want to quickly share the results with attendees or others who didn't make the meeting.

Audio capture

Many popular devices, such as smartphones, make recording sound a snap. Evernote supports these features and turns them into notes. Then, if you use one of the add-ins described in Part V, you convert your voice notes into searchable, taggable text.

Amazing.

Printed and handwritten text

Since Howard Aiken and Admiral Grace Hopper created the Harvard Mark I Computer in 1944, computers have been able to easily understand stuff that someone keys in to a computer. Lots of information, however, is contained in nontextual documents that may never have been typed into a computer, such as business cards and images, even photographs. Think of a picture of New York's Times Square, one of the world's best-known intersections. Any photo of it will include signs, ads for plays and movies, and a wealth of other "hidden" information.

Evernote includes a powerful image-recognition engine. It tries to understand the information in images and to turn what it's read into searchable text that you can use to find things later. That means that it looks at things like a photograph of Times Square and sees text that it tries to use to index the note.

For the most part, handwritten notes are included with the other visual media because you'll often scan notes after jotting them down. For a closer look, check out Parts II and V.

Dine with Evernote. Say that you're in a restaurant. It has a great menu, full of dishes that you'd like to remember. Just use your smartphone to snap pictures of the menu. Evernote will nearly always accurately understand the text in the photos and index it, so later, you can find the dish, read the menu, and remind yourself where you had that great meal.

If you're also enjoying a great wine, snap a picture of the label. Then you can find it any time by any of the words on the label, such as the variety, region, or vintage. No further work on your part is required.

Build your contacts with Evernote. If you snap a photo of a business card with the camera built into your supported smartphone, you've created an image and a note, and have indexed that note, just by snapping a picture.

That's pretty powerful. But it gets better.

When I receive a business card, I jot down some identifying information to jog my ancient memory. Amazingly, Evernote's recognition engine tries to read my handwriting, too, as it does yours. The recognition engine recognizes unrestricted English, German, French, Russian, and Spanish handwriting in a variety of styles. No training is needed.

Retrieving Stored Information

To be useful, information needs to be accessible. Unfortunately, most information systems fail due to their complex and often mandatory protocols for categorizing information to make it retrievable. This isn't because all the information systems' designers are dumb. The designers have just done what they needed to do to make retrieval possible with reasonable search times and at reasonable cost.

Older technology couldn't index everything efficiently and cost-effectively, so it didn't. You had to categorize information yourself so that you could efficiently find it by the categories you created.

Then Google changed everything related to finding and retrieving information from the Internet. In 1998, Google famously began crawling the web, visiting websites to grab and then store all the information the sites contained, which made the data findable instantly when anyone asked Google a question. *Google* became a new and important verb, and the search feature has made all of us a lot smarter. By and by, it also made Larry Page, Sergey Brin, and their friends and backers much richer. Ahh, the rewards of innovation.

Terrific as Google is, and I use it all day long, it isn't nirvana — not for me, at least. Why not? Well, the answer is a paradox:

- ✔ TLI (Too little information)
- ✔ TMI (Too much information)

Evernote is a great tool that's complementary to Google. Google's mission statement since its founding has been "to organize the world's information and make it universally accessible and useful." Google estimated in 2010 that the Internet contained about 5 million terabytes of data (1TB = 1,000GB). That's a lot of information. Too much.

Many searches turn up a lot of what you don't want, making you page through many results to find what you do want. There's also a lot of information Google does not have. Google's information comes only from web pages it has crawled. It doesn't break into the Deep Web, as Mike Bergman, who is CEO of Structured Dynamics and an authority on semantic technologies, called it. (It's also sometimes dubbed Deepnet, the invisible Web, DarkNet, Undernet, or the hidden web). The Deep Web isn't indexed by Google or other standard search engines, but it may contain information that's vital for you.

As with an iceberg, Google can see only the tip of the web. The University of California at Berkeley has estimated that when you include the Deep Web, standard search engines like Google, Bing, and Yahoo! are indexing less than 2 percent of the estimated 90,000TB of information that's available. Google admits that it has indexed only a paltry 0.04 percent of it all!

That's only the half of it. You gather your information from many sources, much of which isn't on the web at all, so Google doesn't know about it.

If you're like me, you're drowning in an overload of information that you already have. More often than not, I already have what I need to know — someplace. But without Evernote, I just can't find it. That's as useless as not having it at all and more frustrating. One way I like to think about Evernote is to consider it to be my own private repository and my own private Google-like search engine for everything I've decided is worthwhile to remember.

And that's the point. Google tries to capture all the world's information as best it can. Evernote lets you keep what you found interesting to you and that *you* may want to find again later. That editing function is what keeps you from being overwhelmed with too much information. It's your own search-able scrapbook of everything you've found and liked and what to be able to instantly find again.

Part III provides the basics as well as the more advanced ways of creating useful searches to help you locate your notes quickly.

For the more advanced user and developer, Part VI explains how to work behind the scenes to customize Evernote and take it to a whole new level.

Titling and tagging makes organizing easier

Evernote remembers information that makes its way in. Many roads lead to Rome, and information gets into Evernote in many ways.

Titling and tagging notes can make the information in them easier to find later. Unlike older systems, in which you have to index and can retrieve data easily only based on the indexes, Evernote makes titling and tagging optional. They just make a good thing better.

Tagging and titling are useful when you want to add information that's not already in a note.

A *title* is almost always created for you automatically when a note is created, such as by web clipping. The title Evernote chooses may not be meaningful. You can always override the automatic title and type in your own more rel-evant one. A note's title is descriptive, and you can call it what you will. For example, if you snap a photo with an Evernote-supported device that has a camera, the note title will not be meaningful, as Evernote knows nothing about the picture unless you tell it.

Any time the automatically generated title isn't a good memory-jogger, con-sider writing your own descriptive title.

A *tag* is a key — a way to relate things with a common name. So although *wedding ceremony, nuptials,* and *hymeneals* all mean the same thing, by tagging notes that include any of those terms with the tag "wedding," you'll be able to more quickly find all notes using the three different terms.

If the phrase *Mary's Wedding* is contained in one or more notes, for example, I can find the notes by using the tag "Mary's Wedding." If I save something about nuptials or about wedding vows and want to find it when I think about Mary's wedding, it may make sense to add a "Mary's Wedding" tag so that I can find the other notes whenever I look at the notes about Mary's wedding.

In a search, put quotation marks around phrases to be searched as a unit, such as "Mary's Wedding," so Evernote only returns matches containing the entire phrase.

As you start to type a tag, all the tags beginning with what you typed are presented to you. Just click your choice to use it as a tag. This prevents you from creating a bunch of separate tags due to typos or different capitalizations.

Obsessing about tagging and titling is both unnecessary and a prescription for madness. You can change these identifiers at any time.

I cover titling and tagging in Chapter 3, but also review Chapter 8 for helping keep tags under control and helpful.

Sorting options

You can quickly retrieve anything in a note, in a title, in a tag, or in content that was indexed automatically by keying the request in the search box. Searching for stuff in Evernote can be as simple or as complex as you like. Most of the time, you just enter your query into the search box, and snippets of matching results are instantly returned.

As your repository of notes is always being updated, you may want to save some searches so that you can do them again and again. Saved searches are treated like notes; they're synchronized to Evernote on the web and, therefore, are available on all your Evernote-enabled devices, including mobile ones.

Furthermore, you can do a simultaneous search in Evernote and on the web, as long as you install the web clipper extension (see Chapter 2). Even though you'll begin to keep more and more of your data in Evernote, you can find some items only with Google, Bing, or Yahoo! On supported browsers, when you do a general web query, you also see the results for the same query to your Evernote repository. There's no need to search twice.

You can also *constrain* (limit) the search in powerful ways (see Chapter 8). Notes, for example, can contain to-do lists with check boxes. You can easily find all the notes with unchecked boxes in a notebook by typing **todo:false**.

You can also limit your search to a single notebook. To limit the results to a notebook called Tasks, for example, type **notebook:Tasks todo:false**. Only notes in the Tasks notebook with unchecked tasks are returned.

Searching options

Evernote's internal structure is formally defined and based on open international standards. It uses many operators and a powerful search grammar. It also uses XML to identify everything and Unicode to support the languages of the world. Many tools have been developed to support XML, so you can use them to write your own programs to extend Evernote, control it remotely, or enable you to read and write to its repository.

Chapter 2

Account Management

*I*n this chapter, you get your own Evernote account, choose the right account type, and get the Evernote products you need for all the devices you use.

Comparing the Types of Evernote Accounts

A basic Evernote account is free, and Evernote promises that it always will be. The free account has two kinds of limitations:

> ✔ **Upload limitations:** Free accounts have a ceiling of 60MB of uploads per month.

> ✔ **File-Size limitations:** The individual file-size restriction is 25MB.

More details on an Evernote accounts is available at www.evernote.com/evernote/.

Evernote also offers a Premium account, which is priced at $5 a month or $45 annually (at this writing). More details on Premium accounts and pricing information is available at www.evernote.com/about/premium.

Sponsored groups have the same features as Premium accounts, but cover multiple accounts on a single bill. More information on Sponsored groups and pricing information is available at www.evernote.com/about/premium/groups/.

Educational and not for profit institutions are eligible for a 50% discount from the standard monthly Premium subscription price. See evernote.com/about/premium/groups/education.php for details.

Table 2-1 lists the differences between the two account types.

Table 2-1	Differences between Free and Premium Evernote Accounts	
	Free	*Premium and Sponsored*
Access to all versions of Evernote	✓	✓
Synchronization across platforms	✓	✓
Text recognition inside images	✓	✓
Note allowance	Upload 60MB/month	Upload 1GB/month, 250 notebooks, 10,000 tags, and 100,000 notes
File synchronization	Limited: images, audio, ink, PDF	Any file type
Search within PDFs		✓
Access to note history		✓
Offline notebooks (iPhone, iPad, iPod, Android device)		✓
Notebook sharing via Evernote Web	Read only	Allow read and edit
Maximum single note size	25MB	50MB
Support	Standard	Premium support
Security features	SSL encryption	SSL encryption
Priority image recognition		✓
Hide promotions		✓
PIN Lock Support		✓
Total Account Size	Not Limited	Not Limited
Cost	Free	$5/month or $45/year

Schools, companies, and other groups become sponsored groups and are eligible for bulk discounted prices; they can make the accounts available as they choose.

Your account and all your notes and notebooks are yours and yours alone. You may share selected notebooks with other Evernote users, but even with Sponsored accounts, no automatic sharing occurs. Your information belongs to you.

Registering for a Free Evernote Account

The first place to start getting organized with Evernote is at the Evernote website where you will set up your account. Don't have a lot of time? Don't worry. The process only takes you a few minutes, then you will be off and organizing in no time. It's much less painful than opening a bank account.

It's a good idea to start with a free account so that you can see just how powerful Evernote is even at the most basic level. Use the following steps to sign up for a free Evernote account:

1. **Navigate to www.evernote.com.**

   The Evernote home screen appears (see Figure 2-1).

Figure 2-1:
The
Evernote
home
screen.

2. **In the top-right corner, click Create Account.**

   A new screen invites you to register (see Figure 2-2).

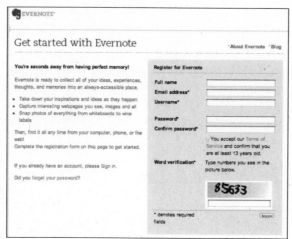

Figure 2-2:
The
Evernote
registration
screen.

3. **Type your full name.**

4. **Type your e-mail address.**

5. **Choose and type a username.**

   Usernames are not case-sensitive.

   Evernote checks username availability as you type. If the username is available, the word *Available* appears below the Username field.

6. **Type a password.**

   Your password must be between 6 and 64 characters long and may contain letters, numbers, and punctuation but not other symbols.

7. **Retype your password in the Confirm Password box.**

8. **Click the check box to accept the terms of service and confirm that you are at least 13 years old.**

9. **In the Word Verification text box, type the numbers you see in the picture.**

10. **Click Register.**

    After you click Register, you receive a message that a confirmation was sent to the e-mail address you supplied in Step 4 (see Figure 2-3).

    An e-mail address created for you by Evernote appears at the bottom of the e-mail.

11. **Click the link in the confirmation e-mail to confirm your identity or supply the access code in the Evernote confirmation screen.**

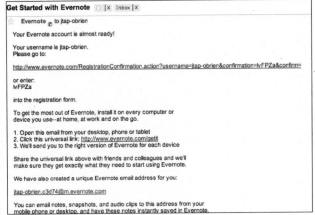

Evernote to jtap-obrien

Your Evernote account is almost ready!

Your username is jtap-obrien.
Please go to:

http://www.evernote.com/RegistrationConfirmation.action?username=jtap-obrien&confirmation=IvFPZa&confirm=

or enter:
IvFPZa

into the registration form.

To get the most out of Evernote, install it on every computer or device you use--at home, at work and on the go.

1. Open this email from your desktop, phone or tablet
2. Click this universal link: http://www.evernote.com/getit
3. We'll send you to the right version of Evernote for each device

Share the universal link above with friends and colleagues and we'll make sure they get exactly what they need to start using Evernote.

We have also created a unique Evernote email address for you:

jtap-obrien.c3d74@m.evernote.com

You can email notes, snapshots, and audio clips to this address from your mobile phone or desktop, and have these notes instantly saved in Evernote.

Figure 2-3:
Click the link
to confirm
your
identity.

If your e-mail client doesn't allow click-through links, type the universal Evernote confirmation address (www.evernote.com/getit) and then type the confirmation code in the confirmation screen and click Confirm.

Whether you used the link or through the confirmation screen, the Welcome to Evernote screen, shown in Figure 2-4, appears.

EVERNOTE

Welcome to Evernote

·Create an account ·About Evernote ·Support

Figure 2-4:
The
Welcome
to Evernote
activation
screen.

Sign in and start remembering everything.

Don't forget, we also have versions available for:
- ○ Windows
- ○ Mac
- ○ iPhone/iPad/iPod Touch
- ○ Android
- ○ BlackBerry

Sign in to Evernote

⊘ Your account has been activated.

Username jtap-obrien
Password

☑ Remember me for a week
Sign In

·Forgot password

12. **Enter your username and password.**

13. **(Optional)** If you want, check the Remember Me for a Week box so that you don't need to re-enter your password on this computer.

14. **Click Sign In.**

You're now signed in to Evernote.

After you complete the registration process, you're immediately taken to Evernote. A welcome note appears in your notebook (see Figure 2-5), with links that can assist you in getting the Evernote products you need.

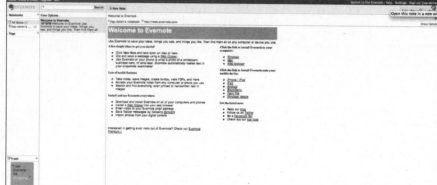

Figure 2-5:
Your initial
view of
Evernote on
the web.

If you're sold on Evernote and want to go ahead and upgrade to a Premium account, access your online account, go to the top bar just below the address, and click Upgrade.

Getting the Correct Version for Each Device

You can freely download the different versions of Evernote at www. evernote.com. Evernote is free of charge for all supported devices, and you can download all the versions you need for all of your devices.

After you create your Evernote account (see the preceding section), you can choose the version for the platform or device you need. Simply click the link for the version you want in the Welcome to Evernote note that was created for you (refer to Figure 2-5).

Evernote has versions available for these products:

✔ Web Clipper (you have to download this feature separately for your web browser of choice unless you're using Internet Explorer, which installs the Web Clipper as part of the Evernote for Windows installation). For

> Apple Safari get it from the Safari Extensions Gallery (Safari 5 or later is required) in the productivity category or download from `www.evernote.com/about/download/get.php?file=SafariExtension`.

✔ Desktops and laptops (Windows and Mac OS X).

✔ Mobile devices (iPhone/iPod touch, iPad, Android, Windows Phone 7, BlackBerry, HP Palm Pre, and Palm Pixi).

If you have an Evernote account, it pays to install Evernote on all your devices. It takes only a few minutes, and there's no cost. Downloading Evernote on all your devices is also the best way to make sure that you have access from anywhere you roam at any time. And it means that no matter where you are, so long as you have your Android device, iOS device, laptop, or other device, even if you don't have Internet access, you can still create and view your notes (Chapter 3 guides you through basic note creation, Chapter 7 provides more detailed instructions for the various devices).

For most devices, with Premium accounts, offline access is supported from the local copy of your notebooks when a network connection is not available; notebooks will be synchronized when you get back online.

Installing a Web Clipper

Web Clipper enables you to save web pages, portions of web-page text, or just web-page pictures using Google Chrome, Mozilla Firefox, Apple Safari, and Internet Explorer.

You can install Web Clipper on your web browser by navigating to `www.evernote.com/about/download/web_clipper.php`. Evernote detects your browser type and offers to download the right one. The download and installation procedures are different for different browsers. If, like me, you work with multiple browsers on one computer, you need to access the link from each browser on your computer to install the corresponding clipper. It's easier than it sounds.

Evernote works with Internet Explorer (available for Windows only), Google Chrome and Firefox (Windows and Mac), and Apple Safari (all versions). All browsers are distributed by their vendors without charge.

I recommend that you use Google Chrome because it's the first browser that Evernote updates, so you'll have greater capability than with the other three browsers. My second browser choice is Firefox because it's updated relatively quickly following Google Chrome updates.

Installing Web Clipper for Google Chrome

Chrome is the preferred browser for Evernote, and improvements are developed for Chrome first. If you don't have Chrome and want to install it, navigate to `http://google.com/chrome`, and click Download Google Chrome.

After you download Chrome, you're ready to install Web Clipper. Follow these steps:

1. **Navigate to `www.evernote.com/about/download/web_clipper.php`.**

   The page shown in Figure 2-6 invites you to install Web Clipper.

Figure 2-6:
Install Web
Clipper
(Chrome
Browser).

2. **Click Install Google Chrome Extension.**

   The Chrome web store appears (see Figure 2-7).

Figure 2-7:
The Chrome
web store.

3. **Click Install.**

   You see the message `Clip to Evernote is now installed.` In the top-right corner of the navigation bar of the Chrome browser, you also see a new button with the Evernote elephant icon, as shown in Figure 2-8.

Figure 2-8:
The Web
Clipper
is now
installed in
the Chrome
browser.

Installing Web Clipper for Safari

Safari comes preinstalled on your Mac, so you need only download Web Clipper. Follow these steps:

1. **Click Web Clipper link in the note provided for you in Evernote or navigate to `www.evernote.com/about/download/web_clipper.php`.**

   You're invited to get the Web Clipper for Safari (see Figure 2-9).

Figure 2-9:
Get Web
Clipper
for Safari
Browser.

In some versions of Safari, you see the message `Drag this to your link bar.`

2. **Drag the clipper to your Safari browser, if you have that option.**

   If you don't have that option, the Evernote Safari Clipper Plug-in package downloads, and the Plugin Installer displays the Welcome to the Evernote Safari Clipper Plugin Installer screen (see Figure 2-10).

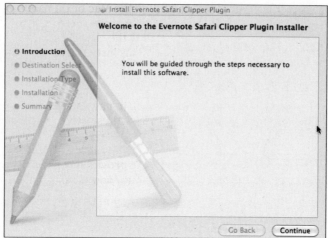

Figure 2-10:
The Safari
Clipper
Plugin
Installer
screen.

3. **Click Continue.**

4. **Select a destination, and click Continue.**

   You're asked how you want to install the software.

5. **Click Install for Me Only, and click Continue.**

   A pop-up window appears.

6. **Click Install.**

   A message appears, indicating that your installation was completed successfully.

7. **Click Close in the message window.**

8. **Close and restart the Safari browser.**

   The Safari browser now has the Evernote Web Clipper button installed to the left of the address bar, as shown in Figure 2-11.

Figure 2-11:
Safari with
Web Clipper
installed.

When installing the clipper for Safari 5.1 on the Mac or on Windows, you need to open the Safari browser and navigate to www.evernote.com/about/ download/web_clipper.php. Then, drag the clipper icon to the link bar and give it a name, like Evernote Clipper. This installs it as a bookmarklet.

Installing Web Clipper for Firefox

If you don't have Firefox and want to install it, navigate to www.firefox. com and download the browser. Then follow these steps to install Web Clipper:

1. **Click the Web Clipper link in the note provided for you in Evernote or navigate to www.evernote.com/about/download/web_clipper.php.**

   If Evernote detects the Firefox browser, you're invited to install the Firefox extension, as shown in Figure 2-12.

Figure 2-12: Install Web Clipper for Firefox.

2. **Click Install Firefox Extension.**

   You're directed to https://addons.mozilla.org/en-US/firefox/ addon/evernote-web-clipper (see Figure 2-13).

Figure 2-13: Web Clipper add-ons for Firefox.

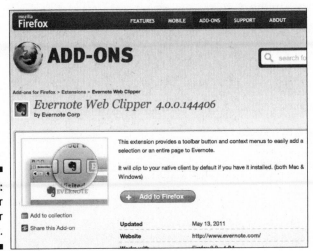

3. **Click Add to Firefox.**

4. **Click Install Now.**

5. **Click Restart Now.**

Firefox restarts, and the Evernote Web Clipper appears on the navigation bar (see Figure 2-14).

Figure 2-14:
The Firefox browser with Web Clipper installed.

Installing Web Clipper with Internet Explorer

The Web Clipper doesn't appear in the Internet Explorer browser bar because it doesn't support add-ons like Evernote. The Clipper is there as part of the native Evernote installation for Windows. You just have to get used to a slightly different way of accessing it.

If Evernote detects Internet Explorer, it installs the Clipper along with Evernote. Although the Web Clipper doesn't work the same way in IE as in other browsers, you can still work most of the Web Clipper options by right-clicking on the website URL and selecting to clip the page to Evernote.

Use the following steps to install Web Clipper for Internet Explorer:

1. **Click Web Clipper in the initial Welcome note that Evernote created for you or navigate to `www.evernote.com/about/download/windows.php`.**

2. **Click Download Now.**

3. **When you're asked whether you want to install Web Clipper, click Yes.**

4. **Click Install.**

5. **Click Finish.**

The Evernote icon appears in your taskbar (see Figure 2-15).

Figure 2-15:
Evernote
icon in the
system tray.

Installing Evernote for desktops

To help you maximize your use, the following sections discuss the different versions by platform.

Installing Evernote for Windows

Evernote supports all versions of Windows 7, Vista, and Windows XP, and they all install from the same download. To install Evernote, follow these steps:

1. **Click Windows in the Welcome note created for you by Evernote or navigate to www.evernote.com/about/download/web_clipper.php.**

2. **Click Download Now.**

3. **Click the downloaded file.**

4. **Click Run.**

5. **If you're asked whether to permit the Windows Installer to install Evernote, click Yes.**

6. **Click Next.**

7. **Click Finish.**

8. **Click Start to start Evernote for Windows.**

9. **Click the Evernote icon.**

   Drag the Evernote icon to your Windows taskbar to pin it so that you can start Evernote easily without any fumbling around.

10. **Close Evernote for Windows.**

    Evernote for Windows is now installed on your desktop.

Installing Evernote on for Mac

To install Evernote for Mac, use the following steps:

1. **Click Mac in theWelcome note Evernote created for you or navigate in your browser to www.evernote.com.**

Evernote recognizes that you're running on a Mac and offers you Evernote for Mac.

2. **Click Download Now.**

   The Mac download page appears.

3. **Click Download.**

   The license agreement appears.

4. **Click Agree.**

5. **After the application is downloaded, drag the Evernote icon into the `Applications` folder (see Figure 2-16).**

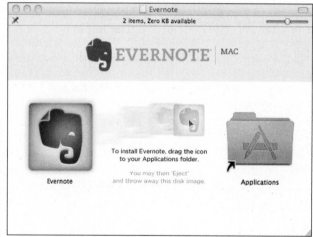

Figure 2-16: Install Evernote for Mac in the Applications folder.

6. **Close the window.**

7. **In the `Applications` folder, click the Evernote icon.**

   You may see a message asking whether you're sure you want to open Evernote.

8. **Click Open.**

   Evernote for Mac opens.

9. **If you see the Welcome to Evernote screen, type your username and password.**

10. **If you like, check Stay Signed In.**

11. **Click Sign In.**

    You've installed Evernote on your Mac.

Installing Evernote for mobile devices

Every mobile device that Evernote supports has a browser. The easiest way to install Evernote on a mobile device is fire up the device's app store or market (Apple's App Store, Android Market, Blackberry App World, Windows Market Place).

Installing Evernote for Android devices

To install Evernote for Android, use the following steps:

1. **Tap on the Market icon.**
2. **Tap Apps.**
3. **Tap the magnifying glass in the top-right corner, enter Evernote in the Search box, and tap the magnifying glass in the lower-right corner.**
4. **Tap Evernote.**
5. **Tap Install.**
6. **Tap Accept & Download.**

   Evernote downloads.

7. **Tap Open.**
8. **Tap Sign In.**
9. **Type your username and password and then tap Sign In.**

   Evernote is successfully installed on your Android device.

Installing Evernote for iPhone, iPod touch, and iPad

To install Evernote for iPhone, iPod, and iPad, use the following steps:

1. **Tap App Store (see Figure 2-17).**
2. **Tap in the Search Box, type Evernote, and execute the search.**
3. **Tap Evernote.**
4. **Tap Install.**
5. **Type your Apple ID and password, and tap Return.**

   The Download Now message appears.

6. **Exit the App Store.**

   Evernote downloads, although it may take a while. You can continue to use the device for other things during downloading.

Figure 2-17:
Download
Evernote
for iPhone,
iPod touch,
or iPad from
the App
Store.

7. **Tap the Evernote icon to launch Evernote.**

8. **Type your username and password, and tap Sign In.**

Evernote may take a few moments to load. Then it synchronizes, downloading snippets of all notes. Patience — this delay happens only once.

Evernote is successfully installed on your iPhone, iPod touch, or iPad.

Installing Evernote for BlackBerry

To install Evernote for BlackBerry, use the following steps:

1. **On your Blackberry, navigate to www.evernote.com, and tap Downloads.**

2. **Below For Mobile Devices, tap BlackBerry.**

You see the screen shown in Figure 2-18.

3. **Tap Available from App World.**

You see the screen shown in Figure 2-19.

4. **Tap Download.**

5. **Log in with your BlackBerry ID, type your e-mail address and password, and tap Login.**

Evernote downloads.

Figure 2-18:
Evernote for
BlackBerry.

Figure 2-19:
Blackberry
for Evernote
download
screen.

   6. Tap Run.

   7. Type your Evernote username and password, and then tap Sign In.

    Evernote is successfully installed on your BlackBerry.

Installing Evernote for WebOS (Palm Pre and Pixi)

Although they don't get as much media attention as other devices, the Palm
Pre and Pixi are nifty little devices that Evernote has added to its arsenal.
The Evernote functionality may be a little less complete, but they're still out-
standing ways to track your information and create notes on the go.

Hewlett-Packard has decided to open source WebOS and Palm Pre and has discontinued manufacturing WebOS devices. As we go to press, it had no hardware licensees.

Perform the following steps on your computer to install Evernote on your Palm Pre or Pixi:

1. **Go to `https://developer.palm.com/appredirect/?packageid= com.evernote.palm.app.evernote`.**

2. **Type your phone number.**

3. **Check I Agree to Terms and Conditions.**

4. **Tap Send to My Phone.**

   An SMS message is sent to your phone.

5. **Tap the SMS message to install Evernote.**

   Evernote downloads. Although this process may take a while, you can continue to use the device for other things during downloading.

6. **Tap the Evernote icon to launch Evernote.**

7. **Type your username and password, and tap Sign In.**

   Evernote may take a few moments to load the first time. Then it synchronizes, downloading snippets of all notes.

   Evernote is successfully installed on your WebOS device.

Installing Evernote for Windows phones

Windows phones are the most recent additions to Evernote, and in mid-2011, Evernote for Windows phones got a serious boost. It went from an extremely basic version for Windows Mobile to a robust, very capable application, which Evernote says is its most powerful version.

To install Evernote for a Windows phone, use the following steps:

1. **Go to `www.windowsphone.com/en-US/marketplace` on your Windows phone.**

2. **Search for Evernote.**

3. **Tap the Evernote app.**

   Evernote may take a few moments to load the first time. Then it synchronizes, downloading snippets of all notes.

   You've successfully installed Evernote on your Windows phone.

Chapter 3

Creating Simple Notes

. . . .

. . . .

*N*o longer do you need to have random thoughts scattered around your brain or colorful sticky notes all over your monitor and desk. To better manage your life, you can take advantage of Evernote's electronic notebooks and notes.

In this chapter, I show you how to create your first notebook and note. Also, because you can install Evernote on multiple devices, I show you several options for getting help, whenever and wherever you need it.

Signing In to Evernote

Before you can do anything in Evernote, you need to create an account and sign in. If you haven't already created an account, go to Chapter 2.

To sign in to your Evernote account, follow these steps:

1. **Navigate to www.evernote.com.**

   If you haven't signed in to Evernote on this computer and asked Evernote to keep you signed in, the Evernote home screen appears (see Figure 3-1).

2. **In the top-right corner, click Sign In.**

   You're invited to sign in to Evernote (see Figure 3-2).

Figure 3-1:
The
Evernote
home
screen.

Figure 3-2:
Sign in to
Evernote.

3. **Type your username and password for your Evernote account (if they aren't filled in) and then click Sign In.**

   Optionally, you can check Remember Me for a Week and then click Sign In.

   After you sign in to Evernote, any notebooks you've created appear in an alphabetical list in the top-left corner of the screen (see Figure 3-3).

Even if you haven't created a notebook, you see a notebook that's named with your user name. This notebook is automatically created for you, using your Evernote account name. You can't change this notebook's name. The Evernote account I created in Chapter 2 is JTAP-obrien, so as you see in Figure 3-3, Evernote created JTAP-obrien's notebook for me.

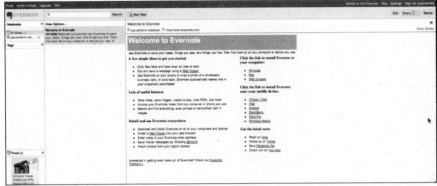

Figure 3-3:
Your
Evernote
notebooks.

In addition to this default notebook and any notebooks you've created, you see shared notebooks.

Accessing Linked Notebooks

Even if you haven't created a notebook yet, you can still access the notebook Evernote created for you, as well as linked notebooks.

A *shared notebook* is a notebook that you're sharing with others and that you can always update because it's yours. A *linked notebook* is created by another user that you can link to your Evernote account and at least view. If the user who created the notebook is a Premium member, you can, with permission, update information in the linked notebook. If not, you have read-only access to the linked notebook.

To access a linked notebook, follow these steps:

1. **Navigate to the notebook you'd like to link to.**

   For this example, I've created a public Evernote notebook that you can link to by going to `http://bit.ly/EvernoteForDummies`. (Please note that the link is case-sensitive.) My notebook is shown in Figure 3-4.

2. **Click Link to My Account.**

   The Access the Shared Notebook dialog box appears (see Figure 3-5). You're asked to sign in, even if you're already signed in.

Figure 3-4:
You can link
to David
Sarna's
*Evernote For
Dummies*
Notebook.

Figure 3-5:
Access
the shared
notebook.

3. **Type your username and password, and click Sign In.**

   Evernote confirms your choice in the Shared Notebook Settings dialog box (see Figure 3-6).

4. **Click Link This Notebook.**

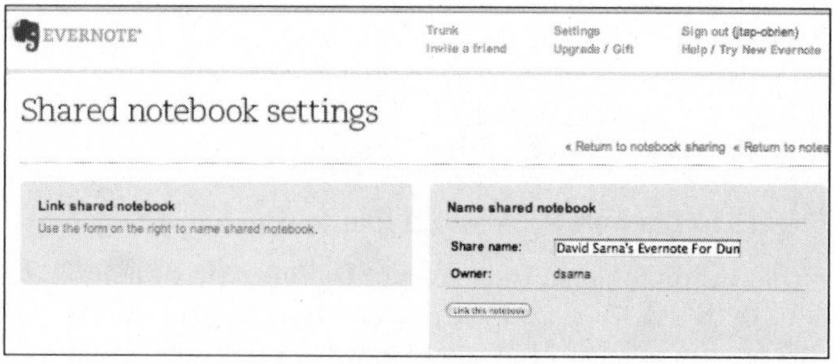

Figure 3-6:
Link to the
shared
notebook.

Evernote lists your shared notebooks (see Figure 3-7).

5. **To access a shared notebook, simply click Linked Notebooks and then the notebook you'd like to access.**

Figure 3-7:
In addition
to any note-
books you
create, you
can access
shared
notebooks.

On web browsers, a linked notebook appears in a separate web tab. On the
desktop implementation, a shared tab is created to the right of Account. For
more information on other public notebooks, see Chapter 18.

Creating a Notebook

Although Evernote creates a notebook for you when you create an account
(see Chapter 2), and you can link to an increasingly large collection of public
notebooks or those shared by your friends (see the preceding section),
chances are that you'll want to create notebooks other than the one that
Evernote supplies. Creating a new notebook is a simple task:

1. **Choose File⇨New Notebook.**

   The Create Notebook dialog box appears (see Figure 3-8).

Figure 3-8:
The Create
Notebook
dialog box.

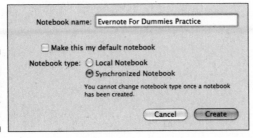

2. **Type a name for your notebook.**

   For this example, I call my notebook `Evernote For Dummies Practice`.

3. **If you want to make this notebook the one that appears automatically when you work in Evernote, click the Make This My Default Notebook check box.**

   If you're following along with my example, you'll be using the Evernote For Dummies Practice notebook just for practice, so don't check the box for this practice notebook.

4. **Choose the type of notebook.**

   You have two choices:

   • *Local Notebook:* The notebook will be available only on this computer.

   • *Synchronized Notebook:* The notebook will be synchronized and available on all your devices.

   For the Evernote For Dummies Practice notebook, choose Synchronized Notebook.

5. **Click Create.**

   The new notebook appears in the list of your notebooks (see Figure 3-9).

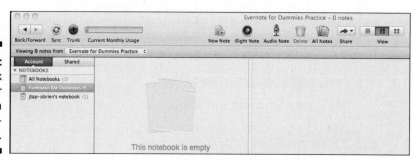

Figure 3-9: Notebook list after creating a new notebook.

Some useful information appears to the right of each notebook name:

✔ The number of notes stored in that notebook is indicated.

✔ The default notebook (where notes are stored if you don't select a notebook) is marked with a star or is highlighted, depending on the type of device you're using.

You can change the names of the existing notebooks in Evernote. Click Edit to add a new notebook or to change the name of a notebook that you created. After you click Edit, you see a small window where you can change the notebook's name.

Creating Your First Note

After you create a new notebook, you can add notes to it. Anything you want to add is fair game; after all, it's your notebook! If you like to make lists, you can create a grocery list or a to-do list. Or perhaps you want to redecorate your kitchen; simply add photos of looks you like, along with links to decorating ideas. Instead of random thoughts wandering around your brain or colorful, tiny sticky notes all over your desk, you can now organize everything in the form of notes in your notebooks. (If you haven't created a notebook yet, see the preceding section.)

The most enjoyable thing about Evernote is that you can capture anywhere, and search and find everywhere. (See Chapter 8 for the scoop on categorizing and finding information.)

When you create a new notebook, Evernote notices that it's empty and even prompts you to create a note by putting a bright red circle around New Note in the menu bar. To create a simple note that contains typed text, follow these steps:

1. **Click the New Note button on the menu bar.**

   A blank note appears (see Figure 3-10).

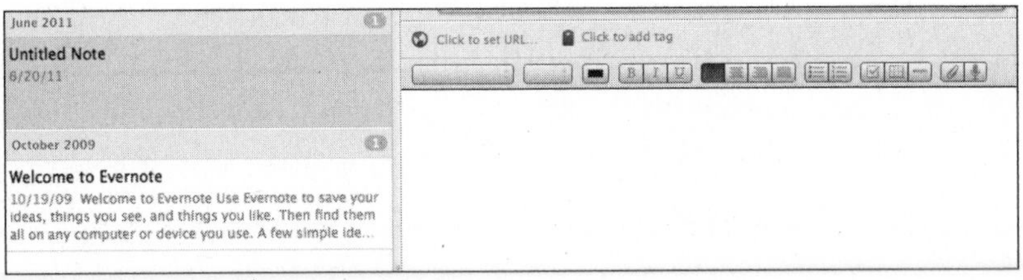

Figure 3-10: Create your new note.

The first time you create a note, a somewhat scary-looking `This is your first note` message appears, in stark black and white, giving you ideas for a note. Don't be alarmed. Evernote is just being helpful.

2. **Click Close in the message.**

   You return to the blank note.

3. **Type your note.**

4. **Give your note a title.**

At the top of your note, above the note text and just above the mini word processor bar, is the place where you give your note a title (see Figure 3-11).

Evernote uses words in the title and tags to search for information, so assign a descriptive title and a tag to the note. For this example, I typed **My first note in Evernote** in the title box and assigned the tag Easy Evernote Things.

5. **Tag your note by clicking Click to Add Tag (refer to Figure 3-10) and typing the tag.**

   Figure 3-11 shows an example of a tag and title.

Figure 3-11:
Title and tag
your note.

6. **Type the contents of the note.**

7. **If a note was created by web clipping, the URL will be assigned for you. Optionally, to assign a URL to a note you type, click to Set URL (refer to Figure 3-10).**

8. **In the window that appears, type a URL and then click OK.**

   Assigning a URL makes sense, for example, if you are abstracting an article and want to refer back to the source.

   Your note is saved automatically as you go along. All your notes are listed in the left pane. Clicking a note makes it active (indicated by the shading) and opens it in the right pane.

Changing the note's look

Depending on the browser you're using, you may be able to change the note's font, font size, and other word-processing features. You may be able to add such formatting as boldface, line justification (left, right, and centered), subscript and superscript, numbers, bullets, and hyperlinks.

Not all devices or browsers support the formatting features. The toolbar will be missing if you use Evernote in a device or browser in which formatting isn't supported.

At this writing, Evernote on my BlackBerry doesn't support formatting (rich text). If you're using a similar device, just create the note. Later, you can access your note on another device and do your formatting then. You can go back and make changes and additions to the note at any time and from any device.

You don't need to open anything to modify a note. Just click the note and make the change. In addition to adjusting your note's text format, you can jazz it up by adding hyperlinks and file attachments.

Adding an attachment

Say that you're using Evernote to simplify your life — what a great idea! — and you find a terrific online article on the topic. You don't have to summarize the article in your note. Instead, you can attach the article to the note.

You're not limited to text. Even if you're using the free version of Evernote, you can still attach an audio clip, picture, PDF file, Microsoft Word document and spreadsheet up to 25MB.

Here's how to attach an item to your note:

1. **Click the paper-clip button in the toolbar.**

   The Select File(s) to Attach dialog box, shown in Figure 3-12, appears.

2. **Select the file(s) you want to attach.**

   In this example, I attached a document called `About Stacks.pdf`, which explains stacks of notebooks (see Chapter 1).

Figure 3-12: Select files to attach.

3. Click Open.

The attachment appears in your note.

Decide that the item you linked to wasn't as great as you'd thought it would be? No problem. You can remove an attachment by clicking the paper-clip button again and then clicking Clear.

Creating a Shared Note

Note links are links to individual notes that you can place almost anywhere. Using note links, you can let anyone you choose see the latest version of a note, no matter what device you use to update it. Anyone who clicks the link or types its URL can see the latest version of the note, delivered directly from Evernote's servers.

No one has access to any of your other notes. Other people can access just the shared link.

Note: Note links are meant to be used within a single Evernote account to connect one note to others — think of it as creating a table of contents. They make sense within the account but you cannot share them with others. If, for example, you create a note link in Evernote for Mac and paste it into an email and send it to someone, nothing happens when the recipient clicks the link.

Creating a note link

Here's how to create a note link:

1. Right-click the note you want to share, and choose Copy Note Link from the contextual menu.

The link appears in your clipboard.

2. Paste the note into another document.

You can paste that link into just about anything: other notes, calendars, to-do lists, third-party apps, and so on. The link is a URL. Whenever you click the link, the note opens.

Shift-clicking (Windows) or Command-clicking (Mac) opens the linked note in its own window.

Creating multiple note links

You can also create a list of links. To do so, select multiple notes; then right-click what you selected and choose Copy Note Links from the contextual menu. When you paste the notes, you see a list of links.

This list is a great tool for building bibliographies, tables of contents, and citations when you're doing research.

As an example, I created a third note with information about the links feature. I highlighted all three notes in Evernote, right-clicked, and chose Copy Note Links. Then I pasted the links into an e-mail to myself. Figure 3-13 shows the e-mail I received.

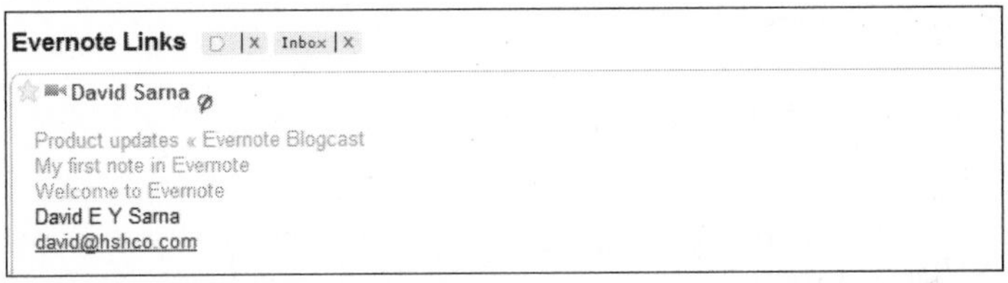

Figure 3-13:
An e-mail
with multiple
links from
Evernote.

Evernote Links ☐ | X   Inbox | X

☆ ◄ David Sarna ⊘

Product updates « Evernote Blogcast
My first note in Evernote
Welcome to Evernote
David E Y Sarna
david@hshco.com

Deleting notes

You can delete any note by clicking Delete. That's so easy that you might think it's really easy to delete things accidentally. No worries. It's just a virtual delete. Deleted notes go to a special notebook called Trash. To undelete, simply click on the note and then click Restore Note. To permanently delete a note, click on it and then click Erase Note.

Changing Your View

Snippet view is the default view of your newly created notes, but you can use the commands on the View menu to change your view. How you control your view is different in Mac and in Windows. Table 3-1 shows which shortcut key does what in each platform.

Table 3-1		Evernote Views	
View	*Mac Command*	*Windows Command*	*What It Does*
List view	Command+1	Ctrl+F5	Gives you a compact, flat view, minus the icons, with just the titles, tags, and summary history, and without the icons (see Figure 3-14)
Snippet view	Command+2	Ctrl+F6	Gives you a snippet of the note, plus a small image, if there is one
Thumbnail view	Command+3	Ctrl+F7	Shows an icon of the note

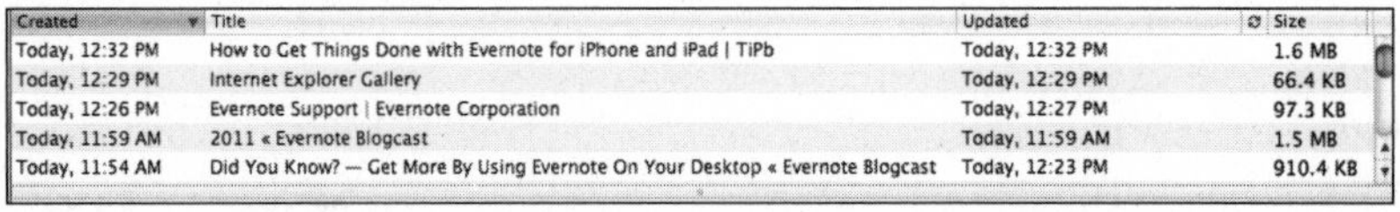

Figure 3-14:
List view.

Created	Title	Updated	⊘ Size
Today, 12:32 PM	How to Get Things Done with Evernote for iPhone and iPad	TiPb	Today, 12:32 PM	1.6 MB
Today, 12:29 PM	Internet Explorer Gallery	Today, 12:29 PM	66.4 KB
Today, 12:26 PM	Evernote Support	Evernote Corporation	Today, 12:27 PM	97.3 KB
Today, 11:59 AM	2011 « Evernote Blogcast	Today, 11:59 AM	1.5 MB
Today, 11:54 AM	Did You Know? — Get More By Using Evernote On Your Desktop « Evernote Blogcast	Today, 12:23 PM	910.4 KB

Getting Help and Support

The good news is that Evernote works nearly everywhere. On the downside, though, you may not have this book with you when you need assistance. Fortunately, Evernote offers several help tools, should you ever get stuck:

- ✔ Instructional videos
- ✔ Support
- ✔ User forum
- ✔ Support inquiry

An abbreviated Getting Started guide is available at www.evernote.com/about/getting_started.

Viewing the instructional videos

Evernote offers you an entire library of videos, including tutorials, stories, tips, overviews, and demonstrations of a whole ecosystem of third-party products, many of which I discuss in Part IV. You can access the Evernote videos at www.evernote.com by clicking the A Quick Introduction to Evernote link (see Figure 3-15).

Figure 3-15:
Watch the
Getting
Started
video.

New features are frequently added to Evernote. Illustrative how-to videos often accompany these feature announcements, and you can access them by clicking the appropriate links (see Figure 3-16). To make things even easier, I've created a direct link to the videos that you can access by visiting http://bit.ly/EvernoteVideos in your browser.

Figure 3-16:
Go to
Evernote's
website to
check out
Evernote's
many
instructional
videos.

You can also access the videos from YouTube. A search for Evernote on YouTube.com shows that more than 1,500 videos about Evernote exist, but you can narrow the choice to about 50 Evernote-produced videos by typing **EvernoteAndrew** in the YouTube search bar. (The *Andrew* in this seemingly strange search phrase refers to Andrew Sinkov, Evernote's vice president of marketing.)

Getting Evernote help and support

Help is only a click away in Evernote. Better yet, Evernote support is free, and in my experience, it's pretty good. Although Premium users receive priority, all requests receive a response.

To get help, go to www.evernote.com, and click Help. You see the main help screen (see Figure 3-17).

Figure 3-17:
The
Evernote
help screen.

At the top of the screen, you can see the most recent status messages relating to the health of the Evernote servers. You can access full details at http://status.evernote.com. You can get the same information as it happens on Twitter by subscribing to @EvernoteStatus.

If the Evernote cloud service is operational (in my experience, it almost always is), you have several options to find answers to your questions:

✔ **Getting Started guide:** You won't ever need this multipart guide (refer to "Getting Help and Support," earlier in this chapter) if you have this book.

✔ **Knowledge Base:** This collection of articles and frequently asked questions is intended for anybody who's interested in finding information about a particular feature of Evernote. (For details on how to search the Knowledge Base, see the nearby sidebar.)

✔ **User manuals:** A PDF manual for the Windows version of Evernote is available at www.evernote.com/about/support/ EvernoteForWindows-UserGuide.pdf. Evernote does not promise to keep this up to date.

Searching the Knowledge Base

If you have a particular question in mind, you can search the Knowledge Base (see figure) for an answer.

1. **Navigate to `www.evernote.com/about/learn_more` and click on Knowledge Base.**

2. **Type a question in the Search box.**

   For this example, I typed **export notes.**

3. **Click Search.**

   Although my question returned more hits than I would have liked, one result is obviously on point (see figure).

You can also browse the knowledge base. Click the any category to browse the Knowledge Base for entries related to that topic. In addition, the same page that contains the search box for the Knowledge Base (`https://support.evernote.com/ics/support/KBSplash.asp`) also shows the most popular and most recent articles. Visit it often.

Search results: 'exporting notes'

Can I send notes to Evernote using Twitter?
Importing Evernote Archives in Evernote for Mac
How do I email multiple notes at once?
Sharing Your Notes and Notebooks with Evernote on the Desktop
Recovering Your Notes after a Hard Drive Failure
Exporting Notes and Notebooks in Evernote for Mac
How can I automatically tag an emailed note and add it to a specific notebook?
An Introduction to Tags
Using Evernote's advanced search operators
How can I see only my 'To Do' notes?
How do I move notes between notebooks?
Connecting Evernote with Your GMail Account
Why doesn't my upload quota reset at the beginning of each month?
How to Install and Use the Web Clipper for Google Chrome
An Introduction to Saved Searches
How can I view the notes I created nearby where I am right now?
How Evernote sync works
Overview of Account Data Limits
Sharing Individual Notes
How can I find notes that I have shared in my account?
What are the keyboard shortcuts in Evernote for Windows?
Sorting Notes
An Introduction to Notebooks
How can I encrypt a portion of a note?
Best Practices for Evernote Image Processing
How many notes, notebooks and tags can a single account accommodate?
How can I synchronize notes between my computer and my mobile phone?
How can I create audio notes?
How can I create additional notebooks?
Using Evernote Peek
An Introduction to Notes

✔ **Getting Started Guide:** A Getting Started Guide is available at www.evernote.com/about/getting_started/.

✔ **User forum:** You can visit the forum from the Evernote support page (www.evernote.com/about/contact/support). For more on the user forum, see the next section.

If all else fails and you can't find what you need, you can contact Evernote's support department. From the Evernote support page (www.evernote.com/about/contact/support/), you can submit a support request. Simply click the Here link or navigate to www.evernote.com/about/contact/support/#inquiry. The Submit Inquiry form appears. Evernote provides two levels of service for support inquiries. The response speed depends on your account. Premium Evernote accounts should receive a reply by e-mail within one business day. Free accounts get a reply as quickly as possible, but no specific timeline is given.

Getting help from fellow Evernote users

Evernote has appointed a group of passionate Evernote users, called ambassadors, who each have a particular specialty. They were chosen for their commitment to teach, share, and help you get more out of Evernote. To meet them, visit www.evernote.com/about/community/. Also read more about them in Chapter 21.

You can use the Evernote user forum to find answers to your questions. Although the Knowledge Base contains official answers from Evernote, answers on the user forum are community-generated, and the results may not be quite as accurate.

You can query or browse the user forum the same way as you do the Knowledge Base:

✔ To query the forum, just type the query in the box, and click Search Forum.

✔ To browse the forum, click the Evernote User Forum link.

The forum is organized by product, as shown in Figure 3-18. Forums cover general discussions, development topics, and *localization* (a community effort to translate Evernote into as many languages as possible).

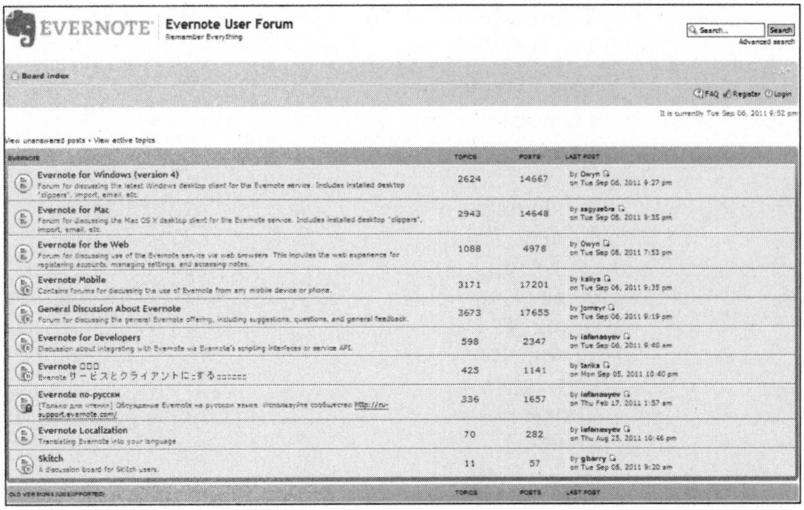

Figure 3-18:
You can
find help
from fellow
Evernote
users at the
user forum.

The Help menu for the web version of Evernote has a Chat with Evernote option that you use by clicking on your account name and then clicking Chat with Evernote.

Part II
Increasing Your Reach

The 5th Wave   By Rich Tennant

"I'm trying to organize the IT guy's documents, and apparently his file system was informed heavily by the Da Vinci Code."

In this part . . .

*P*art II covers how to start creating notes and some of the exciting things you can do with Evernote to capture your memories from a variety of media.

Chapter 4 covers working with notes, dragging and dropping notes, and capturing and clipping web pages (or parts of them). You also find out how to use bookmarklets.

Chapter 5 takes you beyond text to recording voice notes and creating notes from music and from images.

In Chapter 6 you find out how to create notes from other media, which includes creating ink notes, notes from email, and notes from tweets. You can also use scanners, cameras, and e-readers to capture information to store notes.

Chapter 4

Working with Notes

*I*n this chapter, you use several methods of creating notes from existing locations, such as the Internet or images. On way to do this is using the Evernote web clipping tool. You also discover how to create bookmarklets, a tool so handy that you may never bookmark another website again.

Dragging and Dropping into Existing Notes

Creating a note from scratch is easy (see Chapter 3), but what if you already have all the information you need in a file? Or what if that file is a graphic? Those situations are where dragging and dropping come in.

If you've ever moved files and folders around in the Mac Finder or Windows Explorer, you're already familiar with how dragging and dropping works.

You can use drag and drop all files no matter what their extension. If you're a premium member, Evernote can show you previews only of the supported extensions where the platform has a viewer built-in, or for PDF files in Windows, where Evernote developed its own support. Evernote is a great way for keeping your files portable without having to tote around a memory stick or some other device that can get lost or stolen.

Evernote processes `.pdf` files and other supported files for Premium users before it processes them for free users. Scanned PDFs are made searchable for Premium users.

Here's how to create a note by dragging and dropping files:

1. **Click New Note to create a new note.**

2. **Click a file (on your desktop, in the Mac Finder, or in Windows Explorer), and drag it to your Evernote account in your web browser onto the title area of the note.**

3. **Release the mouse button when the file appears in the spot where you want it to be.**

   Seriously, it's that simple. Like magic, your file is saved as a note.

The process is virtually the same if you are working with any one of the desktop versions of Evernote.

By default, in Windows, the name of the file is used as the title of the note; on a Mac, the default filename is `Untitled`. To change the title, click it to highlight it and then type the name you want.

Capturing Part of a Screen or Web Page

When you find something on a web page that you want to keep as a note, maybe you don't want to save an entire everything you see. As often as not, all you need is a portion of a site, maybe just a picture. Evernote makes it easy to pull in as much or as little of a web page as you like.

To capture part of a screen to create a note, follow these steps:

1. **Highlight the part of the web page you want to clip.**

2. **Click the Evernote icon on your browser.**

   Figure 4-1 shows you the screen that appears. This step automatically creates a screen capture and saves it to your Evernote account.

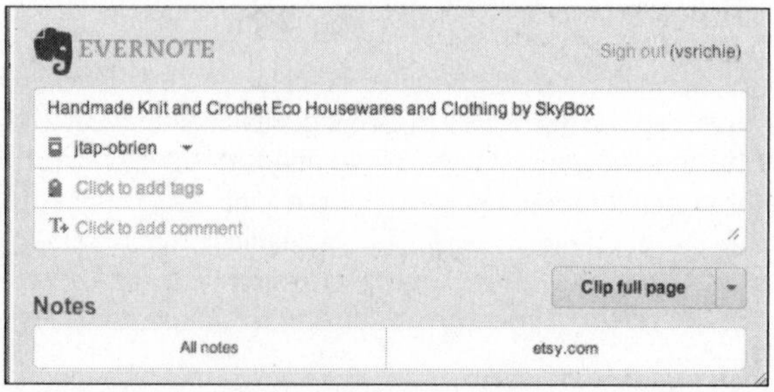

Figure 4-1: Capturing web content into Evernote.

EVERNOTE   Sign out (vsrichie)

Handmade Knit and Crochet Eco Housewares and Clothing by SkyBox

jtap-obrien

Click to add tags

Click to add comment

Clip full page

Notes

All notes   etsy.com

If you prefer to use the crosshair pointer to capture a full screen, try this approach instead:

1. **Highlight an area.**

   You may see a crosshair pointer that you can manipulate.

2. **Right-click the highlighted area and click Evernote Web Clipper,**

3. **Click Clip Selection to save the highlighted area, or Clip URL to just save the URL.**

Check out your latest note to see your clipped area. Don't like it? You can simply delete the note and try again.

It's surprising how easy this feature is to use. Take a couple of trial runs to get a good feel for it. Don't worry — you won't mess anything up on the screen.

You can set up your default capture and clipping settings by using Clipping Preferences from the Tools menu. I go into more detail in the upcoming section "Web clipping."

Saving photos to notes with Webcam Note and iSight

When Evernote for Windows detects that a webcam is installed, the New Webcam Note command is available as on the File menu for capturing photos into notes (in the Mac, it is always present, and is called New iSight Note).

1. **Open Webcam Note using the Ctrl+Shift+W shortcut.**

2. **The New Webcam Note window opens and the video image captured by the webcam is shown in the note.**

3. **Click Take Snapshot to capture the image, or click Cancel to close the capture window (a blank note will be created even if you cancel, and you will need to delete it manually).**

4. **The snapshot is taken (the image is frozen).**

5. **Click Retake Snapshot to go back to Step 3, or click Save to Evernote to load the snapshot into a note. Click Cancel to abandon the task (no blank note is created).**

iSight is the tool Mac users have for taking a quick photograph or screen shot. To take a photo, do the following:

1. **From your desktop version of Evernote, click the iSight icon along the top menu.**

   Alternatively, you can access iSight by choosing File⇨New iSight Note. Either method opens the camera of your Mac, but it may take a minute to access. (This option is not available from the website because no other platform supports iSight.)

(continued)

(continued)

2. **When the camera opens, point it at the object that you'd like to photograph, and click Take Snapshot.**

   If you're not happy with the picture, you can retake it as many times as you like.

3. **When you're satisfied with the picture, click Add to Evernote to save it to your default notebook.**

To take screenshots on the Mac, you have a couple of basic options:

✔ To take a full screen shot, use Command+Shift+3 and save the file to your desktop

✔ To take a shot of a specific area of the screen, press Command+Shift+4, select an area, and then save the file to your desktop

You can do an Internet search to find other shortcuts for taking other types of screen shots on a Mac.

Note: In Windows, the webcam is usually a separate device and faces you. In the Mac the camera is built-in. Images seem mirrored when you look at yourself. On video chats, which iSight was originally designed for, the image is normal to the person at the other end. So you may worry that the picture will be reversed like when you hold up text in front of the bathroom mirror. If you're worrried that the captured image won't be useful if you need text from it, such as an image of a tickets or a receipt, don't be. Evernote flips the picture so that the text is searchable by text recognition, just like in a scan.

Keeping Track of Web Pages

Tracking bookmarks becomes cumbersome because you have to remember where you filed things. Leaving many tabs open in web browsers is problematic for many reasons, especially when your computer shuts down. Evernote, however, makes it easy to keep track of your web browsing in just a couple of steps.

Evernote doesn't support web page extensions, but that doesn't mean that you can't add them to Evernote. You can use a couple of methods to bring information from the web to your external brain.

Internet Explorer doesn't support the Evernote icon near the address bar. For instructions on web clipping with Internet Explorer, see "Browser support for web clipping," later in this chapter.

Web clipping

Web clipping is Evernote's way to clip an entire web page, a URL or just a portion of a web page. Also, you can later edit anything you store in your notes, regardless of platform or browser.

If you have more than a single web page to capture, I suggest capturing each as a separate note. If you like, you can combine them later into a single note. To combine notes in Windows, highlight the notes to be combined (using the Ctrl or Shift keys) and then right-click and click Merge Notes. On a Mac Cmd+click to highlight the notes you want to combine and then Ctrl+click and select Merge Notes.

Ready to make your research faster and easier? Here's how you web-clip to collect all the web pages of interest:

1. **Click the Evernote icon on your tools menu of your Windows desktop and select Clipping Preferences, or on your Mac Ctrl+click and select Options.**

   The Preferences dialog box appears, with the Clipping pane selected in a separate browser tab. (See Figure 4-2 for the Mac Preferences dialog box.)

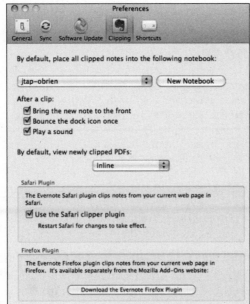

Figure 4-2: Clipping preferences (Mac).

2. **If you want to save your web clipping to a notebook other than the default, choose that notebook from the pop-up menu.**

3. **Set features as you want.**

You can set the sound Evernote makes when it creates a capture, for example, or set whether your clippings will be set inline on the note or as an attachment to the note.

If you use Internet Explorer, web clipping is a little different than described here. Read more about it later in the chapter. Otherwise, it should take you only a few minutes to download the plugin for Google Chrome or Mozilla Firefox.

4. **Go to the website you want to clip.**

5. **If you want to capture only a portion of the website, highlight the portion you want to capture.**

   Otherwise, Evernote captures the entire page.

6. **Click the Evernote icon on the menu bar.**

   A new note appears and is stored in the notebook you set in Step 2.

You can click links in the note to open the web clipping in your default web browser as long as you can connect to the Internet.

Article clip mode

If you want to clip articles or blogs, article clip mode can help you keep them organized. (An article is a portion of a web page.) At this writing, Chrome, Firefox, and Safari are the browsers that support article clipping.

You have to have the Web Clipper extension to use article clip mode. See Chapter 2 for information on installing the Web Clipper.

To clip an article, follow these steps:

1. **To choose what to clip yourself, highlight the portion of the web page you want to clip.**

2. **Click the Evernote icon next to the browser's address bar.**

   If you are using Internet Explorer, you highlight the text, right-click, and click Add to Evernote. (This option is available from other browsers as well.)

3. **A New note is created, and the part of the web page to be clipped is shown.**

4. **Update the note fields to modify the note.**

Chrome, Firefox, and Safari give you the option to change the title, add a tag, select your notebook, and add additional text. Click clip Selection or pull down the menu and click Full Page or Clip URL:

- *Clip Full Page* is the default setting; it saves the entire web page to your notebook. Links on the page still work, but the content is saved so that you can edit it.

- *Clip URL* saves just the link of the article or blog. Although this option may not give you as much information as Clip Full Page, it saves space. You also need to use the drop-down menu and change it from the default option.

That's it. Evernote takes care of all the behind-the-scenes organization for you.

Browser support for web clipping

Just as each web browser receives a different level of Evernote support, the way that web clipping works differs based on the platform you use. Often, Chrome gets features first and then these features are incorporated into the other browsers, but that incorporation could take a while. Some browsers, such as Internet Explorer, have inherent design limitations that prevent them from working identically to the others, so knowing what to look for and how each browser functions is important to clipping the way you want to.

To maximize your web-clipping use, the following sections describe what you can expect from each of the browsers.

Chrome, Firefox and Safari

Chrome is the preferred browser, but Firefox (especially Firefox 6) isn't too far behind. All three browsers are available for Macs and PCs, so you can use your favorite browser with Evernote on Windows as well as on Mac platforms. The options you have when you clip and the appearance of the menus are somewhat different from Internet Explorer.

Chapter 2 gives you instructions for downloading Chrome, Firefox, and their respective Web Clipper extensions. You must have the browser on your computer to use its Web Clipper extension, so start by downloading the desired browser if you don't already have it.

At this writing, Chrome and Firefox give you the most options for storing your notes. Figure 4-3 shows web-clipping options in Chrome, and Figure 4-4 shows you those options in Firefox. To access these options in either browser, click the Evernote icon.

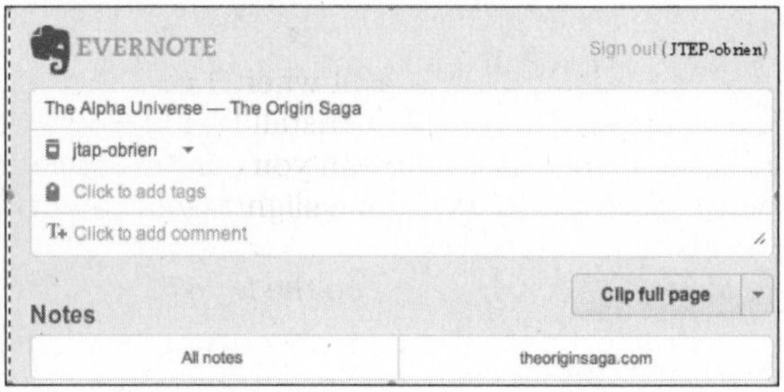

Figure 4-3:
Chrome
Web Clipper
options.

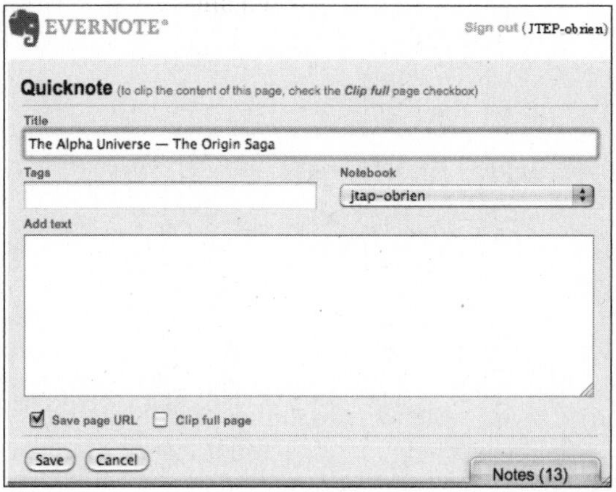

Figure 4-4:
Firefox Web
Clipper
options.

Whatever browser you use, you need to follow the browser instructions to save e-mails to Evernote. If you have Chrome, this process is simple and exactly like clipping any other web page or article.

Safari

Apple's Safari browser is nearly as robust as Chrome or Firefox. It does a decent job of capturing web clippings and allowing for easy drag and drop. It has its own Web Clipper, too, which installs to the left of the URL address bar. It works just like the clippers for the other browsers.

Safari 5.1 is a significant upgrade to earlier versions, and you want to be sure you have the latest version installed. After you have installed it (it comes pre-installed on all new Macs), you need to download the Evernote Safari web clipper at www.evernote.com/about/download/web_clipper.php.

Internet Explorer

Internet Explorer (IE) is the odd browser out when it comes to web clipping. You have nothing to download it when you install IE, but it also doesn't offer you the web-clipping icon. So does that mean you can't use web clipping? Absolutely not. You just have to follow some slightly modified instructions.

To use the Internet Explorer Web Clipper, do the following:

1. **Right-click anywhere on the web page.**

   If you only want a small portion of the web page, highlight the portion you want and then right-click it. Figure 4-5 shows you the options that you get with your right-click.

Figure 4-5:
Internet
Explorer
Evernote
menu.

2. **Scroll down the contextual menu to Add to Evernote 4.0.**

3. **In the box that opens, fill in whatever information you want.**

4. **Save to the notebook of your choice.**

Simplifying Life with Bookmarklets

A *bookmarklet* is combination of a bookmark and an applet, and it's simple to use. You would only use it in a browser lacking support for web clipping. If you like using bookmarks, Evernote's bookmarklet enables you to bookmark pages and also add them to your default notebook.

Bookmarklets are written in JavaScript and are unobtrusive tools that make interaction with the Internet a little easier.

Ready to enable bookmarklets? Here's what you need to do:

1. **Go to www.evernote.com/about/download/web_clipper.php.**

2. **Either drag the icon at the bottom of the web page to your bookmark file or right-click the link and save it to your bookmarks, as shown in Figure 4-6.**

From here on out, you'll be able to save bookmarklets whenever you want to bookmark something as well as add it as a note.

Figure 4-6:
You can
drag the
Bookmarklet
icon to your
web page or
right-click
the link to
save it
to your
bookmarks.

Bookmarklet: Drag the image below into your browser's link bar

DRAG TO YOUR LINK BAR

Chapter 5

Working with Audio and Video

*I*n this chapter, you work with some of the most exciting file types: recordings and images. Saving memories of more important stuff, like visuals and vocals, is how you'll get really attached to Evernote (if you aren't already). Capturing events and conversations for later review and reminiscing has never been this easy.

Answering machines and camcorders got most people over the novelty of recording themselves. But everything was segregated to different devices or files, which meant that locating the right recording was as difficult as locating your tax return from five years ago. Now, Evernote has made it possible for you to centralize all your recordings and images, which is especially important when it comes to meetings or family vacations. Evernote is also awesome for working with files like PDFs and other images containing text because it's capable of "reading" them and then making them searchable.

Recording a Voice Note

Sometimes you're on the go and don't have the time to type and fix notes, particularly with the "help" of autocorrection. You spend more time fighting your keyboard than getting stuff done. If you're hurrying to your next location, voice notes are the perfect way of catching your thoughts before they flit off into oblivion.

The way to record a voice note in Evernote is similar for all devices. The following instructions point out the minor differences.

If you want to add notes or text to any of your recordings, you can do that, too. After you create your recording, just click in the note area and begin typing. Best of all, you can add the text from any device, not just desktop computers or laptops.

Mac desktop or laptop

To record on a Mac desktop or laptop, follow these steps:

1. **Click the File⇨New Audio Note. (See Figure 5-1.)**

File	Edit	View	Note	Format
New Note				⌘N
New Tag				^⌘T
New Notebook				⇧⌘N
New iSight Note				
New Audio Note				
New Saved Search...				
New Evernote Window				⌥⌘N
Sync (DSarna)				^⌘S
Close				⌘W
Save				⌘S
Attach Files...				
Quick Look Attachments...				⌘Y
Import Notes from Archive...				
Export Notes to Archive...				
Page Setup...				⇧⌘P
Print...				⌘P

Figure 5-1: The menu for creating a new audio note.

2. **Click the Audio Note icon, select your notebook, and click OK.**

   The computer starts with your default notebook, but you can select any of your existing notebooks.

3. **Click the Record button when you're ready to start recording your first voice note. (See Figure 5-2.)**

4. **When you are finished, click Save.**

   The recording is inserted as an audio note. Click Play to play it back. Click Done to save the note. Click Delete to send it to the Trash.

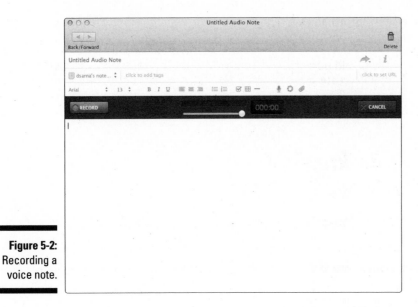

Figure 5-2:
Recording a
voice note.

If you stumble over your words right from the start or get interrupted, don't worry; you can simply click the Cancel button, and the note remains but the recording is deleted. Delete the empty note and start again at Step 1. You can also delete your recording later, as described in Step 7.

5. Click Play to determine whether your recording is a keeper.

Take the time to review your recording (see Figure 5-3). If you like what you hear, you're done. If you want to take another crack at it, go to the next couple of steps.

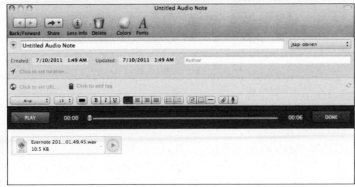

Figure 5-3:
Audio note
options and
menus.

6. **(Optional) Click Delete.**

This option is only visible after you have saved a note and clicked Done. The note is sent to the trash. From there, you can click Erase Note to erase the recording permanently, or, if you deleted it in error, Restore Note to reinstate it.

7. **To rerecord your note, click the Record Audio icon.**

The icon is on the toolbar just above the notes.

iPhone or iPod touch

To record on an iPhone or iPod touch, follow these steps:

1. **Launch your Evernote app.**

2. **Create a new note, and select the Voice option. (See Figure 5-4.)**

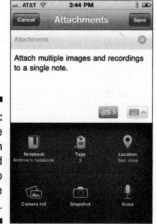

Figure 5-4:
Using the Voice option to record an audio note on the iPhone.

The app starts recording 3 seconds after you tap the Voice option. The recording icon flips over to the recording bar, so be ready to talk.

3. **Begin talking.**

4. **Tap Stop when you're finished.**

If you stop the recording instead of saving it, you can listen to what you have. By stopping, you also can try as many recordings as you want.

5. **When you're satisfied with the recording, tap Save.**

   Your recording is saved to the note.

iPad and Android tablet

Recording on an iPad or on an Android tablet works basically the same way. Here's what you need to do on either type of device:

1. **Touch New Note.**

   The editor appears.

2. **Touch the microphone icon, and start speaking.**

   Recording starts as soon as you tap the icon, so make sure that you're ready.

3. **Touch Stop when you're done recording.**

   On an Android device, when you touch Stop, the audio automatically attaches to the note. If you want to listen to your recording, just tap the audio portion of the note.

   On an iPad, after you stop recording, you can either save or delete the recording. You should be able to listen to it from the note if you want to make sure that you got it right before you save.

4. **(iPad only) Touch Save to add the clip to the note or touch Discard to delete it.**

BlackBerry

To record on a BlackBerry, follow these steps:

1. **Touch Audio Note on the menu screen.**

   Figure 5-5 shows you the screen for creating the note. Figure 5-6 shows you the information you can add to the note.

Figure 5-5: Creating an audio note.

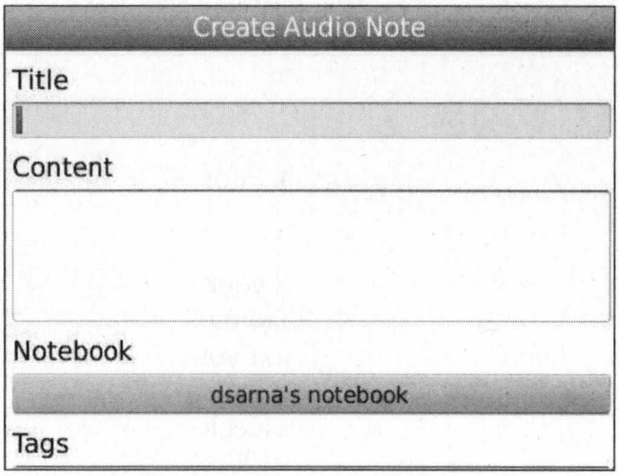

Create Audio Note

Title

Content

Figure 5-6:
Add an
audio note
title and tag.

Notebook

dsarna's notebook

Tags

2. **Touch Record.**

   The recording starts as soon as you clip the icon, so make sure that you're ready.

3. **Touch Stop when you're done recording.**

   You can play the audio back by clicking the audio portion of the note. Then you can decide whether to rerecord or save what you have.

4. **When you're satisfied with your recording, press the BlackBerry button and then press Save Note.**

   The audio is saved to the new note. You can add a title, tags, and text.

Creating Notes from Music

You can record music through the audio recording, but it will come out sounding muffled and distant. For most people, saving music as a note makes sure that you have all the music you want to listen to on every device. Yes, you can sync some of it, but if you have crossover devices, odds are that it will be easiest to save your music to Evernote so that you don't have to resync a device for your music every time you get a new phone, MP3 player, or even computer. For best results, plug a professional microphone into your device and the quality will be great.

Essentially, the best way to add a music file to Evernote is to drag and drop your music files from iTunes or your favorite music player (Songbird,

MediaMonkey, Foobar2000, TouchCopy09, or whatever music application you use on your computer) to an Evernote notebook. This method does have a few limitations, however:

✔ The maximum note size is 50MB for a Premium account and 25MB for a free account.

✔ Note size is limited by account type, and that limit applies to recordings, so keep it in mind when you start moving files over.

Music files can be large, meaning that you may save only as many music files as will fit within your note-size limit. Still, this capability is very handy, and here's how you do it:

1. **Click New Note to create a new note.**

2. **In the Finder (Mac) or Windows Explorer, go to the location where you store your music, and drag it to your Evernote account in your web browser.**

✔ The default location for Macs is the Music folder inside your Home folder. The default location for PCs is the My Music folder on the C drive.

✔ On the Android the default location for music is user music.

✔ The default location for iTunes on Mac OS X is `/Users/username/Music/iTunes/`.

✔ The default location for iTunes on Windows XP is `C:\Documents and Settings\username\My Documents\My Music\iTunes\`.

✔ The default location for iTunes on Windows Vista is `C:\Users\username\Music\iTunes\`.

✔ The default location for iTunes on Windows 7 is `C:\Users\username\My Music\iTunes\`.

After you complete this step, you can rest assured that your music is where you want it.

Creating Notes from Images

Saving images is similar to saving recording files (see the earlier section "Recording a Voice Note,"); you can save multiple images in a single note. Chapter 4 offers basic instructions on working with images on a website, which you can clip into a note, but here, I focus on individual image files.

Essentially, the best way to add an image file is to drag and drop it, but this method has limitations. As with audio notes, you can save as many files as you want to a note, but each note has a note size limitation based on your account type, so make sure that you're aware of that when you start to add images. (Check out Chapter 2 for details on your account type limitations.)

Here's how you get your cool images saved to Evernote:

1. **Click New Note to create a new note.**

2. **In the Finder (Mac) or Windows Explorer, go to the location where you store your image, and drag it to your Evernote account in your web browser.**

   Refer to Chapter 4 if you need a refresher on dragging and dropping files.

   The default location for Macs is the Pictures folder inside your Home folder. The default location for PCs is the My Pictures folder on your C: drive.

   When you complete this step, your image is in Evernote.

Saving Pictures from a Mobile Device

You can also save images taken from your cellphone camera or — with Eye-Fi Pro X2 — from any electronic camera that supports a memory card compatible with SDHC (see Chapter 19).

Taking pictures on an iPhone or iPod touch

To take and save pictures on an iPhone or iPod touch, follow these steps:

1. **Launch your Evernote app.**

2. **Create a new note, and select the Snapshot option.**

3. **Take the picture when you're ready.**

   This feature operates the same way as simply taking a picture.

4. **Click Retake or Save, depending on whether you're happy with the picture.**

   Retake allows you to try again. If you're satisfied with the picture, go ahead and save it to the note by tapping Save.

Taking pictures on an Android device

To take and save pictures on an Android device, follow these steps:

1. **Touch New Note on the menu screen.**

2. **Touch the camera icon in the top-right corner.**

   This step takes a picture.

3. **Touch Save when you're satisfied with the picture.**

   The picture automatically attaches to the note.

Mac users have the additional iSight feature for taking pictures and saving them to a note. Check out Chapter 4 for a refresher on adding camera shots.

Adding screen-shot images to a note

You probably have a million pictures that you want to save into Evernote. In this case, you can get a screen shot of an existing picture and save it. If you'd like to save an image from a screen capture, the steps are short and sweet, but (of course) they vary based on whether you use a Mac or a Windows PC.

This method works just as well for capturing screens from applications you're running as it does for saving photos you've taken.

Mac method

To create a screen shot of a picture for a new note on a Mac, follow these steps:

1. **Open the image you want to add to Evernote.**

2. **Press Cmd+Ctrl+C to create a new note with the image you want to save.**

   Drag the crosshair pointer to make a rectangle over the portion and click to create the note. Whatever is inside the rectangle will be captured in the new note.

3. **Click the note area, and add text.**

   Go wild. Add whatever text you need to help you remember what the note means and why it is important.

4. **Save the note.**

   You have a screen shot in your new note.

Windows method

To create a screen shot of a picture for a new note in Windows, follow these steps:

1. **Open the image that you want to add to Evernote.**

2. **Press the Print Screen button on your keyboard.**

   You get a screen shot of everything on your monitor (or monitors).

3. **Click New Note to create a new note.**

4. **Drag and drop your image into the note area.**

   You can drop the image in a current note the same way that you do in a newly created note.

5. **Crop the unwanted portions out of the screen shot.**

   If you want to make adjustments, you need to right-click the image and open it in a new program.

Attaching a Video

There are a couple ways to reference video files in a note. For example, you can link to Facebook, YouTube, or other media sites if you want to reference video in a note. (Check out Chapter 4 for information on clipping from the Internet.)

All users can also save video files as attachments to notes, subject to the note size limitations. Using an attachment may not be quite the same as having the item readily available on the notes screen, but it really requires only one extra click to have them play. Simply follow the steps for dragging and dropping, and you're good to go with your existing video.

Currently, a note is limited to 50MB, so it's suitable only for relatively short video clips. If you use an iPhone, you can record a short video and e-mail it directly to your Evernote account or use iTunes as the conduit. (When you sync iTunes, the video will be copied and you can drag it into a note.) For longer video, use one of the low-priced, nifty pocketcams and then transfer it via a computer to your Evernote account or use an Eye-Fi card (see Chapter 19).

It all adds up!

Although you aren't limited to how much data you can store in your Evernote account, monthly uploads are limited. Currently, free accounts are limited to 60MB a month, and premium accounts are limited to 1GB. Although that amount of storage sounds like a lot, be aware that videos eat upload capacity. Be conscious of your monthly limits.

To see where you stand with regard to your monthly upload limit, do one of the following things:

✔ On a desktop Windows PC, choose Tools⇨Account Info to see how much storage you've used and how much remains before the next cycle.

✔ On a desktop Mac, check out the bar on Current Monthly Usage. Click Account Settings on the Help menu to bring up your account details. How much of your allowance you have used and how much is available is shown under Usage. (You need an active Internet connection, as you're being connected to `www.evernote.com/User.action#summary`.)

✔ On `www.evernote.com`, log in, and click Settings. Your numbers appear in the middle of the page.

If you have limitations on e-mail size, transfer longer video from your iPhone to your computer and then to Evernote to circumvent the size limitations of e-mail. I do this often. But keep in mind that the file plus any additional info in the note still needs to be less than the note limit for your Evernote account type.

You also need an application on each computer or device that can play the file type you're storing. Evernote is your extended memory; it stores the clip, but it doesn't inherently play anything.

You can increase your note allowance for a single month by 5GB for a small fee (currently $5.00) and you can do this up to five times a year. Increases are temporary and expire at the end of the month in which you bought the upgrade, whether you've used it or not.

Reading Images and Image Recognition

One of the coolest things about Evernote is its ability to read images. If there's text in an image, including images embedded in PDFs, Evernote can read and catalog the information.

Grill shopping made easy

Evernote's image-recognition feature can simplify your life — even when you're out and about. When I was shopping for a new grill, I used my BlackBerry to photograph grills, their product descriptions, and price tags and then put all that information in a note in Evernote (see figure). If you aren't sure how to go about tagging a note, check out Chapter 8 for the most efficient way to use tags.

The note made its way into my Evernote account, and Evernote read the picture, even though I took it sideways. When I searched for *Brinkmann*, Evernote found the picture instantly, even though I inadvertently tagged the note incorrectly by leaving out the second *n* in *Brinkmann.* Because Evernote recognized the name in the photograph, the search instantly retrieved what I was looking for.

Evernote does not make images in PDFs searchable. Evernote's image recognition is performed on image files (jpg, gif, and so on). PDFs are a separate case. For Premium users, Evernote uses optical character recognition to scan PDF documents. This process is optimized for making text documents searchable.

So where are the instructions for running this cool feature? That's where the program is really neat. Image recognition is automatic. Any image you add is automatically scanned for recognition. You don't have to do anything other than add the image to your computer.

Want to remember the name of that dish you had in New York at that quaint little restaurant? Snap a picture of the menu with your mobile device, and you'll have it forever and be able to search for what you need. (For another example of how Evernote's image-recognition feature can make your life easier, see the nearby sidebar "Grill shopping made easy.")

Yes, image recognition even works on handwritten stuff, but it's limited by the neatness of the handwriting. If you can't make out what you wrote, don't expect Evernote to be able to read your writing either.

Read Chapter 8 for tips on searching Evernote.

Evernote does not run the recognition software locally over the application, but within its servers, so there'll be a delay from when you store the note until it's read. If you store a note and search for it immediately, you may not find what you just stored. Patience. A subsequent search will recognize it.

You don't need to stay online for the file to process. After you store the note, Evernote recognizes that you've added a file for recognition. That file gets queued and processed. The next time you sync your account, the local database will be updated, so a search from a web client (which synchronizes automatically) may see it first.

The amount of time it takes to process image recognition depends on file size and the load on the Evernote recognition service. Premium members' requests are processed ahead of requests from free accounts, so their files can usually be completed within a few minutes (in my experience, often in a few seconds). If you have a free account, expect it to take hours for the recognition servers to get around to indexing your documents. But hey, remember that you're getting the service free.

If you have only a paper copy of a document, simply scan it to move it over to Evernote. Chapter 6 has more details on scanning.

Chapter 6

Creating Notes from Other Media

. . . .

. . . .

*I*n this chapter, you explore applications and devices that you may not normally have thought of in connection with Evernote. But if you've ever sunk time into trying to locate an e-mail in your Inbox or in your Sent Mail folder, or you have a plethora of faxes, you know just how frustrating keeping track of everything can be. In this chapter, I tell you how to create notes from many programs, apps, and devices.

Exploring Evernote's Diversity

Information comes in many forms and from many sources. Evernote helps you get it all together. It's a repository for your useful information — the type of information you will want to refer to again.

One of the reasons Evernote is useful is because it handles diverse media, originating from diverse sources, and not just because it works with a plethora of computer and mobile types. Here are some examples of ways you can use Evernote with different media:

✔ If you're linked to a scanner, you can send the scanned document directly to Evernote as a PDF, and, if you are a Premium subscriber, Evernote's servers will make the PDF searchable for you.

✔ If you have a tablet with a tool for taking notes, you can send the notes right into Evernote.

✔ Use your mobile device to take a picture and send that photo right into Evernote to save your memories instantly — and easily find them again later.

✔ Forward or carbon-copy (cc) important e-mails and deliver them as notes, with all the power of Evernote for searching and retrieving them.

✔ Tweet to Evernote or save tweets from other people that you'd like to keep.

✔ Save information straight from your Nook or Nook Color to Evernote.

Use discretion. Evernote is for keeping important and useful stuff that you'll likely access again. It's easy to end up with too much of a good thing if you're not careful. If you signed up for lots of RSS feeds and direct them indiscriminately to your Evernote account, for example, you may find yourself with too many notes to handle — and may also exceed your monthly upload allocation. (You can click Settings to see where you stand in terms of your monthly upload allowance.)

Evernote has such a large following (more than 20 million registered users as of January 2012) that many manufacturers and developers, both of hardware and software, are eager to make their products compatible. The possibilities are exciting and almost endless, but there are still some limitations. In this chapter, I discuss how to get your information safely stored into a note.

Application users can now share notes to Facebook and Twitter via the iOS app or from Windows by pulling down Share on the menu bar and clicking Post to Facebook or Post to Twitter. By choosing to share a note, the user is making the contents of the note publicly accessible. It's a small but important update that furthers Evernote's social direction, which is discussed in greater detail in Chapter 11.

For other platforms, you can still use the old web-clipping method to get content from the site into a note.

Creating an Ink Note (Windows 7 and Mac OS X)

Chapter 5 covers how to use image recognition and how to take pictures of notes that you hurriedly scribble. If you have an app for taking handwritten notes, or a graphics tablet connected to a PC or a Mac, or a tablet supporting Windows 7, you can go one better by scribbling the note right into Evernote — no camera necessary.

Evernote for Windows lets you create an *ink note* — a note written on a graphic tablet — right inside Evernote. Click the Ink Note option and then start scribbling with your Wacom or other supported tablet. After you're done, that ink note syncs to all other versions of Evernote that you use.

You can also use the ink technology built into Mac OS X. For detailed instructions, see `bit.ly/w90a3r`.

To create an ink note on a Mac, follow these steps:

1. **If you haven't done so already, connect your tablet to Evernote.**

2. **Start writing on your tablet.**

   What you're doing in this step is working with Evernote to teach it your handwriting.

3. **Create a doodle.**

   This step is mostly for practice, but sketching something helps Evernote differentiate when you're writing and when you're drawing.

4. **Go to System Preferences and click the Ink icon.**

5. **Make sure Handwriting Recognition is set to On and select Open Ink Help.**

   You're ready to start showing Evernote what all your chicken scratching or flowing lettering really says.

Using notes in graphic (pen) tablets

You can use Evernote with most devices you can think of: PCs and Macs, mobile phones, tablets, and scanners. What's left? The Wacom pen tablet (see Chapter 19) is another unique device tightly interfaced with Evernote that enables you to write a note that goes straight into Evernote, just like scribbling in your journal.

This cool little device means that you can wake up, scribble notes, and return to sleep without worrying about losing any of your ideas. And the Wacom tablet isn't the only one out there. Do a little research to see whether you can find one that's within your budget.

WritePad

iPad users can use WritePad for iPad by Stan Miasnikov (available at `http://itunes.apple.com/us/app/writepad-for-ipad/id363618389?mt=8`). WritePad lets you take notes in your own handwriting with an iPad stylus pen or even your finger. The state-of-the-art handwriting-recognition software adapts and learns your style of writing. You can use simple gestures to select text, cut, copy, paste, and insert special characters.

WritePad has a spell checker with its own custom dictionary, a context analyzer, an auto-corrector, and a shorthand feature that fills in words and phrases you frequently use and have entered into the Shorthand Editor.

WritePad lets you save and transfer files over Wi-Fi from your iPhone or iPad to another iPhone or iPad.

Other than as described above, Ink on Mac or iOS (iPhone and iPad) and on Android devices isn't yet supported as this book goes to press. Some support is provided by third-party applications such as Awesome Note (`http://bridworks.com/anote/en/ipad/features/index.php`), which is described in the Evernote Trunk (`www.evernote.com/about/trunk`) and Notability (see `http://gingerlabs.com/` or the App Store). Sadly, it does not sync directly with Evernote. PhatPad, another option, is described in Chapter 15.

An option I use myself is Evernote's Skitch application (read more in Chapter 19) to create a note or drawing and then drag it into Evernote (Mac and iOS only).

Creating and Forwarding Notes by E-mail

Similar to the way you clip a web page (see Chapter 4), you can create an e-mail note. Evernote has made creating an e-mail even easier than clipping a web page, however, because you can have your e-mails delivered into the application as notes.

Creating an e-mail note

To create an e-mail note, follow these steps:

1. **Click on Settings on your Evernote for Web home page and write down your incoming e-mail address, which is shown under Emailing to Evernote.**

   When you created your account, Evernote generated an e-mail address for you (see Figure 6-1). If you're using a desktop version of Evernote, you can find your e-mail address as follows:

   - **Mac:** Choose Evernote⇨Account Info.

   - **PC:** Choose Tools⇨Account Info.

   - **iPhone and iPod touch:** Tap Settings⇨Evernote e-mail address.

   - **iPad:** Tap the Settings gear button at the bottom right; scroll down and tap Evernote e-mail address under Settings.

   - **Android:** Tap the Evernote menu, select Settings and scroll down until you see your Evernote e-mail address.

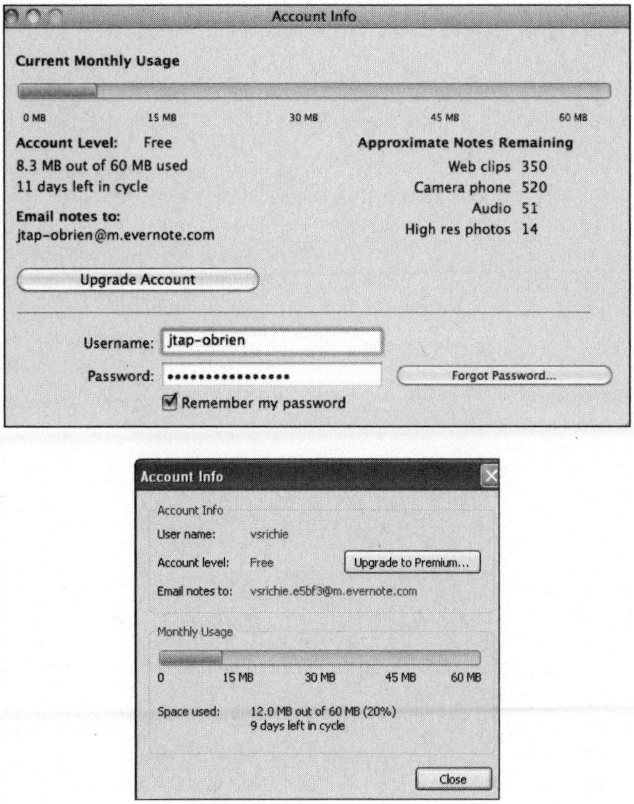

Figure 6-1:
You can find your Evernote-generated e-mail address in Account Info on a Mac (top) or a PC (bottom).

Evernote enables you to designate the target notebook and tags for an emailed note in the email's subject line. For example, if you want your emailed note to appear in your Cooking notebook, simply append @Cooking to the email subject. If you want to tag the note, just add tags to the email subject by preceding them with the hash (#) sign, like this: #recipes #vegetarian #sometag. Note that when you want to designate the target notebook and also use tags when sending or forwarding an e-mail to Evernote, you have to enter the notebook name before typing the tag names. Precede each tag with a space and a #, as shown in the preceding example. Of course, any notebook or tags added to the email's subject must already exist in your Evernote account; you can't create new ones this way.

2. **In your regular e-mail account, add the Evernote-generated address to your contacts list or white list for your regular e-mail address to be sure e-mail from Evernote is not filtered out.**

   You might create a contact called Evernote with the e-mail address associated with your Evernote account. If you're setting up your note on an iPhone, you can tap Add to Contact below the e-mail address when you look it up.

3. **Create a new e-mail, add your Evernote e-mail address, enter** Test Email **as the subject, and type** Test email **in the e-mail body. Click Send to e-mail it.**

   The first part of your subject is the title of the note. After the title, type @ and the name of the notebook where you want the e-mail to be stored (see Figure 6-2). If you'd like to add a tag as well, type # before the tag name. Even better, you can add multiple tags to the e-mail.

Figure 6-2:
Sending a
test e-mail
to your
Evernote
account.

4. **Click the Sync button to resync your account and verify that the e-mail was filed properly.**

If you want to add items, such as tags, that require specific syntax, you may have to practice a couple times to get the notes just the way you want them. The extra effort is well worth the time.

Your Evernote-generated e-mail address

Evernote generates a unique but random address for your account. For your own protection, you can't choose your own. Allowing you to do so means that Evernote would have to let you know that an address you've been craving — say, `JenniferLopez@evernote.com` or `MarcAnthony@evernote.com` — is already taken. So Evernote decided that the best solution was to provide a random e-mail address created by Evernote.

You can use one of the many free e-mail services, such as gmail.com, to create a "friendly" e-mail address and have the e-mail forwarded automatically to your Evernote e-mail address.

You're not stuck with the original Evernote-generated address. If you need to generate a different random e-mail address for some reason, click Reset Incoming Email from the browser version of Evernote Account Settings.

You can use the @ and # symbols only for existing notebooks and tags, so make sure that they're set up before you try to e-mail them. Also, always include the title of the e-mail first.

In addition, if you have the @ or # symbol as part of the name of a notebook or tag, consider changing it. If you don't, you won't be able to file the e-mails the way you'd like.

Forwarding mail to another e-mail account

You may want to have your incoming e-mail forwarded automatically to Evernote for archiving and for rapid search. Gmail and some other e-mail systems let you forward incoming mail to another address automatically, if you like. Consult the help documentation of your e-mail provider for specific instructions.

Creating a Note by Tweeting

If you're a Twitter user, you can create notes from tweets. The feature you use to turn tweets into notes is called *myEN*.

If you're not familiar with Twitter, consider it to be the highest-tech diary you can make, whether it's about you or about the things you love to follow.

If you're wondering why you'd ever need to create a note by tweeting, consider that Twitter already holds a lot of your information nicely on the Twitter site, and Evernote is where you compile information so that it's all in one place. If you tweet something and find that you want to make it searchable later, getting it into Evernote means you won't have to spend time later combing through Twitter — especially if you're like me and have trouble remembering what you did yesterday, let alone last month.

Linking your Twitter and Evernote accounts

To create tweet notes, first you need to link your Twitter and Evernote accounts. Follow these steps:

1. **Access your Twitter account at** www.twitter.com.

2. **Click Who to Follow.**

3. **Type** myEN **in the search box, and click Search (see Figure 6-3).**

Figure 6-3:
Set up your
Twitter
account
to follow
myEN.

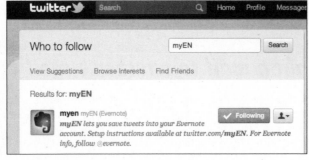

4. **Click Follow.**

   myEN reciprocates the follow and sends you a linked direct message (DM) (see Figure 6-4).

   If you've protected your Twitter account, you can still access it. All you have to do is accept myEN when it sends the follow request and then send a DM back to myEN.

Figure 6-4:
myEN's
e-mailed
DM.

5. **Click the link myEN sent you.**

6. **Go to your Evernote account and connect your Evernote and Twitter accounts.**

Tweeting your first note

After you link your Twitter and Evernote accounts, you're ready to tweet your first note. Fortunately, myEN makes that easy. All you have to do is enter your tweet in the What's Happening? text box, including @myEN anywhere in the text (see Figure 6-5). Click the Tweet button, and your note is sent straight to Evernote. Your public tweet automatically bounces over to your Evernote account and includes any pictures posted to the tweet, which will be visible to all of your followers.

Figure 6-5:
You can
tweet to
Evernote.

> What's happening?
>
> Test Tweet @myEN
>
> 100   Tweet

To send to Evernote from Twitter directly, create a DM for myEN. The tweet will be delivered as a new note.

When another Twitter user tweets something that you'd like to save to a note, you can retweet it and include @myEN to save it to Evernote.

The note appears as quickly as Twitter can process the request. Usually, processing is relatively fast, but if Twitter is experiencing heavy traffic, it can take a half hour or longer for your note to arrive.

If you want to tweet something from your mobile phone or tablet, just send the following text to 40404 (U.S. only):

d myEN and the note

You can send Twitter only simple text messages without attachments, and, of course, Twitter limits you to 140 characters.

Creating a Note by Scanning

You can create a note from scanned documents in several ways. The method you use doesn't necessarily depend on what computer you have. You must have a scanner for these steps to work, of course.

If you're not sure whether your scanner is directly supported by Evernote, navigate to www.evernote.com/about/trunk, and click Hardware.

If you have a scanner but no software (it does occasionally happen), you can find several programs that you can download and use. Make sure to read the information on them for compatibility with your computer before you download.

Scanning into Evernote on a PC

Scanning into Evernote is as varied as the number of scanners out there, but you can generally apply the following instructions to most scanners. If you're in the market for a new scanner and want to make working with Evernote as easy as possible, see the nearby sidebar "Evernote-compatible Scanners."

Before you scan your first note, you should spend some time making sure that your scanner is set up properly and ready to go.

To scan a note into Evernote, follow these steps:

1. **Find your scanner settings (located in the Control Panel or a stand-alone program).**

2. **Look for a way to configure the hardware buttons on the scanner.**

3. **Set a button to launch Evernote by pointing it to Evernote.exe (in most cases, in C:\Program Files\Evernote).**

4. **Save the settings.**

5. **Start scanning.**

   Evernote knows what to do with files sent to it from a scanner, such as image or PDF files. If Evernote isn't running, it launches and creates a new note from the received file.

Using Image Capture to scan into Evernote on a Mac

Image Capture is the technology built into Mac OS X that transfers images from your digital camera or scanner to your Mac for use in iPhoto or Automator. Maybe you're already familiar with this feature. If so, life is good, as Image Capture automatically works with whatever scanner you've set up to work with your Mac. Image Capture is a default program, so you don't have to download anything to start scanning your note.

To scan your note with Image Capture, follow these steps:

1. **Start Image Capture.**

   This free application comes with OS X and is located at `/Applications/ Image Capture`.

   If your scanner is supported and turned on, you see a window similar to the one shown in Figure 6-6.

Figure 6-6:
Image
Capture.

2. **Select the area you want to scan by dragging a rectangle around the preview of the scan.**

3. **Set the quality of the scan to B/W or Color Photo, depending on what you are scanning.**

4. **Give your scan a title.**

5. **Choose PNG or JPEG as your scan's format.**

   If you'd rather scan to PDF, keep in mind that Evernote's image recognition doesn't recognize images but makes PDFs searchable for Premium subscribers.

6. **Select Evernote as the Automatic Task.**

   This step is the key step in this process.

7. **Click Scan.**

8. **Go into your Evernote account, and check out your newest note.**

Evernote-compatible scanners

If you're looking to buy a new scanner, and you plan to use Evernote a lot, consider purchasing one that's Evernote-compatible. The following list includes some that you may want to investigate:

✔ **Fujitsu ScanSnap:** In my opinion, the Fujitsu ScanSnap is the front runner for Evernote-compatible scanners because it works very well with Evernote and allows you to choose Evernote as the destination for your scans instead of a location on one of your drives. It works with both PCs and Macs. You can find a video tutorial that guides you through using it with Evernote at www.documentsnap.com/scansnap-evernote-chocolate-peanut-butter. The video shows the Mac version, but Windows uses the same concepts.

✔ **Canon imageFormula P-150:** This Canon scanner can run up to 15 pages of scans at a time, and it still fits comfortably on a desktop. After just a few seconds of working in the optimization menu, you can make Evernote your default location for scans. From then on, everything goes into Evernote without your doing anything more than adding the page and pressing Scan.

✔ **Lexmark SmartSolution:** This little scanner from Lexmark lets you scan right into

Evernote. What's more, you can scan, convert, and post from the scanner's touchscreen without turning on your computer.

✔ **Apparent Corp. Doxie:** This ultra-portable, fully automatic scanner scans directly to Evernote. Just insert your paper, and Doxie sends your scans right into Evernote to share, sync, and access on the go.

✔ **Pathway Innovations & Technologies, Inc. HoverCam:** This scanner combines a scanner and a camera, and enables you to take high-resolution image scans in less than a second. Using the HoverCam Flex software, you can send your scans to your Evernote account with a single click.

✔ **Visioneer and Xerox:** Mobility Air and the Strobe series are scanners that come with a utility that enables you to send scans directly to Evernote's cloud-based service with just one touch, even if the computer you're using doesn't have Evernote for Windows installed.

Many other scanners are just as friendly, so keep an eye out for one that fits your needs and budget. Being Evernote-compatible is a convenience that you may not want to do without.

For more on scanners, see Chapter 19.

Whatever options you choose the first time (scanner, image type, and automatic task) are retained as your default settings.

Scanning handwritten notes

Scanners save images usually as PDF files or JPEG files. Many scanners also are bundled with software that can do optical scan recognition for you, too. None of this software will process handwritten text, but Evernote can help. If you are scanning pages of printed or handwritten notes, Evernote's image recognition servers can read them and make them searchable.

Image recognition on the Evernote servers can take time (less if you are a Premium subscriber); don't expect to discover that your scanned notes are searchable immediately after you synchronize. Eventually, though, scanned notes are read and are made searchable using the Evernote Indexing System. This system was designed to extend Evernote's search capabilities beyond text documents into media files. It goes through your uploaded files and makes any textual information searchable.

Currently the Evernote Indexing System processes images, PDFs, and digital ink documents. Evernote has stated its intention of extending the service to other media types. The index produced by the servers is delivered back to you in the form of an XML or PDF document the next time you sync. It contains recognized words, alternative spellings, associated confidence levels, and their location rectangles.

Creating a Note from Cameras by Using Eye-Fi

Today, most devices — BlackBerrys, Android devices, iPods, iPads, and Mac and PC laptops — have digital cameras built into them. The quality of the cameras varies from very good to blah, but few take pictures with the quality of a good digital camera and a high-quality lens. (See Chapter 19 for a full discussion.)

To take high-quality digital pictures, you need a quality digital camera. Until now, to get pictures into Evernote, you had to remove the card from the camera and insert it into the card reader on your computer, or you had to take along a cable and transfer files from the camera to your computer. No longer. A company called Eye-Fi has made it possible to hook up your camera with Evernote, even without hooking up the camera to your computer.

An inside look at Eye-Fi

Eye-Fi created the Eye-Fi Pro X2, a neat little Secure Digital (SD) card. This nonvolatile memory-card format developed by the SD Card Association is for use in portable devices. The SD technology is used by more than 400 brands across dozens of product categories and more than 8,000 models and is considered to be the industry standard.

SDHC (Secure Digital High Capacity, SD 2.0) is an extension of the SD standard, which increases the card's storage capacity up to 32 GB.

The Eye-Fi Pro X2 can slip into most digital cameras, enabling Wi-Fi or wireless attachment to

a host of devices that accept the SD format. It looks and works just like a regular SD or SDHC card used in digital cameras.

On top of that, the Eye-Fi card has built-in Wi-Fi to transfer photos and videos to your iPhone, iPad, Android device, or computer.

You can still use your mobile device's camera to take pictures and store them in Evernote, but with the Eye-Fi Pro X2 card, you can more easily use your much better camera for special occasions and family trips, and still load the photos to Evernote or social-media site as soon as you take the pictures.

Despite the rhyming name, Eye-Fi using Direct Mode doesn't require that you have a Wi-Fi connection for it to work, When you put the Eye-Fi X2 card in your camera, it creates its own Wi-Fi network and then uses a free app (which you can download from `http://support.eye.fi/features/direct/mobile-applications/`) to transfer pictures and other files to your computer or mobile device.

For a "hands-on" independent review of Eye-Fi, see `http://sevenbyfive.net/hardware/eye-fi-full-review`.

Preparing to use Eye-Fi mobile apps for Android

To use Eye-Fi Direct Mode on your Android device, you need to have the following items before you begin:

- ✔ Eye-Fi Center version 3.3 or later
- ✔ Eye-Fi Card with firmware version 4.5021 or later
- ✔ Computer with an Internet connection

✔ Android device running Android 2.1 or later

✔ Eye-Fi app for Android

For instructions on setting up Eye-Fi Direct Mode with an Android phone or tablet, navigate to `http://support.eye.fi/mobile-applications/eye-fi-android-app`.

Preparing to use Eye-Fi mobile apps for iPhone, iPod touch, or iPad

To use Eye-Fi Direct Mode on your iOS device, you need to be sure that you have the following before you begin:

✔ An iPhone, iPod touch, or iPad with iOS 4.0 or later

✔ Eye-Fi app for iPhone or iPad

For instructions on setting up Eye-Fi Direct Mode with an Apple iOS device, navigate to `http://support.eye.fi/mobile-applications/ios-eye-fi-app`.

Using Eye-Fi mobile apps

The Eye-Fi card comes ready to be configured in a USB reader. The software you'll need to get started is included.

1. **Follow the instructions that come with the Eye-Fi card to set up an Eye-Fi account.**

2. **Insert the Eye-Fi card into your camera.**

3. **Power on your camera.**

4. **Add the wireless networks the Eye-Fi card will use to upload your media.**

   You can add up to 32 networks, even if they're not in range, but you need IDs and passwords to add them.

5. **Choose your destinations and customize which computer and folders are used to store media. If your Eye-Fi card supports Online Sharing, you also need to customize where on the web your photos are wirelessly transferred. Link the Eye-Fi card to your Evernote account as a destination (probably as the preferred destination).**

6. Take pictures.

Eye-Fi and Evernote do everything else.

After you're done taking hundreds of pictures of baby's first step or a collection of business cards or receipts, go into your Evernote account, and start determining which photos are keepers and which ones you don't need.

Be mindful of monthly upload limits — 60MB for free accounts and 1024 MB for Premium. Digital photos, especially from higher resolution cameras, can chew up bandwidth. For example, 6MP images with low compression allow for only about 464 pictures per GB. In months when you're on vacation and may be taking lots of high-resolution pictures, you may want to increase your upload allowance, 1GB at a time, with a limit of 5 increases in one month and up to 25 additional gigabytes in a single year. You can easily check usage by clicking Settings in Evernote Web and looking at Usage. Click Increase Upload Allowance to add more bandwidth.

The notes created retain the filename assigned by the camera as the note title. As with any other note, you can retitle the note, add descriptive information, and add tags at will.

Using E-Readers with Evernote

E-readers such as the Kindle and Nook are lightweight and optimized for book reading. They are very popular and can also interface with Evernote.

Using the Kindle with Evernote (PC and Mac)

Although the Kindle and Evernote are a match made in heaven, no one remembered to tell the designers. As a result, getting information from Kindle into Evernote can be a bit of challenge because the Kindle doesn't directly support copy and paste functions, but a new free service, ClippingsConverter.com (http://clippingsconverter.com) lets you easily pull quotes and text from your Kindle and save them to Evernote as notes.

In this section, I assume that you have a basic knowledge of how to use the Kindle.

If you're new to the Kindle, *Kindle For Dummies,* by Greg Holden, and *Kindle Fire For Dummies,* by Nancy Muir (both from John Wiley & Sons, Inc.) are great books for discovering how to get the most out of your Kindle.

Clipping quotes and text using ClippingsConverter.com

Have you ever been reading a book or a newspaper on your Kindle and wanted to clip a few words to refer to later? You can do that.

Creating clippings on your Kindle depends on the generation of the device. For detailed instructions, see `http://clippingsconverter.com/kindle-clippings-faqs`.

Here's what to do:

1. **Select Add a Note or Highlight from the menu.**

2. **Highlight the content you want to clip by using the five-way controller.**

   The highlighted text has a slightly darker background than the surrounding text.

3. **Press the five-way controller to save your selection.**

   The clipping you highlighted is saved in a file called My Clipping.txt that is also accessible at `kindle.amazon.com/your_highlights`.

4. **Access your clipping file by connecting your Kindle to your computer via the supplied USB cable.**

   Click Open in response to the invitation to open the device and look for a directory named documents.

5. **Copy the My Clippings.txt file to your computer.**

6. **Navigate to `http://clippingsconverter.com/Upload` and upload the My Clippings.txt file you saved in Step 5.**

   This free site lets you publish your clippings to Evernote with one button press after you have authorized ClippingsConverters.com to access your Evernote account.

   The clippings are added as Evernote notes.

You can review your clippings later, search for words or terms you clipped, and transfer the My Clippings file to your computer. This clipping technique is a great way to capture your favorite quotations to share with others.

Creating notes directly from the Kindle

The Kindle Fire has a version of Evernote that you can download from the Amazon Apps for Android store at no charge.

For older Kindles, you can also create notes directly from the Kindle using the Kindle's experimental basic browser and Evernote's mobile application.

Be sure that your Kindle's wireless mode is on.

To create notes on the Kindle, follow these steps:

1. **Click Home on the Kindle.**

2. **Click Menu.**

3. **Click Experimental.**

4. **Click Launch Browser.**

   You might need to press OK if your wireless connection isn't turned on already. The basic browser, where you can enter any URL, appears.

5. **Type `evernote.com/m`, and press Enter.**

6. **Log in to your Kindle account.**

   You see the normal Evernote basic web view.

   Although the Evernote mobile version isn't much to look at on a Kindle, it does load up reasonably quickly. You can also search and view any existing note.

   You can navigate to the full Evernote website at `www.evernote.com`, but I don't recommend doing so because the site takes quite some time to load and is awkward to navigate on the Kindle. In my own tests, I found it impossible to use such buttons as New Note, Edit, and Delete.

7. **Press the Next Page button until you reach the bottom of the screen.**

8. **Click Quick Note.**

   The easiest way to create a quick note is to navigate to `http://evernote.com/mobile/CreateNote.action?targetUrl=%2Fmobile%2FCreateNote.action` (I suggest bookmarking this so you can find it easily).

   You see the screen shown in Figure 6-7.

Figure 6-7:
Creating a
new note
(any note)
on the
Kindle.

note from kindle	dsarna

Click to set source url... 🔒 kindle Click to add tag...

Tahoma ▾ 10 ▾ **A** ▾ **B** *I* U ╤ ≡ ≡ ≡ ≡ ≔

note typed from a kindle

9. **Type the note's title.**

10. **Move the cursor down to Body.**

11. **Type a note and/or paste what you copied.**

12. **Type Tags.**

    You can enter the first tag directly; if you want to add additional tags, click Click to Add Tag for each additional tag you ant to add.

13. **Click Save.**

Sending Kindle content to Evernote by e-mail

One huge disadvantage of the mobile Evernote website is that although you can create a new note, you're able to apply a title and tags to it only on the latest Kindle. Currently, you can't place or input any text in the main section of a note.

If you want to be able to use your Kindle to add notes to Evernote, the best method is to send notes via e-mail. Here's how:

1. **Locate your Evernote e-mail address.**

   If you're not sure what your Evernote e-mail address is, on your PC or Mac, go to www.evernote.com, and click Settings. The Evernote e-mail address is located below Emailing to Evernote.

2. **On your Kindle, log in to your online e-mail account however you usually do it from the web.**

3. **Use the Kindle web browser to compose your note.**

   The subtitle section of your e-mail is the note title, and the content of your e-mail becomes the body of the note after you open it in Evernote.

4. **Copy and paste each note into your Evernote account.**

5. **Send the e-mail to your Evernote e-mail address.**

How you organize your notes is entirely up to you. If you want to store all your notes in a single notebook, great. If you want to create a separate notebook just for the books you read on your Kindle, great. If you want to create a notebook for each book you read (which seems a little excessive!), you can certainly do that.

You can also save your `My Clippings` file. Hook your Kindle up to a computer, and simply copy the file into Evernote.

Using the Nook and Nook Color

The Nook Color is a 7-inch tablet based on the Android platform, and the Nook is a similar black-and-white version. Both models support Evernote. All Evernote features for Android tablets should work the same way on the Nook and Nook Color. See Chapter 15 for more on using Evernote with an Android device.

You can't do anything on the Nook or Nook Color involving GPS or camera features, but you can still do the other regular Evernote stuff.

Go to `www.barnesandnoble.com/w/evernote-evernote/1102538597`, and download the free Nook App for Evernote.

Nook is based on an Android platform and uses an Android app to run Evernote. It enables you to do most of your regular Evernote activities, such as syncing to your other mobile devices, creating a secured PIN lock, and using Evernote's support tools. Evernote for Android, even when it's running on the Nook or Nook Color, always requires an SD card to function.

Part III
Managing Information

The 5th Wave   By Rich Tennant

"The funny thing is he's spent 9 hours organizing his computer desktop."

In this part . . .

In Part III, you find out how to manage all of the information you want to capture, save, and retrieve. Chapter 7 gets you started by helping you customize your Evernote experience and extend Evernote to mobile devices.

Chapters 8 and 9 cover some of the most important things you'll do with Evernote: categorizing, finding, securing, and synchronizing information. Chapter 10 explains how you can use Evernote for group projects by sharing notes with others. Chapter 11 expands on the sharing theme by covering how to import and export notes and how to securely encrypt notes so that only certain people can read the contents.

In Chapter 12 you learn how to interface Evernote with other tools you use, such as Twitter, email, and RSS feeds. And, for the times you hit a bump in the road, review Chapter 13 for tips on easy ways to troubleshoot problems.

Chapter 7

Customizing Evernote at Home and Away

*I*n this chapter, you discover how to work on Evernote from your desktop and how to get yourself organized. Organization is the whole point of Evernote, of course, so I show you how to move and organize your notes.

You also find out about working from your mobile devices. I tell you about texting, taking snapshots, working with camera rolls, and recording on the different types of mobile devices.

Working with Evernote on Your Desktop

You love working on Evernote wherever you go, but what happens when you hit an area without an Internet connection or your Internet connection is down? Or perhaps you just want to do a few things and don't want the temptation of checking e-mail or surfing the Net.

In both situations, Evernote has you covered. When you signed up, you downloaded Evernote to your computer, so you can work right from your desktop or laptop even if you don't have an Internet connection.

Evernote's approach is unique. In cloud computing, nothing is stored locally; in classic desktop computing, everything is stored locally. Evernote is a unique blend. Everything is stored on Evernotes servers, but many devices on which Evernote runs also store local copies. The two copies — your local store and the notes stored on Evernote's servers — are synchronized, as discussed in Chapter 9.

If you find yourself without Internet access (by choice or not!), enjoy being on your little desert island for a while, and take some time to get yourself organized. When you return to the busy, civilized world of Internet access, Evernote syncs everything you did, so what's on your local device and what's on Evernote's servers are once again identical.

Exploring your view options

One of the first organizing tasks you'll want to tackle is personalizing Evernote on your desktop. You can change Evernote's look and feel by choosing the settings that work best for you.

When you open Evernote and go to the View menu, you see several options that you can customize (see Figure 7-1). Table 7-1 describes the different options available on the View menu.

Figure 7-1: You can change several settings on the View menu (left, PC; right, Mac).

Table 7-1	Options on the View Menu	
Command	*Shortcut Keys*	*Description*
Hide Toolbar (Mac only)	Alt+Command+T (Mac)	Hides the toolbar. (The default setting is for the toolbar to show.)
Customize Toolbar	Right-click the top toolbar and choose Customize Toolbar	Allows you to add any features of note manipulation to the bar, such as the Sync button or All Notes.

Command	*Shortcut Keys*	*Description*
List View	Ctrl+F5 (PC); Command+1 (Mac)	Provides a view of your notes in a list (see Figure 7-2). You can drag the window down to show more notes. The right side has more details on the note highlighted in the list.
Snippet View	Ctrl+F6 (PC); Command+2 (Mac)	Shows you part of the title, the note date, a few more details, and a thumbnail of your notes (see Figure 7-3).
Thumbnail View	Ctrl+F7 (PC); Command+3 (Mac)	Shows you a thumbnail of the note and the first few words of the title (see Figure 7-4). You can drag the window to the right to see more thumbnails.
Hide Search Explanation	Ctrl+F10 (PC); no shortcut for Mac	Hides the main icon toolbar — the one that helps you manipulate notes.
Hide Unassigned Tags	No shortcut for PC; Shift+Command+A (Mac)	Hides all the tags on the left side that don't have notes. The right side has more details on the note highlighted as a thumbnail.
Hide Note Info	F8 (PC); Shift+Command+I (Mac)	Hides the note's details, such as when you created the note and when you last updated it.
Go to Selected Note (Mac only)	Command+L (Mac)	Takes you to whatever note you select. It's the same thing as clicking it with your mouse.
Back	Command+[(Mac)	Returns to the previous screen.
Forward	Command+] (Mac)	Becomes enabled after you click the Back button; returns you to the screen from which you backed out.
Show Editing Toolbar (PC only)	Ctrl+F8 (PC)	Shows you the font and other editing elements for your selected note under the tag information.
Show Status Bar (PC only)	None	Shows the details about your note at the bottom of the screen (see Figure 7-5). Details include word count and characters for the notebook you have highlighted.
Show Note History (PC only)	None	Shows you the history of your notes. This feature works only for Premium members.

Personally, I like Snippet View best. It gives you the most details, even if it does show you fewer notes at a time. You can drag the window farther to the right to see more details. You can find more details on your selected note below the list.

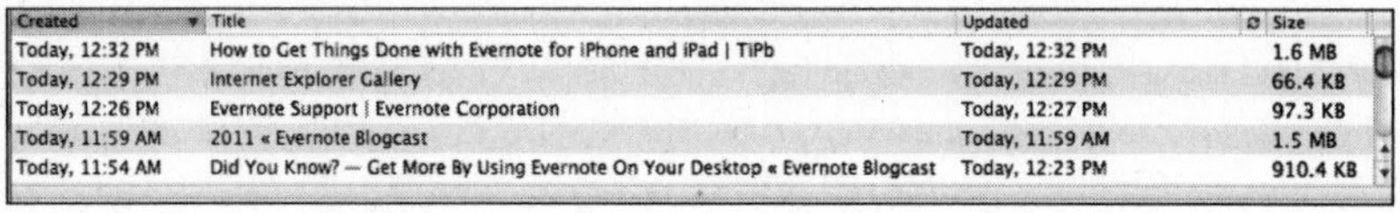

Figure 7-2:
If you like
lists, List
View is
for you.

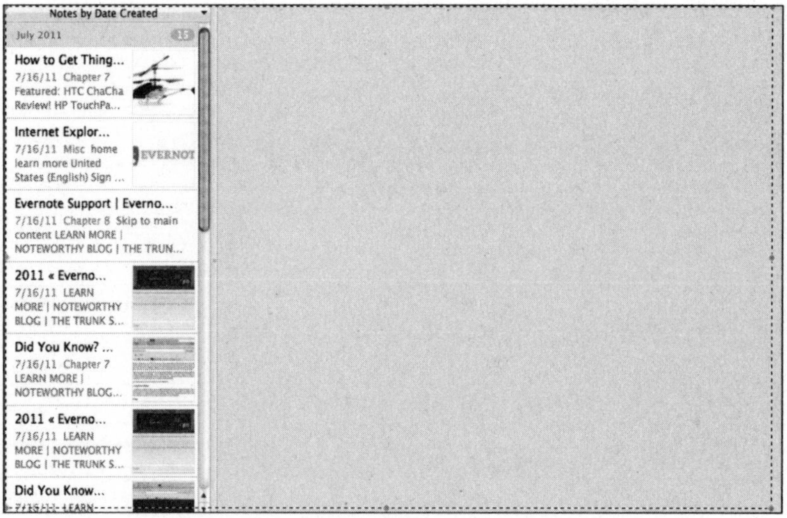

Created ▼	Title	Updated	⊘ Size
Today, 12:32 PM	How to Get Things Done with Evernote for iPhone and iPad	TiPb	Today, 12:32 PM	1.6 MB
Today, 12:29 PM	Internet Explorer Gallery	Today, 12:29 PM	66.4 KB
Today, 12:26 PM	Evernote Support	Evernote Corporation	Today, 12:27 PM	97.3 KB
Today, 11:59 AM	2011 « Evernote Blogcast	Today, 11:59 AM	1.5 MB
Today, 11:54 AM	Did You Know? — Get More By Using Evernote On Your Desktop « Evernote Blogcast	Today, 12:23 PM	910.4 KB

Figure 7-3:
Snippet
View is my
favorite
view, thanks
to all the
detail.

Notes by Date Created

July 2011

How to Get Thing...
7/16/11 Chapter 7
Featured: HTC ChaCha
Review! HP TouchPa...

Internet Explor...
7/16/11 Misc home
learn more United
States (English) Sign ...

Evernote Support | Everno...
7/16/11 Chapter 8 Skip to main
content LEARN MORE |
NOTEWORTHY BLOG | THE TRUN...

2011 « Everno...
7/16/11 LEARN
MORE | NOTEWORTHY
BLOG | THE TRUNK S...

Did You Know? ...
7/16/11 Chapter 7
LEARN MORE |
NOTEWORTHY BLOG...

2011 « Everno...
7/16/11 LEARN
MORE | NOTEWORTHY
BLOG | THE TRUNK S...

Did You Know...
7/16/11 LEARN

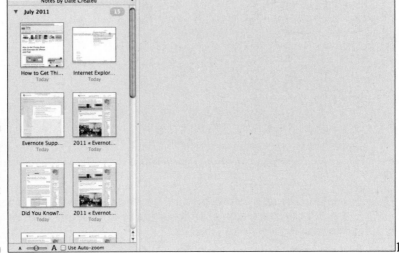

Figure 7-4:
Thumbnail
View shows
you the first
few words
of each
note.

Figure 7-5:
The status
bar lets you
see where
you stand
on word
count.

Making changes to your toolbar

Looking at the installed version of Evernote, you may be wondering whether there's any way to make the icons on the top bar appear more personal, focusing on items that you'd like to see, not just the defaults. There is, of course! The process is simple and takes you only a matter of moments. To customize the Evernote toolbar, follow these steps:

1. **Open the View menu.**

   The menu (Figure 7-6 shows the Mac version) gives you options to customize your toolbar.

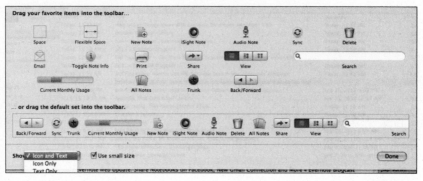

Figure 7-6:
Drag and
drop the
icons you
want to
appear on
the top bar.

2. **Drag the default setting toolbar into the toolbar area if you're satisfied with it; otherwise, drag the icons that you want on your toolbar into the toolbar area.**

3. **(Optional) Click Use Small Size to shrink your icon sizes.**

   The smaller size isn't much of a change for most computers, but it is noticeable. If you're like me and want to maximize what you see on the screen (especially your note area), you have the power to shrink those icons.

4. **Change your icon view and text (Mac only).**

   The defaults are Icon and Text, so you see both. If you want just the icons, change the setting to Show Icon Only. If you prefer text, select Show Text Only.

5. **Click Done.**

   Ideally, your toolbar is just the way you want it. As time goes by, remember that you can always adjust the appearance here if you no longer like the way your toolbar looks.

Organizing Your Notes

If you've been clipping, taking pictures, scanning, and recording without any attention to organization, your notes may look as bad as your office desk. Whether you keep your notes online in Evernote or on sticky notes around your desk, you won't be able to find what you need without organization.

A note on organizing

Moving notes isn't so difficult, but keeping everything up to date can be difficult, especially if you're concerned about attachments. Thanks to one very cool Evernote feature, you can edit with a note. Drag a Word doc into an Evernote note and then double-click it from inside Evernote to open it in Word. Now, if you make any changes to that file and click Save, the version saved in Evernote is updated, and the attachment reflects your latest changes.

One key to staying organized is using tags. Chapter 8 gives you the details on how to use tags to maximize your organization.

Lose something? All notebooks show all the notes you have saved. If you have multiple notebooks and aren't sure where you saved something, start by checking each notebook (that is, if you haven't already generated a ton of notes!).

To keep your notes organized, you can move them, copy them, and (if you're a Premium member) even refer to an older version of the note.

Moving and copying notes

Fortunately, even if you didn't start off organizing your clips, pictures, and more, you can still do so now. You can move notes from folder to folder in the same way that you move files around in Windows Explorer and the Mac Finder.

In Evernote, you can move a note in several ways:

- Drag and drop your note into the appropriate folder.
- Highlight the note, and choose Note⇨Move to Notebook (see Figure 7-7).

Figure 7-7:
You can move notes to a new folder.

Note	Format	Window	Help
Open Note in Separate Window			
Share ▶		All Notebooks – 58 notes	
Copy Note Link			
Move To Notebook ▶		Evernote	
Copy To Notebook ▶		Emails	
Move/Copy Again		Holiday Pictures	

Either way, the note moves from the original notebook into the new notebook.

To copy the note to another folder instead of moving it, choose Note⇨ Copy to Notebook.

Referring to a previous version of a note

If you're a premium member, you can check out an older version of a note. After opening the note for which you want to retrieve the older version, follow these steps:

1. **Choose Note History⇨Export.**

   Evernote retrieves the most recent version in the history.

2. **Go to your desktop Evernote, and choose File⇨Import.**

   The version of the note that Evernote exported from the history has been restored to your notebook. Be aware that it overwrites your previous version, so if you've made changes to the note, you lose them.

 If you have content that you don't want to lose, copy the content of the target note and paste it into a new note. This option saves your newest version and keeps the old one.

Using Evernote on Your Mobile Phone

Evernote has a pretty standard view that it displays on mobile devices, whether you're looking at an iPhone, Android phone, BlackBerry, Windows 7 phone, or Palm Pre or Palm Pixi. Tablets are slightly different, but the standard setup pretty much holds.

In the following sections, I offer a general discussion of each feature and point out the different functionalities of various mobile devices.

 Although the iPod touch isn't a phone, it can do almost anything that the iPhone can do, so the iPhone instructions work for the iPod touch, too.

Except for texting, the following methods save attachments to your note. When you open Evernote, you see the new note you just created from your mobile device. Attachments and their extensions are added to new notes.

Texting

If you want to text, you need your Evernote-generated e-mail address. (See Chapter 6 if you're not sure what yours is.) If your mobile device doesn't have texting, of course, you can ignore this section.

To text a note to Evernote, follow these steps:

1. **Go to the device you use for texting, and enter your Evernote-generated e-mail address.**

   Although the iPod touch doesn't come with texting, you can download a free app, such as TextNow from the App Store, that doesn't require a data package. This app lets you send pictures and text without paying a dime. You do need a Wi-Fi connection to send texts.

2. **Type** Test.

3. **Tap Send.**

After your Evernote account syncs up, you receive the nifty note that you texted to yourself.

See a recipe you want to try? Snap a photo, give a little detail, and text it right into your notes.

Adding pictures to notes

Most people have adopted their phone as their primary camera because — let's face it — people are rarely without their cellphones. This is one of the ways that Evernote really shines. If you're in the bookstore and want a book, but want to check the price online, simply snap a picture of the cover in Evernote, and voilà — you have an image when you need it.

To add a picture to a note, follow these steps:

1. **Go into Evernote on your mobile device, and tap New Note or tap the + sign on iOS devices.**

   If you have an Android phone or a BlackBerry, cut right to the chase: Tap Snapshot, and skip to Step 3.

2. **Tap Snapshot.**

3. **Take a picture.**

Just like with the regular camera feature, you have the opportunity to retake the picture if you don't like the first, second, or tenth try. You can take as many pictures as you need until you're satisfied or have used up your battery.

4. **Tap Save (Android) or Use (iOS).**

Evernote saves your photo right to your default folder. Evernote even displays the picture as soon as it's done saving the new note.

Using the camera roll

If you've already taken pictures with your mobile device, you can still send them to Evernote from your camera roll. Here's how:

1. **Go into Evernote on your mobile device, and tap the plus sign to create a new note on iOS and Windows 7. On other devices, tap the icon labeled New Note.**

2. **Tap Camera Roll, and select the desired picture.**

   You see every picture that's currently saved to your mobile device.

3. **Tap Camera Roll again, and select as many pictures as you like (up to the limit for a note of 50MB for premium users and 25MB for others) until you've posted all the pictures you want from your camera roll to your new note.**

4. **Tap Save.**

When adding images from your Camera Roll, you can choose to attach multiple images to a single note (probably up to 5 or 10) or create a note for each image. To select multiple notes, tap on the arrow in the lower-left corner of the Camera Roll note screen. If you decide to make multiple notes, the title, notebook, and tag settings associated with the note you are creating will be automatically be applied to all of the new image notes.

iPhone/iPod touch users can also highlight more than one photo at a time by following these steps:

1. **Click the iPhone Settings icon and then from the menus, select General, Location Services, and finally Evernote.**

   This mandatory step sets your geolocation, which Camera Roll is tied into, and lets you select multiple photos.

2. **Exit Settings.**

3. **Tap the Camera icon.**

4. **Tap Camera Roll.**

5. **Tap the Send To icon, hold your finger on an image until it turns white, and swipe your finger to choose your photos instead of tapping each individually. Select up to five photos.**

   Check marks appear next to all your selected pictures.

6. **When you finish selecting your photos, choose either Single Note or Multiple Notes along the bottom of the screen.**

7. **Tap Single Note or Multiple Note at the bottom of the screen.**

   As soon as you select a single note or multiple notes, Evernote loads your selected photos all into one note or into individual notes, one per picture. Pretty sweet.

   You can use two fingers to tap Camera Roll to get photo folders. You shorten the amount of time it takes you to locate your pictures if you know which folders you put them in.

Creating a voice recording

Unfortunately, the Voice feature isn't supported on the Palm Pre or Palm Pixi as of this writing. If you're using other mobile devices, however, you can create voice recordings in Evernote. Follow these steps:

1. **Go into Evernote on your mobile device, and tap the plus sign (for New Note).**

2. **Tap Voice (iPhone and iPod touch), the microphone icon (Android phone), Record (BlackBerry), or the cassette icon (Windows 7 phone).**

   You're now free to begin your voice recording.

   The iPhone and iPod touch may have a short delay, so wait for the time counter to start incrementing before you start talking.

3. **Tap Recording Tap to Stop.**

   The recording stops. You can stop your recording once and then start a new recording inside the same note if you need to. You can also tap Edit to delete notes that just don't work for you.

4. **When you're ready, save the new note.**

Chapter 8

Categorizing, Finding, Sorting, and Securing Information

*W*ith Evernote, you have several ways to get your notebook or notebooks situated for easier searching and storing. In this chapter, I give you the keys that make Evernote the one-stop shop that has made it award-winning software and the external brain for so many. After all, if you aren't organized with Evernote, what's the point? In this chapter, you find out everything you need to know to become more organized and start password-protecting your notes.

Tagging

Evernote offers several fantastic methods for organizing your notes. (See Chapter 7 for a preview of some of these tools.) Tagging is one of those many methods, and a very important one. (For more on tagging and titling, see Chapter 1.)

 The ways to tag a note are as numerous as Evernote-compatible devices and apps. Because you have so many choices in how you can tag a note, I group the types of devices and the best method of tagging for each type. Regardless of which device you're using to access Evernote, you need to look for the tag icon.

Tagging is meant to be helpful; that's why you are able to apply multiple tags to every note. However, if you tag every note with a unique label, go overboard on tagging, or add the same tags to every note, you'll find that the feature doesn't work very well. Before you begin tagging notes, consider how you want to set up your tags based on the types of notes you know you'll use most often (such as by research project, book you're reading, list or chore type, note type, and so on).

Here are a few tips I've found useful when tagging:

- **Don't overtag.** Evernote has a great and speedy full-text search engine. You usually don't need to tag words in the note's title,

- **Tag related notes with the same tag.** Tagging is most useful for making sure that notes containing different words for the same thing are retrieved together, even if only one of the terms appears in any single note. I suffer from chronic kidney disease, and I use Evernote to save information I come across that's related to the disease, which is sometimes referred to as CKD ESKD (end-stage kidney disease) or renal failure. I tag all related notes with the CKD tag.

- **Keep the tags short.** Brevity is the soul of wit, and short tags reduce typing and make it easier for you to tag as you go along.

- **Words in the document or title will be found by a search without the need to tag them specifically.** I use the tag Medical David for all prescription and lab test results because the phrase isn't in the body of the note and wouldn't be found when I just use a text search for Medical David.

- **Notes can have more than one tag**. Up to 100 tags per note are supported; 2-3 are usually adequate.

When you start typing the tag, Evernote automatically provides tags that begin with the same letters you've typed. The feature is kind of like autocorrect except that it doesn't try to replace what you've done; it just helps you along by reducing how much new material you have to type. Also, if (like me) you're a poor typist or have an inexact memory, Evernote's helpful suggestions let you click to select tags you've already saved, which prevents you from having multiple similar tags for the same thing.

Tagging on PCs, Macs, and tablets

Tagging is fundamentally similar for all platforms and is extremely useful as you dash about trying to enter notes with whatever device you're using at the time.

To create a tag for a note using a PC, Mac, or tablet, follow these steps:

1. **Highlight the note you want to tag.**

   If you're creating a new note, refer to the "Creating Your First Note" section in Chapter 3 and work your way to Step 5.

2. **Click the Tag icon or the Click to Add Tag link.**

   A small window opens as shown in Figure 8-1.

Figure 8-1:
Adding tags
to a note.

Evernote Dummies Account info	
Created: 6/18/2011 1:57 PM	Updated: 6/18/2011 3:41 PM
Click to set author...	✈ Click to set location...
https://mail.google.com/mai... ▼ 🔒	

3. **Enter your tag name.**

   Your tag name can be a new tag or an existing tag. If you create a new tag, Evernote includes it in its collection of possible tags.

4. **Click anywhere outside the area (or press Enter/Return), and save the note.**

As you create more and more tags, you may lose track of tags you've already created. The side panel labeled Tags, shown in Figure 8-2, shows you all the tags you have and how many notes are associated with each one.

Figure 8-2:
The side
panel helps
you keep
track of your
tags.

▼ TAGS
Psychic Fraud 1
Pump-and-Dump 10
Purchase Order Fraud 1
PyLog 1
Python 3
Quotes 53

Tagging on phones

Tagging is a little more difficult to do on a phone because of the smaller keys and the need to tap just the right spot to get the tag added, but in the long run, tagging keeps your notes properly organized. Don't worry. With a little practice, you'll become adept at getting the tags set up.

The tagging feature for phones is pretty universal, regardless of what device you use. Follow these steps:

1. **Tap New Note.**

2. **Enter whatever information you need, including pictures, recordings, and so on.**

3. **Tap the i, then the Tag icon, and add your tag.**

4. **To add tags, tap I and then tap the Tag button.**

   You can create a new tag or use the name of an existing tag. Tap Select from All Tags below the text box, and check the tag or tags you want to add.

5. **Complete your note and save after you've added your tag.**

Tagging is just like adding a title, but it gives you a little more information to narrow the results of your searches.

From the Home menu, you can check out all your tagging options. Tap the Tag icon, and review the notes specific to each tag.

Sorting Lists of Notes

Evernote provides several criteria by which you're able to sort a list of notes. The group of notes in question doesn't make a difference, whether you're viewing the contents of a notebook or the results of a search. Any group of notes is sorted the same way.

Sorting on PCs

To sort a group of notes in Evernote for Windows, click Notes by Created. The default setting sorts notes by the date they were created. Several other sorting options are available, including title, size, and author (see Figure 8-3). To re-sort, click the down arrow next to Notes by Created and choose another sorting option.

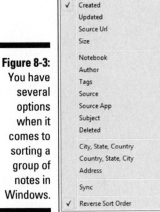

Figure 8-3:
You have
several
options
when it
comes to
sorting a
group of
notes in
Windows.

Sorting on Macs

Sorting notes in Evernote for Mac works similarly to sorting on the PC. Clicking Notes by Date Created shows the list of potential sort criteria that you can select. Your sorting options, shown in Figure 8-4, include date created, source URL, and size.

Figure 8-4:
Sort options
for the Mac
are similar
to those for
a PC.

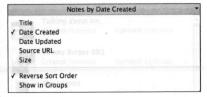

Sorting on an iPhone

When you view a collection of notes on an iPhone, you can tap the View Options button, shown in Figure 8-5, to access the various sorting options available. Your options are pretty much what you'd expect from a sorting method, such as title, dates, or sizes.

Figure 8-5:
Tapping
the View
Options but-
ton shows
you your
sorting
options on
an iPhone.

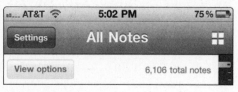

Sorting on an iPad

When you're working on an iPad, tapping View Options shows you a list of sorting options (see Figure 8-6). You can sort by note creation date or the last time notes were updated, for example.

Figure 8-6:
Tapping
View
Options
shows you
your sorting
options on
an iPad.

Sorting on an Android phone

On an Android phone, you can tap the small gray down-pointing arrow (see Figure 8-7) to the left of the list of notebooks to see the available sorting options.

Figure 8-7:
Clicking the
gray arrow
reveals the
notebooks.

Then tap the Choose Sort Order menu to see your sorting choices, including date created, title, and notebook (see Figure 8-8).

Figure 8-8:
You can
choose your
sort order
when you
tap Choose
Sort Order.

All Evernote devices have an All Notes feature, which is the easiest way to access all your notes in one place. As the number of your notes grows, you probably won't want to view them all at once, but this chapter shows you a lot of ways to search, merge, manipulate, and tag with all notes available so that you don't have to work through multiple notebooks.

Merging Notes

If you've captured notes that are similar in content from different devices that you plan to use on the same project, you can use Evernote's merge feature to put them all in one place. However, you can merge only on desktops, laptops, and Apple and Android tablets.

After you merge notes, you can't unmerge them. Make sure that merging is truly the best option.

To merge your notes, follow these steps:

1. **Open the notebook with the notes you want to merge.**

   If you're not sure what notebook contains the notes you want to merge, open All Notebooks on the side panel so that all notes are visible.

2. **Highlight the notes you want to merge.**

   To highlight the different notes on a PC, Ctrl+click. If you're working on a Mac, Command+click.

3. **Right-click the highlighted note and choose Merge Notes from the contextual menu.**

   Alternatively, instead of right-clicking, you can choose Note➪Merge Notes on either a PC or a Mac.

Conducting a Simple Search through Your Notes

You can search through your notes in many ways, some of which are more effective than others. You can start by doing a simple search by keyword, title, or tag.

A *simple search* is exactly as it sounds — pretty simple. Regardless of your device, you can quickly type a keyword or phrase and run a search over all your notes or notes in a specific notebook.

Keep these tips in mind when conducting a simple search:

✔ If you want to review the notes that include your simple search by tag, check out the Tags pane on the left side of your screen. If you have a tag called Projects, all the notes that have that tag (and only the notes that have that tag) appear when you click that tag.

✔ If you want to run a simple search on more than one topic, go to the search box, and type the word you're searching for. To find notes with both the words *Android* and *iPhone,* for example, type **Android iPhone**. Evernote returns everything that has both words in it.

 ✔ Don't type extra words in your search. Words such as *the, and, or,* and *a* will be highlighted and will be part of the search requirement. So if you want *A Comparison* between Android and iPhone, go ahead and type **A Comparison**. Evernote returns only the messages that contain all these words.

When you're done with a search, you need to clear it by either deleting the text or clicking Reset at the top right. If you go to the search box and delete all text from the search box, you see all existing notes because you have cleared the contents of the search box.

The following sections give you the tools you need to run rudimentary searches on different platforms.

Doing a simple search on a PC, Mac, or tablet

To do a simple search on a PC, Mac, or tablet, follow these steps:

1. **In the search box, type the word you want to search for.**

   Suppose that you're getting a new phone and have researched Android devices and iPhones. You can run a search on *Android* just to see what notes you've already saved by typing **Android**. Evernote displays your notes down the side of the panel for all the notes in this particular notebook that contain the word *Android*. And yes, these results include anything that has *Android* handwritten in it. So cool!

   The search isn't case-sensitive, so don't worry about including both *android* and *Android* in the search. Misspelling is another issue. If you type **Androd**, you're not likely to have any results displayed unless you also misspelled the word in your notes.

2. **Press Enter or Return.**

3. **Start reviewing the notes.**

   Evernote highlights all instances of *Android* in each note. This search includes any notes that have *Android* in the title or in the tag.

Doing a simple search on phones (iPhone and Android)

To do a simple search on a mobile device, no matter which type it is, follow these steps:

1. **Open your Evernote app.**

2. **Tap the magnifying glass at the top right of the screen.**

   The search area opens. If you haven't previously run a search, you won't have much to look at. If you have run a search, you see a list of all words that you've searched on, as well as the notebooks that you included in the search.

3. **Type the words you're looking for in the search box, and tap the magnifying glass beside the box.**

   If you type **Android iPhone,** the search returns all notes from all notebooks with the words *Android* and *iPhone,* or *android* and *iphone.*

Searching by title or tag is even easier. Follow these steps:

1. **Click the magnifying glass.**

   You return to the search area.

2. **Click the clock (title search) or the tag (tag search).**

   If you searched for *iPhone* and *Android,* the clock looks for notes with *iPhone* and *Android* in the title. If you click the tag, the tag looks for notes with *iPhone* and *Android* in the tag.

Searching on Autogenerated Attributes

Autogenerated attributes are labels placed on notes that provide information about its creation, such as the date the note was created or updated, where it was created, or in what notebook it was saved and that you don't have to enter yourself. Evernote lets you search on those autogenerated attributes.

Searching on a PC or Mac

Whether your collection of Evernote notes runs in the hundreds or thousands, the text-search feature provides instant results. In fact, almost as quickly as you can type just a few letters of your search keyword(s), Evernote filters the display to show the found notes, displays the count of how many notes it found (in the left portion of the status bar at the bottom of the screen), and highlights the keywords found.

To find words contained anywhere within the note, follow these steps:

1. **In the search box, type the words you're searching for.**

   For this example, I typed **Android iPhone**.

2. **Press Enter or Return.**

3. **If you're using a PC, go to the list on the left sidebar and click the Attributes option; on a Mac, go to the list of notes titled Notes by Date Created, and click the drop-down list.**

   Your PC lets you search by several options, as shown in Figure 8-9.

Figure 8-9: You can search by several autogenerated attributes.

On a Mac, Notes by Date Created is the default, but you can sort by several autogenerated fields, as shown in Figure 8-10.

As soon as you change what you're sorting on, the view is reordered to suit your revised preference.

Evernote creates or updates these attributes automatically every time you create or update a note.

Figure 8-10: Mac autogenerated fields.

Sorting by attributes

The attributes you can sort on are the following:

- ✔ **Title:** Sorts by — what else? — the note's title.

- ✔ **Date Created:** Sorts by date creation, is the default, and the simplest to understand.

- ✔ **Date Updated:** Sorts notes in order of the most recently updated.

- ✔ **Source URL:** Sorts by source URL. (If you return to a website often or have a few locations you're using for research, this option makes life a lot easier.)

- ✔ **Size:** Lists a range by 100KB (10KB to 200KB, 200KB to 300KB, and so on), making it easier to isolate merged notes, notes with attachments, or notes with images or recordings. Smaller notes are grouped by 10KB or solo because most people don't tend to have as many of them.

Sorting by organization

You can also sort on organization of the notes:

- ✔ **Reverse Sort Order:** The default is in descending order, so clicking this option gets the opposite order from what you usually get for a search. (It's a binary switch; every time you click, the search order is reversed.)

- ✔ **Show in Groups:** If you don't want your files grouped, you can show them all as stand-alone notes.

Searching attributes on phones

Running a search from your phone is just as easy as running a search from a desktop or laptop, and the directions are similar across the different supported phones. Follow these steps:

1. **Open your Evernote app.**

2. **Tap the magnifying glass at the top right of the screen.**

   On the iPhone, the magnifying glass is on the bottom right.

3. **Tap the drop-down arrow next to Notes Found For.**

   On an iPhone, you don't need to do this step. Skip straight to Step 4.

   The Display Options menu appears. If you want to see a List View of results, you can switch to the less detailed view. Otherwise, Snippet

View is the default; it shows you a thumbnail with the title and date. (For more on the different types of views, see Chapter 7.)

4. Tap Choose Sort Order, and select your preference.

You have a bit wider range of choices than in Step 3. Date Updated, Date Created, and Title are pretty self-explanatory. Notebook lets you search by which notebook the notes are in. City lets you sort by the location of the source of your note, which is useful if you clip articles from newspapers or magazines to read later. Country is a slightly expanded version of City.

Now you can go through your search results and find the note or notes you need.

City and Country display notes with an unknown location first, which isn't very helpful if the vast majority of your notes don't have known origins. Most notes created from mobile phones include geo-location information, which notes created on desktops do not include. If you have a notebook just with geotagged photos from a phone, or from a digital camera that captures geo-location information or uses an Eye-Fi card (see Chapter 19), it can be very helpful indeed.

After the notes are reordered as you like, you can do anything you want with them: e-mail them, print them, move them, and so on. It's just another view of your note collection.

Why can't I find it?

Sometimes it happens: You know you saved information in a note, yet a search doesn't turn it up.

What happened?

We humans have an amazing capability to intuitively abstract important information from what we see and to relate similar but not exactly identical things. Even a small child learns to recognize his or her name, for example, and understands intuitively that David is the same whether it's written in small or large letters, bold, plain, or italic typeface, and in a variety of fonts, or even in no font at all when the name is handwritten.

For computers, it's not so easy. Computers are good at making exact matches because, of course, computers are digital, which means that they store numbers only. Text is stored by assigning codes to numbers.

Early computers (using punched paper tape for input) used 69 codes and could distinguish only 69 unique characters. The ASCII format expanded that to 256. Currently, with memory costs much lower, the preferred internal coding uses an industry-standard technique called Unicode. It comes in flavors of 8, 16, and 32 bits per character. The most expansive form, UTF-32,

(continued)

(continued)

can represent 2^{31} or 2,147,483,648 unique characters, a large number that is more than sufficient to represent text in most of the world's writing systems, but that's only part of the story.

Printed and handwritten words contain a lot more information than just characters. Size, color, font, and emphasis are only a few attributes that we intuitively understand. A popular method of encoding this additional information is Rich Text Format (RTF), which nearly all versions of Evernote support, as do most word processors. Under the covers (the encoding is usually hidden), RTF surrounds text with codes. The following code

```
{\rtf1\ansi{\fonttbl\f0\
    fswiss Helvetica;}\f0\pard
This is some {\b bold} text.
    \par
}
```

will be rendered as

This is some **bold** text.

For searching, this additional coding is fine, and if there is an exact match between the text you've stored in Evernote and what you're searching for, Evernote finds it irrespective of size, font, and other attributes.

With documents that begin as pictures, it's another story because they enter Evernote either as scanned documents, which means that they're really just pictures (technically called raster images), or as various picture formats (such as JPEG, PNG, and BMP, which are all just technical jargon for describing a collection of dots). Evernote also supports and reads documents in Portable Document Format (PDF), an open standard pioneered by Adobe, in which images are stored as vector graphics, similar to PostScript. In each case, Evernote has to "read" these images by using an image recognition technology engineered by Evernote, reverse-engineer the dots into letters, and then assign the letters to the appropriate text symbols.

This process is still imperfect.

So although Evernote, in my experience, does an amazing job of reading most documents accurately, even those that started out being hand-printed, it's not guaranteed and not foolproof. If you want to be 100 percent sure that a term in a scanned document can be retrieved in a search, you can tag it yourself.

Note: Evernote doesn't give you direct access to the text that it reverse-engineers through its OCR servers. If you're unsure whether something was indexed correctly, you can enter a specific query and see whether the note pops up. Keep in mind, though, that indexing isn't instantaneous and that premium users are served first.

Doing a Simultaneous Search in Google, Bing, and Yahoo!

One of the coolest things about Evernote is that you can search any of the three big search engines and your notes *at the same time*. The feature works in Chrome, Firefox, and Safari. Here's how:

1. Open the desired search engine.

2. Click the Evernote icon next to the address.

The sign-in page appears — the page where you go to log in (see Figure 8-11). Notice the top check box? It tells you that you can search Google, Bing, or Yahoo!.

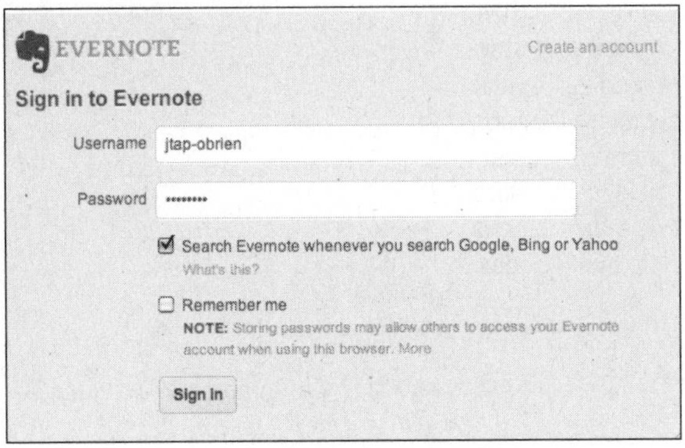

Figure 8-11: Simul- taneous search setting.

3. Check the box titled Search Evernote Whenever You Search Google, Bing, or Yahoo!.

Now whenever you run a search in one of these search engines, you see a window showing the number of notes in your notebooks that contain the same information. (Check out Figures 8-12, 8-13, and 8-14 for examples in each search engine.)

Bet you didn't see that trick coming! It's simply amazing, the number of things you can do with Evernote, and this is just about the pinnacle of getting yourself organized and comparing what you have with what you can find online.

Figure 8-12: Simul- taneous search results in Google.

Figure 8-13:
Simul-
taneous
search
results in
Bing.

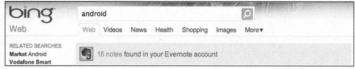

Figure 8-14:
Simul-
taneous
search
results in
Yahoo!

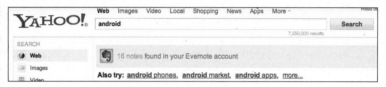

Doing an Advanced Search

An advanced search is for the times when you have an idea what you're looking for but don't remember exactly how you stated it. This type of search
relies on the use of syntax to find what you need.

Syntax means the parameters and words you use to execute a search, allowing the search to work like an Internet a search in Microsoft Word. Tag syntax
looks like this:

```
Tag: "name of tag"
```

A basic search starts at the beginning, but when you add the syntax (everything that appears up to the colon, like Tag), you free Evernote from the con-
straint of matching the exact text.

You can run these types of searches on titles or tags, your to-do list, and
many other items. Table 8-1 lists some of the most basic and useful syntax.
The best way to learn the most up-to-date syntax is to check out bit.ly/
udURQk. For now, I focus on the advanced search that you're most likely to
want to use first: the initial search.

Table 8-1	Basic Syntax
Syntax	**Description**
Intitle	Executes and returns notes based on the titles.
Tag	Executes and returns notes according to their associated tags.
-Tag	Executes and returns notes that are not associated with tags.
Source	Executes and returns notes based on the source where the notes were generated, such as e-mail, picture, or typed.
Any	Executes and returns notes based on any of the criteria entered in the search.
Todo	Executes and returns notes that have a check box.

The advanced search is nearly identical across platforms, with the method of accessing it matching the type of device, as discussed in the earlier section "Searching on Automatically Generated Attributes." For example, in the search box you could type **intitle:bills** to pull up every note within a highlighted notebook that has *bill* in the title.

Don't add punctuation if you didn't originally include it in the title. The colon is the only piece of punctuation that you should use. You also should avoid adding spaces.

Saving Searches

At first, the simple and advanced searches are enough to cover what you need for your notes. After several years, however, you'll have so many notes that you'll find yourself periodically running searches repeatedly. Well, you probably don't want to have to remember exactly what you typed two months ago. If you soon realize that you're using the same searches, saving them can really speed your ability to find notes quickly, particularly if you're running advanced searches often.

Saving Searches on PCs

To save your searches on a PC, follow these steps:

1. **Type the text you'd like as your criteria in the search box.**

This view looks just like the regular search.

2. **Click the blue arrow next to the search box.**

   After you click the arrow, a pop-up window appears, giving you the details of the search you're about to save.

3. **Click the blue magnifying glass with the plus sign in the bottom-right corner.**

4. **Enter the name you want to give the search. (See Figure 8-15.)**

Figure 8-15:
The Create
Saved
Search win-
dow.

5. **Click OK.**

   Your search is saved. Evernote stores your saved searches down the left side of the window (see Figure 8-16).

Figure 8-16:
Location
of saved
searches
(PC).

Saving Searches on Macs

To save your searches on a Mac, follow these steps:

1. **Type the text you'd like to use as your search criteria in the search box.**

2. **Press Return.**

   Figure 8-17 shows you how a search for the word *Bills* looks.

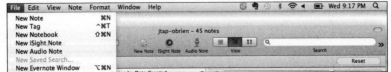

Figure 8-17:
Create a
new saved
search
(Mac).

3. **Choose File➪New Saved Search.**

   A Create Saved Search window appears for you to enter the new name of the search and also the query.

4. **Enter a new name for the search — one that you'll remember later.**

5. **Click OK.**

   The note is saved. Evernote stores your saved searches down the left side of the window (see Figure 8-18).

Figure 8-18:
Location
of saved
searches
(Mac).

Saving Searches on Phones and tablets

Tablets automatically save your searches, so the first time you run one, you've saved a search. So all you need to do is discover how to find searches. Follow these steps:

1. **Open your Evernote app.**

2. **Click the magnifying glass at the top right of the screen.**

   On an iPhone, the magnifying glass is on the bottom right.

   You see the old familiar search area. It shows you searches you've recently run on your phone as well as the notebooks that you included in the search. Better yet, even if you run a simple search, Evernote saves an advanced search.

Viewing Notes in a Text-Only View

All devices have a way to display a text-only view of your notes. This view is helpful because it maximizes the number of notes you can see.

Unfortunately, the text-only view is unavailable on the iPhone, iPod touch, and iPad. On those devices, Snippet View is the default view.

Here's how to change the view on different devices:

- ✔ **PC:** Open Evernote on your desktop. Select List View or press Ctrl+F5.
- ✔ **Mac:** Open Evernote on your Desktop. Select List View or press Command+1.
- ✔ **Android phone:** Open your Evernote app. Tap All Notes or Notebooks (if you know which notebook you need to check). Tap the menu across the top, titled All Notes or next to the notebook name. Tap the drop-down arrow below Choose Information Level, and choose List View.

Now you can see more notes at a time.

For Windows and Mac, the full note displays in the note area if you highlight it. You can maximize the number of notes you see by extending the list area to the right, shrinking the amount of a single note you see on the side.

Working with Multiple Notes

Evernote makes it possible to work with multiple notes. Working with multiple notes is extremely useful if you have notes spread over several notebooks that you need to merge into a new notebook or want to print for a meeting, export, or combine into a single note.

Tagging Multiple Notes on PCs

You can work with multiple notes at a time in several ways on a PC. Here's how you can see what is available on a PC:

1. **Open Evernote on your desktop.**

2. **Highlight the notes that you want to work with, and right-click the highlighted note.**

TIP

To highlight notes out of sequence, hold down the Ctrl key, and click the notes you want to highlight.

3. **From the contextual menu, choose what you'd like to do with the notes you have highlighted.**

You have several options, as shown in Figure 8-19:

New Note	Ctrl+N
Open Notes	Ctrl+Enter
Print Notes...	Ctrl+P
Export Notes...	
Save Attachments...	
Copy Note Links	
Email Notes...	
Delete Notes	Delete
Merge Notes	
Move Notes	▶
Tag Notes...	Ctrl+Alt+T

Figure 8-19: Menu for working with multiple notes.

- **New Note:** Creates a new note. This one really isn't for working with multiple notes, but it's there anyway, just in case you need it.

- **Open Notes** (Ctrl+Enter): Opens all the highlighted notes in new windows.

- **Print Notes** (Ctrl+P): Prints all the highlighted notes.

- **Export Notes:** Creates new files (.enex, .html, .mht, or .html) from the highlighted notes. Check out Chapter 10 for more details on exporting notes and what the different formats do.

- **Save Attachments:** Saves attachments for the highlighted notes. Check out Chapter 7 for more details on working with attachments.

- **Copy Note Links:** Saves all the links within the highlighted notes.

- **Email Notes:** Sends the notes to an e-mail account, whether personal or professional. You get something that looks like Figure 8-20, with the subject being the title of the first highlighted note. You can change the subject. Don't forget to add the e-mail address, and feel free to add a message to your notes. Check the box titled CC Me on This Email if you're sending the notes to someone else.

- **Delete Notes:** Deletes all your notes. You also can just press Delete without right-clicking for the same effect.

- **Merge Notes:** Merges your notes. See the section "Merging Notes," earlier in this chapter, for the details.

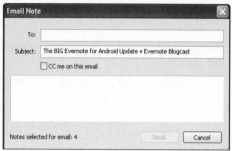

Figure 8-20:
E-mail
options (PC).

- **Move Notes:** Gives you options on where to move the files. Check out Chapter 7 for details.

- **Tag Notes** (Ctrl+Alt+T): Tags several notes at a time. This feature is the coolest of all. The pop-up window, shown in Figure 8-21, lists your tags. (For more on tagging, see the sidebar "Tagging multiple notes.")

From here, you can start working with the notes.

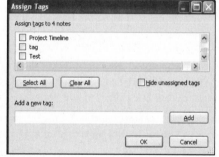

Figure 8-21:
You can
assign tags
to multiple
notes.

Tagging Multiple Notes on Macs

On a Mac, you have several ways to work with multiple notes at a time. What's available on a Mac is essentially the same stuff you get when you check out the Note menu on the menu bar.

To work with multiple notes on a Mac, follow these steps:

1. **Open Evernote on your Desktop.**

2. Highlight the notes that you want to work with, and Ctrl+click to open a contextual menu.

To highlight notes out of sequence, hold down the Command key and click the notes you want to highlight.

3. From the contextual menu, choose what you'd like to do with the notes.

Figure 8-22 shows you your options:

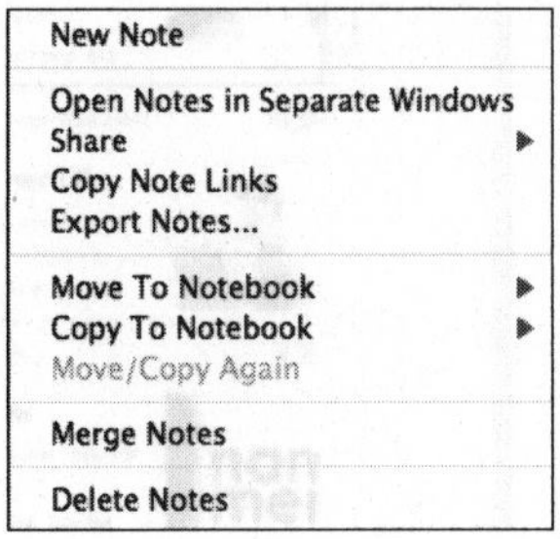

Figure 8-22: Menu for working with multiple notes.

- **New Note:** Creates a new note. This one really isn't for working with multiple notes, but it's there anyway just in case you need it.

- **Open Notes in Separate Windows:** Opens all the highlighted notes in new windows.

- **Share:** Has several different options that help you share your notes with others (see Figure 8-23). Check out Chapter 10 for more information on sharing.

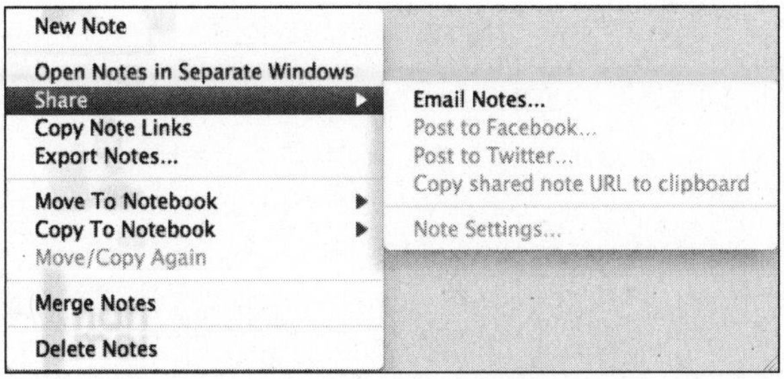

Figure 8-23: Sharing notes (Mac).

- **Email Notes:** Sends the notes to an e-mail account. You get something that looks like Figure 8-24, with the subject being the title of the first highlighted note. You can change the subject. Don't forget to add the e-mail address, and feel free to add a message to your notes. Check next to CC Me on This Email if you're sending the notes to someone else.

Figure 8-24:
Email
options
(Mac).

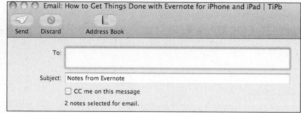

4. **Click the check box to indicate what you'd like to do with your notes.**

   You have several options:

   • **Post to Facebook:** Posts your notes to Facebook.

   • **Post to Twitter:** Posts to Twitter.

   • **Copy Shared Note URL to Clipboard:** Saves all the links within the highlighted notes.

   • **Note Settings:** Helps you set up defaults for sharing by note. You can only modify settings after you've executed one of the other elements of the Share menu that have setting options.

   • **Copy Note Links:** Saves all the links within the highlighted notes.

   • **Export Notes:** Creates new files from the highlighted notes (.enex, .html, .mht, or .html). Check out Chapter 10 for more details on exporting notes.

   • **Move to Notebook:** Gives you options on where to move the notes. Check out Chapter 7 for more details.

   • **Copy to Notebook:** Gives you options on where to copy the notes. Check out Chapter 7 for more details.

   • **Move/Copy Again:** Gives you options on where to move or copy your notes again. You can only use this option after you have executed Copy to Notebook for the highlighted notes.

   • **Merge Notes:** Merges the notes you've selected. For more details, see the earlier section "Merging Notes."

   • **Delete Notes:** Deletes the highlighted notes. You can also just press Delete without right-clicking for the same effect.

From here, you can start working with the notes.

Tagging multiple notes

If you choose to tag multiple notes at the same time on your PC or Mac, you have a few things to do after you choose the Tag Notes command:

1. **Select all the tags that you want to apply.**

2. **Choose what you'd like to do with the tags:**

   ✔ If you want to apply all your tags, click Select All.

   ✔ If you want to clear the selected tags, click Clear All.

✔ If you want to hide the tags not currently applied to the notes, click Hide Unassigned Tags.

✔ If you want to create a new tag, use the Add a New Tag: field.

3. **Click OK.**

Evernote incorporates the tags into whatever tags are already applied. (To add a tag, click Click to Add Tag.)

Printing a Combined List

Have you ever wanted to print several to-do lists so that you can easily review them at a glance (say, while running errands) but still keep those lists as separate notes for updating? It's not only easier to work with a single list of errands, but also, you can help save trees by avoiding unnecessary printing.

The obvious solution is to merge the note, but because you can't undo a merge, here's a simple workaround suggested by Brad Berens (http:// bradberens.com/2011/06/17/new-evernote-trick-combine- print-notes): Print a combined list, which still keeps the note unmerged. Just make a copy of the notes in a temporary location and merge them.

Here are the detailed steps:

1. **Create a new notebook called** Combine Lists.

   For this example, I assume that you keep all your to-do lists in a notebook called To Do to distinguish these pressing items from all the other important things that Evernote keeps for you.

2. **Select the notes in the** To Do **notebook one at a time by highlighting each note.**

3. **Right-click (PC) or Ctrl+click (Mac) the highlighted note, select Copy Note and then select the notebook you created in Step 1.**

4. **Go to the** Combine Lists **notebook; press Ctrl+A (PC) or Command+A (Mac) to select the contents; then select Merge Notes**

from the Note menu (Mac) or right-click and click Merge Notes (PC) to create a single combined note from the copy you just created.

The original notes remain untouched.

5. (Optional) Edit the combined list to make it more readable by increasing the font size and selectively highlighting.

6. Print (Ctrl+P for PC or Command+P for Mac) your list.

7. Delete the merged note so that you're ready to combine and print again at a later time.

Chapter 9

Synchronizing Notes

*O*ne of the nicest things about Evernote is that it lets you save items individually on all supported devices and then access everything you've saved on any device. The only requirement is that all your devices be in sync, which usually occurs without your needing to do anything.

In this chapter, you get the inside scoop on Evernote's synchronization mechanisms, settings, and methods. This chapter contains fewer directions than the other ones in this book. Think of this chapter as an information download so that you can better understand how Evernote works and why you can be confident of its ability to work for you.

Working with Evernote Servers

The core of the Evernote service is a farm of servers that Evernote calls *shards*. Each shard handles all data and all traffic (web and API) for approximately 100,000 registered Evernote users. Because more than 20 million people use Evernote (at this writing), the math translates into around 200 shards.

Because each user's data is completely localized to one (virtual) shard host, Evernote can run each shard as an independent island with virtually no crosstalk or dependencies. As a result, the issues on one shard don't snowball to other shards.

Despite all the precautions and redundancies, problems are bound to happen occasionally because nothing is foolproof. Evernote understands these odds and has created a web page for you to check the status of its network: `http://status.evernote.com`. If you're having issues with syncing, you may want to check out this page to make sure that it isn't something on Evernote's end.

An in-depth look at Evernote shards

Physically, a shard is deployed as a pair of SuperMicro computers with two quad-core Intel processors, 64GB of RAM, and a full chassis of Seagate enterprise drives in mirrored RAID configurations. On top of each box, Evernote runs a Linux (Debian) host that manages two Xen virtual machines. The primary virtual machine (VM) on each processor runs Evernote's core application stack: Debian + Java 6 + Tomcat + Hibernate + Ehcache + Stripes + GWT + MySQL (for metadata) + hierarchical local file systems (for file data). (You can find details on the Evernote architecture at `http://blog.evernote.com/` `tech/2011/05/17/architectural-digest.)`

All user data on the primary VM on one box is kept synchronously replicated to a secondary VM on a different box using software called Distributed Replicated Block Device (DRBD) designed as building blocks to form high-availability (HA) clusters. The system accomplishes this task by mirroring a whole block device via an assigned network. DRBD is a network-based RAID-1, which means that each byte of user data is on at least four enterprise drives across two physical servers and is backed up nightly.

Automatically Synchronizing Notes

A primary benefit of Evernote is that it enables you to access the most recent version of all your notes, regardless of what device you're using — even when you're logged in to a library computer to double-check a grocery list because your phone battery is dead and you're between chores. Evernote's ability to synchronize notes on all devices is a reliable service, and you no longer need to try to cram everything into your smartphone. This ability to have synchronized devices and a centralized network to store everything is probably the main reason why you chose Evernote in the first place.

Best of all, this automatic synchronization usually happens for you under the covers; Evernote saves you having to really do anything most of them time. Because the default setting is automatic synchronization, Evernote automatically syncs your notes on the web, regardless of your device or platform. (I discuss how to change these options in "Setting Sync Preferences," later in this chapter.)

Evernote can juggle so much information supported by so many devices because it operates on what is called a *hub-and-spoke system*. The Internet or web serves as the hub — a single, centralized location for all the data, files, and information to be stored. The spokes are your devices that you access to update your notes, and you can have as many spokes as you need.

Suppose that you have a desktop PC, a MacBook Pro, a BlackBerry for work, an iPhone for personal use, and one of each tablet. In that situation, you're really experiencing the marvel of Evernote's system. Every time you sign-in to work on your notes, Evernote syncs the hub to the spoke you're using to ensure that the next time you access your account, you have everything at your fingertips. When you're at the grocery store an hour later, the grocery list you typed on your PC is on the iPhone you're toting, even though the systems are ordinarily notorious for being pretty standoffish with each other.

Synchronization considerations

Synchronization is a fundamental and powerful feature of Evernote. Most of the time, it just happens for you automatically, and you need not give it a second thought. This section covers some considerations you need to give to synchronization.

Premium subscribers can save notebooks locally and work offline on Android devices, iPhones, iPod touches, iPads, and BlackBerry devices. All users can work offline on Mac and Windows computers.

Ordinarily, you want all of your notes to be synchronized and to be accessible from all your devices. Sometimes, though, you may want to limit synchronization. Suppose that you have a notebook dedicated to keeping your online passwords. Clearly, you don't want this information stored anywhere that it may be accidentally posted or shared. If you were to lose your cellphone, someone might find it and be able to access information in your Evernote account, especially if you chose an easy-to-guess password. No matter how secure Evernote is and no matter how good the encryption is, you may not be comfortable with posting that type of personal information live outside your own device. This is a universal truth — famously, government secrets have been compromised when laptop and cell phones were carelessly left in taxicabs. Thus you might have some information that you never want to have synchronized to your portable devices. You can choose not to synchronize a particular notebook.

Choosing whether a notebook is synchronized is a one-time election that you make when you create a notebook; it cannot be changed after you create the notebook.

If you do make the choice not to sync, this information is not synced by Evernote, and you're on your own with regard to backing up the notebook. (A USB dongle that you carry on your keychain is an obvious possibility for an alternative backup.)

Not syncing certain notebooks limits synchronization, but make sure that you understand that there's no backup on the Evernote server before you choose to create a notebook that won't be synchronized. Limiting synchronization in what Evernote calls local-only notebooks removes a primary reason for using Evernote, so consider whether it's something you actually want to do before you save local-only notebooks.

Having visited Evernote personally, I'm satisfied with its security measures. I use Evernote to sync even my most sensitive data. (I have no secret Swiss bank accounts, so I'm not overly sensitive.)

Personally, if I have especially sensitive information to protect, I use the encryption feature. When you encrypt text within a note, which is based on a passphrase to decrypt, Evernote derives a 64-bit key from your passphrase and uses this to encrypt the text. 64 bits is the longest key length permitted by U.S. export restrictions without going through a complex process to gain export approval. (See Chapter 11 for more on encrypting notes.)

Working on a note when the network is down or when you're not connected to the Internet means that whatever you work on is saved locally and synchronized after connectivity is reestablished. You may want to initiate a sync manually as soon as connectivity is reestablished to make sure that you get those changes back up to the secure Evernote servers ASAP.

Managing conflicting changes

If you edit a note from a second device before sync occurs, you may accidentally create two versions of one note. Perhaps you edit a note from your phone just as you leave work, and the phone goes dark before the sync. When you arrive home, you get on the computer and start updating the note with links without having given your computer time to sync.

I wanted to explore what can happen in such situations, and I was able to create exactly this situation and can give you a firsthand account of how I was able to deal with it. In my test, I updated a note from my Android phone and saved it. While the phone was thinking and syncing, I bounced over to my MacBook Pro and started adding information to the same note, knowing full well that the copy on my Mac was unsynced. Moments after I saved the note, I got a message from Evernote (see Figure 9-1). Evernote noticed the conflict and put the note in a new notebook called Conflicting Changes.

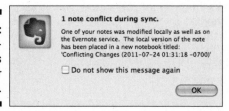

Figure 9-1:
Conflicting-
changes
error
message.

On my Notebooks menu, Evernote reminded me of my faux pas. So now I had a bit of an intentional mess on my hands that I needed to set right.

If you ever are in a situation in which you have conflicting versions of a note, here's what you do when you need to resolve the conflict:

1. **Open the note in the new `Conflicting Changes` notebook in another window.**

   Evernote gives you a date and time stamp on your `Conflicting Changes` folder (see Figure 9-2) so that you know exactly when you made the unsynced change. In Figure 9-2, notice the icon next to the notebook; it lets you know that this notebook is unlike the others (in case the extra-long title didn't catch your attention).

Figure 9-2:
This note-
book has
conflicting
changes.

2. **Go back to the notebook where the original note is stored, and open the now-synced note in another window.**

   You should now have the updated version of the note and the older version.

3. **Compare the two notes.**

   You have to do this comparison manually.

4. **Copy and paste anything that has changed into the synced version of the note.**

   You want to get rid of the conflicting note.

5. **Delete the `Conflicting Changes` folder after you're satisfied that you've resolved the issue.**

   Evernote asks you a couple of times whether you're sure you want to delete, so please do make sure that you're ready to delete before you do so.

Avoid having multiple `Conflicting Changes` folders. You can easily end up with a half dozen versions of the same note or so many conflicting notes over several notebooks that Evernote is harder for you to follow.

Check out Chapter 13 or the Evernote User Forum (`http://forum.evernote.com`) if you're still experiencing syncing issues.

Setting Sync Preferences

One of the most useful features of Evernote that runs in the background is the automatic syncing of your files. As with nearly every other aspect of Evernote, you can personalize the sync preferences to occur as often as you feel is necessary.

If you don't spend much time in Evernote, you probably aren't going to need the notes to be synced often, so the default setting is probably adequate. If you spend hours in Evernote, you probably want to sync a little more often to make sure that your changes aren't lost.

Syncing on PCs and Macs

The default setting on a PC is for the sync to occur every 30 minutes, whereas on the Mac, synchronization occurs automatically every 5 minutes. You can go into the sync preferences and make changes to the default and a couple of other settings. Here's how:

1. **Open Evernote on your computer.**

2. **On a PC, choose Tools⇨Options; on a Mac, choose Apple menu⇨ Preferences.**

   The Options dialog box appears.

3. **Click the Sync tab.**

   You see the Sync Preferences screen (see Figure 9-3).

Figure 9-3:
The Sync
tab of
the Mac
Options dia-
log box.

4. **Adjust the amount of time between syncs by clicking the up/down key. You can choose Manually or Every 5, 15, 30, or 60 minutes.**

5. **Optionally, you can also update your shared-notebook sync times individually:**

   On a PC, double-click the notebook you want to update. Figure 9-4 shows the pop-up menu and the options you have to set up the sync preferences for that notebook.

   On a Mac, you also have to update your shared notebooks one at a time by clicking the area next to the notebook you want to update (see Figure 9-5). Use the drop-down menu to select the update frequency.

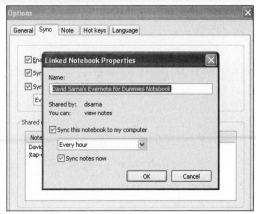

Figure 9-4:
PC note-
book sync
options.

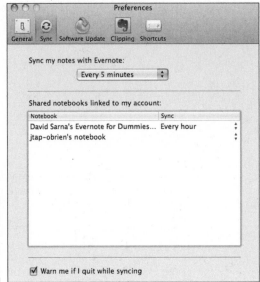

Figure 9-5:
Mac note-
book sync
options.

6. Close the window when you're done setting sync options.

On the Mac, you have the option to stop Evernote from warning that syncing is not complete when you close (refer to Figure 9-5), but to me, it would be just plain silly to clear that check box.

Evernote's default is to sync automatically when you open it, so if you usually work on one device and then open Evernote on another, you may end up spending a good bit of time waiting for the sync to complete. If you have shared notebooks linked to your account that are frequently updated, you may want to set those to update manually. If you keep Evernote open (but minimized) then Evernote synchronizes in the background while you work on other things. I leave Evernote open all the time.

Syncing on Android devices

Setting up the sync settings on an Android device is quick and easy. The default setting is every 60 minutes. If you'd like to change the setting, follow these steps:

1. Tap the Settings button on the bottom of your phone.

This button is on the phone, not the screen.

2. Tap the Settings icon.

3. **Scroll down to Sync Automatically, and select one of the times available on the menu.**

    You have five choices:

    - No Background Sync

    - Every 15 Minutes

    - Every 30 Minutes

    - Every 60 Minutes

    - Every 1 Day

    I don't recommend choosing No Background Sync because you have to sync your information manually every time you need to have your notes synced to the system (see the next section).

4. **Exit the Evernote Settings screen by pressing the back key on your phone.**

    In addition to changing auto sync (see Step 3), you have several other sync options in the Settings screen:

    ✔ **Wi-Fi Sync Only:** You can make your Android device sync only when it's hooked up to Wi-Fi.

    ✔ **Sync Data on Power-Up:** This option begins syncing your phone as soon as you turn it on — very cool if your phone battery drains while you're updating notes.

Manually Synchronizing Notes

Sometimes, you need to update your notes manually, particularly from your mobile devices. Regardless of the device you're using, you look for the same standard Sync icon. On iOS devices, the dish antenna icon shows when the device is communicating.

You don't need to sync Evernote when you access it from a web browser.

Here's how to synchronize your notes manually:

✔ **PC:** Click the sync icon or press F9.

✔ **Mac:** Click the sync icon or press Control+Command+S.

✔ **iPhone/iPod touch:** Tap the Settings button at the top of the screen and then tap Synchronize Now.

✔ **Android phone:** Press the Settings button at the bottom of your phone and then tap Sync.

✔ **Windows 7 phone:** Click the Sync button to sync all your changes.

You should use the sync feature over Wi-Fi to extend your bandwidth, which will speed the process.

Maximizing Sync Performance and Robustness

Syncing often can tie up your phone and slow everything else you're doing. It can kill your phone battery and create a lag in getting your information into the hub.

Evernote has been working diligently to ensure that syncing is not only stable and reliable, but also convenient. Synchronization is efficient on all platforms but is limited by the communication speed of the device.

Android phones and iPhones have the best syncing performance of smaller mobile devices. The latest BlackBerry release is much improved, too.

Running sync in the background means that it runs much faster. The more often you sync, the less data your phone has to transfer at a time. After all, you aren't going to be able to update 250 notebooks in the amount of time you've set for autosync (refer to "Setting Sync Preferences," earlier in this chapter).

The sync feature is also robust, which means that you're less likely to encounter problems with conflicting notes. In my example in "Automatically Synchronizing Notes," earlier in this chapter, when I wanted to force a problem, I had to move very quickly and deliberately to update my note on an Android phone and a laptop to successfully create a conflict and get the conflict message. As long as you keep your autosync set to a time limit that's reasonable for the number of updates you make in a day, you're very unlikely to have much of an issue with duplicate saved notes. (For more on this topic, see "Managing conflicting changes," earlier in this chapter.)

Sync handles really large databases. The sync feature does have a few limitations, but only a handful of users have ever hit them. If you ever do hit a limit, please write and tell me what you're doing that exceeded an Evernote limit. The restrictions are mostly theoretical and shouldn't be an issue as long as you keep autosync running in the background on your devices:

✔ **You can sync only 100,000 notes.** If you have autosync set to function daily, this limitation shouldn't be a problem. If you turned off autosync, however, you could have issues. (The average Evernote user has fewer than 5,000 notes, so in all likelihood, you won't have an issue.)

✔ **Evernote can't sync more than 250 notebooks.** That amount should be more than ample, but be aware that you don't want to get crazy with the number of notebooks you create if you sync among several devices.

✔ **You can sync only 10,000 tags.** That number is certainly more tags than I'd be able to follow, and odds are that you won't have nearly that many tags either. But that limitation is something to keep in mind when you're getting organized.

✔ **Evernote syncs up to 100 saved searches.** If this limitation is a problem, consider organizing your notebooks to reduce the number of saves you need. If you keep your bills organized, keep them in one notebook, which means that you don't need to save as many searches.

Seeing Your Sync Status

The sync status displays on the lower part of the screen on the right. The *sync status* messages let you know that the sync is working as you expected, running in the background storing your updates without your having to do a thing.

The following list describes how you know a sync happened on the various devices:

✔ **PC:** Your PC generates messages along the way and a pop-up window after every sync, manual or automatic, has completed.

✔ **Mac:** The arrows on the Sync icon rotate when a manual or automatic sync is occurring.

✔ **iPhone/iPod touch:** With Evernote active, tap the Settings button at the top of the screen. The first option in the Settings screen shows you the date and time of the last update and whether sync is occurring.

✔ **Android phone:** When you update a note, the Evernote icon appears in the top-left corner of your screen with a check mark. You can click and pull down to see which notes you have uploaded. When your Android phone is loading, it shows you a downloading bar across the bottom of your screen. When it's complete, you see Last Sync, followed by the month, day, and time.

Chapter 10

Sharing Notes and Notebooks

● ●

In This Chapter
▶ Sharing over many platforms and media
▶ Putting an end to sharing
▶ Sending notes to others
▶ Sharing over the Internet
▶ Working with RSS feeds
▶ Indexing your notes

● ●

*I*n this chapter, you find out about the many ways of sharing your notes with family, friends, and professionals. Evernote gives you numerous options, from e-mail to social media, for getting your lists, research, and pictures out to a wider audience. Evernote isn't just about organizing yourself; it's also about making it easier to share what you know with others.

What kind of application would Evernote be if it didn't let you share information with the major social networks? No more just talking about that big fish you caught. You can actually take a picture from the lake while the fish is still on the line, record an audio note to go, and post it to any number of places.

Sharing information is by far one of the most exciting aspects of Evernote. Mom always said you need to learn to share; Evernote has given you a means to do as she said.

In this chapter, I tell you what you need to know to share and publish notebooks and work with RSS feeds.

Sharing Notes on Social Networks

You can share notes on social networks in several ways, which means that you're not limited by the network or to sharing with just one friend. The only limitations are the number of networks you've joined and the number of contacts you have.

The mobile devices have different apps to accomplish different types of sharing as well. Check out Chapter 11 to see all the cool apps developed specifically for sharing Evernote on the go without having to share with the world or over e-mail.

Connecting to Facebook and Gmail

To share a note on Facebook or Google, you need accounts. After you've set up the accounts on these networks, hooking them into Evernote is fast and easy. Follow these steps:

1. **Go to your Evernote account, and click Settings near the top.**

   The Settings page, shown in Figure 10-1, appears.

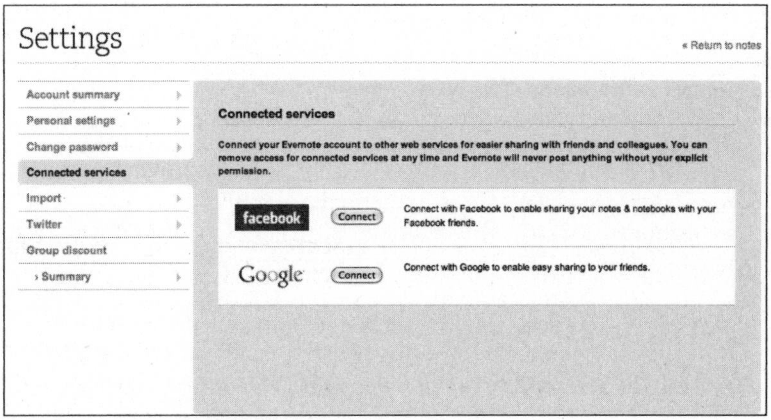

Figure 10-1:
Click
Connected
Services
to access
either
Facebook or
Google.

Settings   « Return to notes

Account summary ▸	**Connected services**
Personal settings ▸	Connect your Evernote account to other web services for easier sharing with friends and colleagues. You can remove access for connected services at any time and Evernote will never post anything without your explicit permission.
Change password ▸	
Connected services	
Import ▸	facebook (Connect) Connect with Facebook to enable sharing your notes & notebooks with your Facebook friends.
Twitter ▸	
Group discount	Google (Connect) Connect with Google to enable easy sharing to your friends.
› Summary ▸	

2. **Click Connected Services.**

3. **Next to Facebook or Google, click Connect.**

   This completes everything you need to do to connect Evernote and Google, but you have a little more work on Facebook to complete the connection there.

   The Facebook login screen appears.

4. **Enter your Facebook username and password.**

5. **Click Allow Access.**

   Now your account is linked to Facebook, and you can start sharing.

If at any time you want to unlink the account, return to the Connected Services page, and click Disconnect.

Sharing on Facebook using PCs and Macs

Sharing a note with Facebook is easy from both Windows PCs and Macs. Follow these steps:

1. **In the Note panel, highlight the note you want to share.**

2. **Click the Share button, and select Post to Facebook (see Figure 10-2).**

Figure 10-2:
You can share your notes through Facebook by using your PC or Mac.

3. **Enter your Facebook password.**

   When your Facebook page appears, you're free to update information as you normally would before sharing the link on your wall.

4. **Click the Share Link button.**

Sharing on Facebook using iPhone, iPod touch, or iPad

With just a few simple steps on your Apple mobile device, you can share any note you like. Follow these steps:

1. **Open the note you want to share.**

2. **Tap the Forward/Reply button at the bottom of the screen.**

3. **Tap Facebook.**

4. **Tap OK.**

   If you realize that you've selected the wrong note, you can tap Cancel and start again from Step 1.

5. **Enter your Facebook information.**

6. **Tap Allow.**

7. **Enter text (if you have something you want to say about the note) and then click Share to share the information or else Cancel to back out if you realize that you have the wrong note or have decided against posting it.**

   Share posts to your wall.

Sharing on Facebook using Android devices

Starting with the Gingerbread version, Android enables users to share notes and notebooks (groups of notes). Use the following steps to share notes with Facebook from Evernote for Android.

To share on Facebook from an Android device, follow these steps:

1. **Press and hold the note you want to share until the editing menu appears.**

2. **Tap Post to Facebook.**

3. **Enter your Facebook login information.**

4. **Enter any text you'd like to post with your note.**

5. **Tap Share.**

   You're done.

You may be happy to know that after you've posted your first note to Facebook, the sharing process becomes much simpler. If you're already in a note and have previously shared with Facebook, the steps for sharing your notes are much faster:

1. **Tap the Menu button on the bottom of your Android device.**

2. **Tap Post.**

   If you have a notebook that you have previously shared that you'd like to share with your Facebook friends, then go to the Sharing options for that notebook and you see a Post to Facebook button in the Share with the World section. Clicking that button takes you through Facebook sharing process described earlier.

Sharing notes with Gmail (Evernote Web only)

To configure Evernote to work with your Gmail account, follow these steps:

1. **Log in to your Evernote account.**

2. **Click the Settings link at the top of the page.**

3. **Choose Connected Services from the options on the left.**

4. **Click the Connect button next to the Google logo.**

   Google gives you the following message: "A third-party service is requesting permission to access your Google Account." Click Continue. If you have multiple accounts, it offers to connect you to the currently active account. To connect to a different account, click Sign in to Another Account.

5. **Click Continue.**

6. **Click Allow Access.**

   Google advises you that "Evernote is requesting permission to: Manage your contacts" and asks you if it's okay to perform these operations when you're not using the application. Click Allow Access to permit or No Thanks to terminate the connection.

After completing this process, Evernote Web has access to your Gmail contact lists.

To share a note, use the following steps:

1. **Click Share and, if Email is not the default, click the down arrow and select Email.**

   A window, Email note *<Title of Note>* opens. Under Sent To, start typing the email address and Evernote autocompletes it based on the matching entries from your Gmail contacts. Select the entry.

   You can send the note to multiple people by separating the addresses with commas.

2. **Click Email to send the note.**

   The e-mail is sent as soon as you click the Email button, so type a message, if you want to include one, prior to selecting the recipient(s).

Sharing notes on Twitter

Sharing a note is really easy to do regardless of what device you are using. Of course to do this, you will need to get them talking. The following sections will walk you through linking your Evernote account to Twitter, then will help you tweet a note.

One thing to keep in mind about Facebook and Twitter is that they provide links that anyone can follow. Unless you have a secure account for them, anyone will have access to the notes you post. It is best to follow common sense for posting information to social networks and keep all private notes off of these types of sites.

Linking Evernote and Twitter

Before you can tweet a note, you need to link your Evernote and Twitter accounts. Follow these steps:

1. **Access your Twitter account at** www.twitter.com.

2. **Click Who to Follow.**

3. **Type** myEN **in the search box, and click Search.**

   This step is to set up the connection between Twitter and Evernote, with myEN being the entry you need to follow.

4. **Click Follow.**

   myEN reciprocates the follow and sends you a linked direct message (see Figure 10-3).

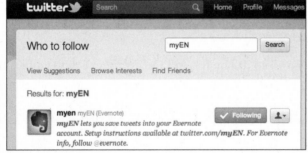

Figure 10-3:
myEN's
emailed DM.

5. **Click the link that myEN sent.**

6. **Sign into your Evernote account to connect your Evernote and Twitter accounts.**

If you've protected your Twitter account, you can still access it with Evernote. All you have to do is accept myEN when it sends the follow request and send a direct message.

Tweeting on PCs and Macs

To share to Twitter from your desktop or laptop, follow these steps:

1. **Highlight the note you want to share in the Note panel.**

2. **Click the Share button, and select Post to Twitter.**

3. **Enter your Twitter username and password.**

4. Update the text you want to tweet.

Evernote automatically inputs your note's title, so if you have something else to say, make sure that you update it before you tweet (see Figure 10-4).

WARNING!

When you post to Facebook or Twitter, you are creating a public link to a note that anyone with access to the link is able to view. On Twitter (and Facebook, to a lesser degree) anyone, not just followers, is able to view your posts, so by posting to Twitter or Facebook you are, in effect, making your note completely public. *Be sure this is your intention.*

Figure 10-4:
Tweet text.

> Share a link with your followers
>
> Spent the day out toward the desert checking out the sites.
>
> You are sharing https://www.evernote.com/shard/s97/sh/3c586bd8-40b0-40e2-b2... using Twitter's 81 [Tweet]
> URL shortener, t.co.

---

5. Click Tweet.

That's all. You get a note similar to Figure 10-5.

Figure 10-5:
Tweet success!

> Your Tweet has been posted! View it on Twitter →
>
> All done.
>
> ← Go to Twitter   Get a Tweet Button for your own website!

Tweeting on iPhone, iPad, and iPod touch

To share to Twitter from your iPhone, follow these steps:

1. Open the note you want to share.

2. Tap the Forward/Reply button at the bottom of the screen.

3. Tap Twitter.

If you realize that you've selected the wrong note or don't want to share on Twitter, you can tap No Thanks.

TIP

You need to do the next step only if you haven't ever linked to your Twitter account from your phone. If you have shared before, skip to Step 5.

4. Enter your Twitter information, and tap Allow.

5. Tap **Send to Twitter.**

6. Go to your Twitter account to check out your post.

Tweeting on Android devices

You aren't exactly out of luck if you want to share a note through Twitter on an Android device, but at this writing, it's a bit more difficult than it is on other platforms. To share with Twitter, make sure the Twitter application is installed on your Android device. Then, to share, tap the Menu button and then tap More and choose Share. Twitter is one of the options. Check out Chapter 6 for more on using Twitter to work with notes on your Android device.

 You've probably noticed another option for Windows and Macs called Copy Note URL to Clipboard. The command for this feature, located in the Share-button menu, allows you to share the note's URL easily if you just want to send a link to a friend or colleague.

Sharing Notes with SMS on Android Devices

Android users can share notes with SMS, assuming, of course, that your Android device can support SMS. Here's how:

1. Tap a note that you'd like to share.

2. Tap the Share icon.

3. Tap Other App.

4. Tap Messaging.

5. Enter the contact information.

6. Tap Send.

   Evernote sends a link to the note to the cellphone number you provide in Step 5.

Sharing Notebooks

When you share notebooks, the principles are the same as when you share notes, but sharing a notebook is a little more complicated. You need to do it either from your desktop or laptop.

Additional sharing options for Premium subscribers

Premium subscribers have an incredible advantage when it comes to sharing: They can save notebooks that others can modify. So if you have a project that you need to coordinate, and you divvy up the tasks, everyone on the project can make changes without a network. You can be at the store snapping pictures and uploading them while your friend records and loads some audio and a third friend is adding text and

websites from home. Better yet, only one of you has to be a Premium subscriber to make this happen. The Premium subscriber grants the other users access so they can start loading into the notebook.

Here's a nice bonus: Additions made by other users don't count toward the Premium subscriber's 1GB monthly allowance for uploads.

To share a notebook, follow these steps:

1. **Right-click the notebook you want to share, and choose Share Notebook from the contextual menu.**

2. **Click Start Sharing with the World or Invite Individuals to Access This Notebook.**

   The left side of the resulting Shared Notebook Settings pane (see Figure 10-6) shows you the information you need to enter to complete a universal share. The right side of the figure shows you the information you need to enter to complete individual sharing.

Only notes, and not entire notebooks, can be shared from mobile devices.

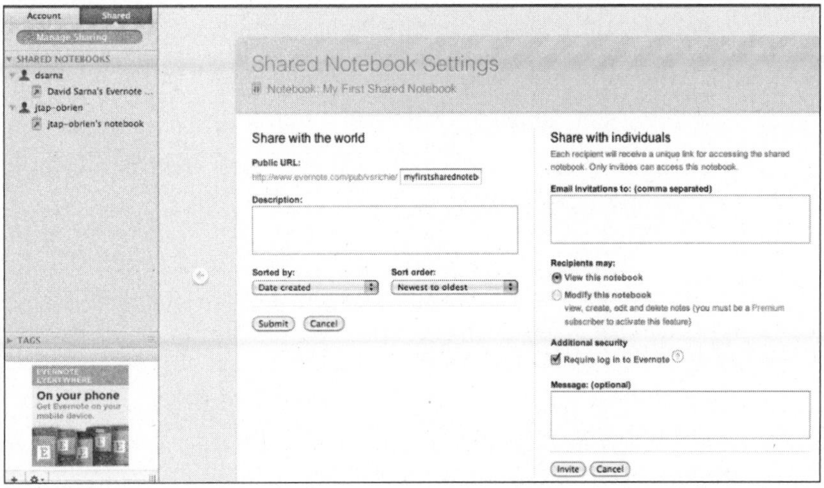

Figure 10-6: Choose public or private sharing.

3. **Depending on whether you're creating a universal share or sharing only with select people, enter the required information and then click Submit (for a universal share) or Invite (to invite specific people to access the notebook).**

That's all you have to do to share your notebook with whomever you want.

Stop Sharing

There are times when you'll want to stop sharing things. No matter what device you're using, it won't take you long to stop sharing.

Stop sharing with a PC or Mac

To stop sharing on a PC or Mac, follow these steps:

1. **Highlight the note you want to stop sharing.**

2. **Click the Shared button.**

You see a note like Figure 10-7.

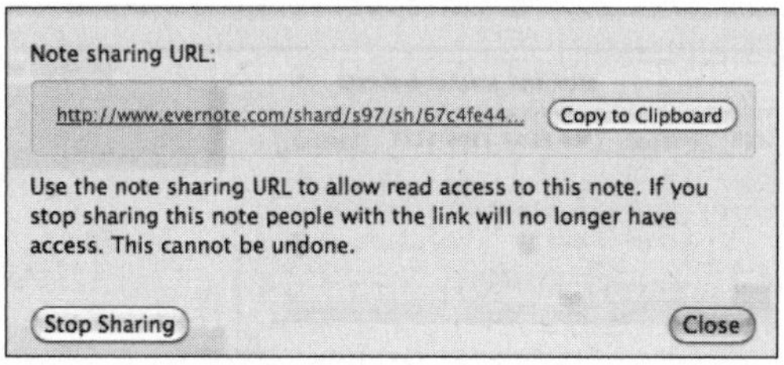

Note sharing URL:

http://www.evernote.com/shard/s97/sh/67c4fe44... [Copy to Clipboard]

Use the note sharing URL to allow read access to this note. If you stop sharing this note people with the link will no longer have access. This cannot be undone.

[Stop Sharing]   [Close]

Figure 10-7: Stop sharing.

3. **Click Stop Sharing.**

Evernote asks you to verify that you really want to stop sharing.

4. **Click Stop Sharing again.**

You can also take the long route by choosing Note⇨Share⇨Note Settings⇨ Stop Sharing, but it takes you a little longer than simply clicking the button that does the same thing.

Stop sharing on an iPhone, iPad, and iPod touch

To stop sharing on an iPhone, follow these steps:

1. **Open the Evernote app.**

2. **Tap Settings.**

3. **Scroll down to Linked Accounts and tap on it.**

   You have the choice to disconnect from both Facebook and Twitter in this area.

4. **Tap on Disconnect from Facebook or Disconnect from Twitter.**

Stop sharing a notebook

If you want to stop sharing a notebook, right-click on the shared notebook (PC) or Cmd+Click (Mac). Click Share Notebook. If the notebook is shared, the public URL is visible and you can see Edit Share and Stop Sharing links. Click Edit Share to edit how and with whom you share. Click Stop Sharing if you no longer want to share the notebook. An "Are you sure" message displays. Click OK to stop sharing and Cancel to abort.

E-mailing Notes

Sometimes you have notes that would be perfect to e-mail. Thank goodness Evernote has taken that fact into account and has made it very easy to e-mail your notes to anyone.

E-mailing using a PC or Mac

To email from a desktop or laptop, follow these steps:

1. **Highlight the note you want to e-mail in the Note panel.**

2. **Click the Share button, and choose Send by Email (Windows) or Email Note (Mac).**

3. **Enter your intended recipient.**

   If you're e-mailing someone who is in your contact list, just pull that contact up from the address book. Otherwise, type the full e-mail address.

4. **Click Send.**

   Your note is sent, and you're good to go. If you decide against emailing, just close it and all is forgotten.

To email yourself a cc of the shared note, simply check the box next to CC Me on This Email.

E-mailing using an iPhone, iPad, and iPod touch

To e-mail from your iPhone, follow these steps:

1. **Open the note you want to share via e-mail.**

2. **Tap the Forward/Reply button at the bottom of the screen.**

   A screen of choices slides up.

3. **Tap Email, and fill in the fields just like you would for any other e-mail sent from your phone.**

4. **Enter your intended recipient.**

   If you're e-mailing someone who is in your contact list, just tap the plus sign to the far right of the To box. Otherwise, type the full e-mail address.

5. **(Optional) Change the subject line and add text, if you like.**

6. **Tap Send.**

If you want to cancel, tap the Cancel button any time before you tap Send in Step 6.

E-mailing using an Android device

To e-mail from an Android device, follow these steps:

1. **Press and hold the note you want to e-mail until the editing menu appears.**

2. **Tap Email.**

   You're now on a screen where you can e-mail, just like you would from your mailing app.

3. **Enter the e-mail addresses of the intended recipients.**

   If you're e-mailing someone who is in your contact list, just start typing. Your device lists people whose addresses start with the letters you enter. Otherwise, type the full e-mail address.

4. **(Optional) Change the subject and add text, if you like.**

5. **Tap Send.**

Sharing Notebooks: The Basics

In this section, I focus on sharing notebooks from the Internet. You don't have to worry about platforms or devices to charge. As long as you have Internet access, you're good to go to share your notebooks.

To share a notebook that can only be viewed by people you invite to see it, follow these steps:

1. **Log in to Evernote.**

2. **Highlight the notebook you'd like to share, click the Share button, and choose Share Notebooks from the drop down menu (see Figure 10-8).**

   Figure 10-9 shows you the screen that appears after you choose Share Notebooks. When you share from Evernote Web, you can share more than one notebook at a time.

   To the right of Share, there is a down arrow. When you click it, it opens a small window where you can choose the sharing destination.

Figure 10-8: Getting to the Share Notebooks on the drop-down menu.

Figure 10-9: Notebook sharing panel for linking notebooks.

3. **Click Start Sharing next to the notebook you'd like to share.**

   The Shared Notebook Settings page appears, as shown in Figure 10-10. You have two choices:

   - **Share with the World:** Enables you to share your new notebook with anyone who has an Evernote account. You can even share your notebook on Facebook. All you have to do is check the Share on Facebook box in the next screen.

   - **Share with Individuals:** Enables you to share your notebook only with selected e-mail addresses (whether or not the invitees have Evernote accounts).

   Figure 10-11 shows you the information you need to provide for each type of sharing.

   If at any time you decide that you no longer want to share the notebook, repeat steps 1 through 3. There is an option to stop sharing next to notebooks currently being shared (keep reading for more details to stop sharing).

4. **If you're sharing with individuals, indicate who you're inviting to have access to the notebook, and click Send Invitations; if you're sharing with the world, click Save.**

   If you're sharing with the world, you can also modify the name of your notebook and add a description to give people basic information about the notebook. Set the notebook to sort notes by date created or date updated, and by newest to oldest or oldest to newest.

   Unless you're a Premium subscriber, invitees can only view this notebook. If the person initiating the invitation has a Premium account, you have the ability to edit as well (keep reading for more on sharing with a Premium account).

   If you are using Evernote web, you see a screen where you can check out your notebook sharing status, which indicates if the notebook is being shared, as well as see notebooks that others are maintaining (see Figure 10-12).

5. **Manage sharing of your notebooks.**

   If you want to share any of your other notebooks, the easiest way to access your notebooks at one time is through the Notebook Sharing screen.

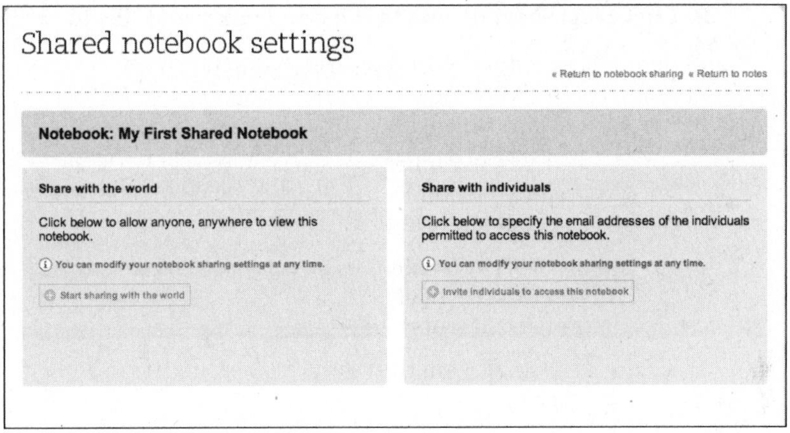

Figure 10-10:
You can
share your
notebook
publicly or
privately.

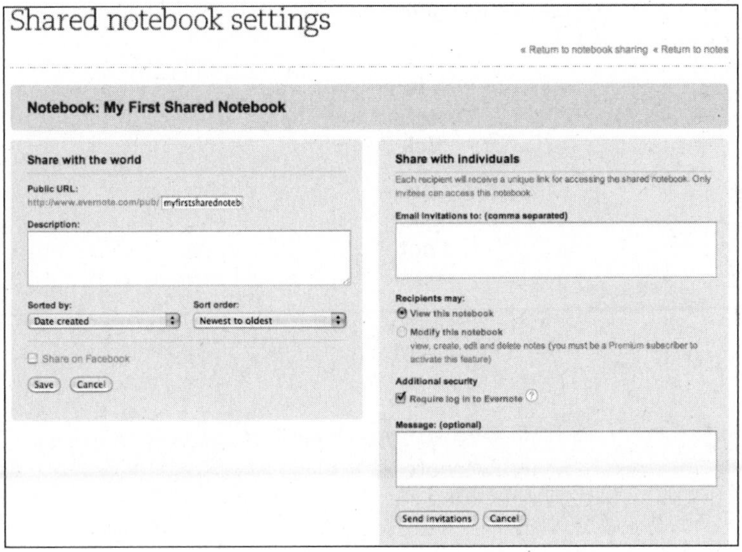

Figure 10-11:
Sharing
options
after you've
selected
your
notebook.

Sharing on mobile devices

Mobile devices may not be able to share notebooks — at least, not yet — but numerous apps enable you to share notes in real time.

To see the many apps specially designed for mobile devices, go to www.evernote.com/about/trunk, and choose your device. You can come here to see all kinds of apps for everything that can work with Evernote. Apps that you probably didn't even think were possible are just waiting for you to download them and make your life easier. Read Chapter 17 to learn more about third-party applications.

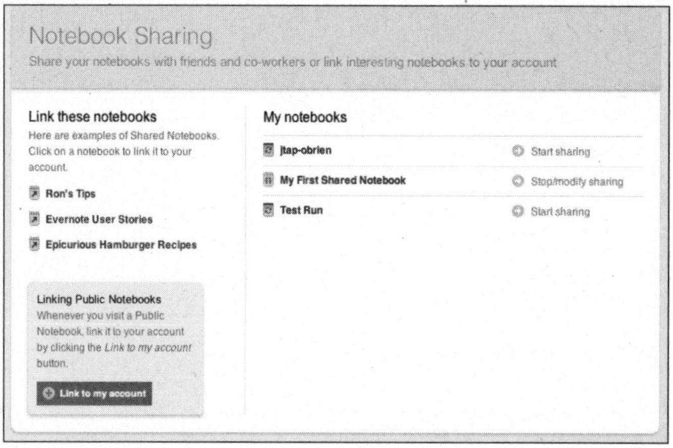

Figure 10-12:
Notebook
Sharing
manager.

Notebook Sharing

Share your notebooks with friends and co-workers or link interesting notebooks to your account

Link these notebooks
Here are examples of Shared Notebooks. Click on a notebook to link it to your account.

Ron's Tips

Evernote User Stories

Epicurious Hamburger Recipes

Linking Public Notebooks
Whenever you visit a Public Notebook, link it to your account by clicking the *Link to my account* button.

Link to my account

My notebooks

Jtap-obrien   Start sharing

My First Shared Notebook   Stop/modify sharing

Test Run   Start sharing

Publishing Notebooks on Facebook

This section helps you to publish (share) entire notebooks on Facebook. Just make sure to check Share on Facebook when you choose to share with the world (refer to Figure 10-11).

After you check the button and click Save, the notebook, along with the description, instantly appears on your Facebook Wall. Anyone that can view your Wall is able to click the link and view all notes in the notebook. Examples of notebooks you might want to share on Facebook include notebooks of recipes, movie reviews, book reviews, or other similar content.

Follow these steps to post a notebook to Facebook:

1. **In Evernote, right-click the notebook name and then choose Share Notebooks.**

2. **Click Start Sharing next to the notebook you'd like to share.**

3. **The Shared notebook setting dialog box opens. Click Start Sharing with the world.**

4. **Click Share on Facebook.**

5. **Click Save.**

6. **Click Post to Facebook.**

   The Facebook login screen, shown in Figure 10-13, appears.

Figure 10-13:
Logging in
to post a
notebook to
Facebook.

7. **Log in to Facebook.**

   You see the Post to Your Wall page, shown in Figure 10-14.

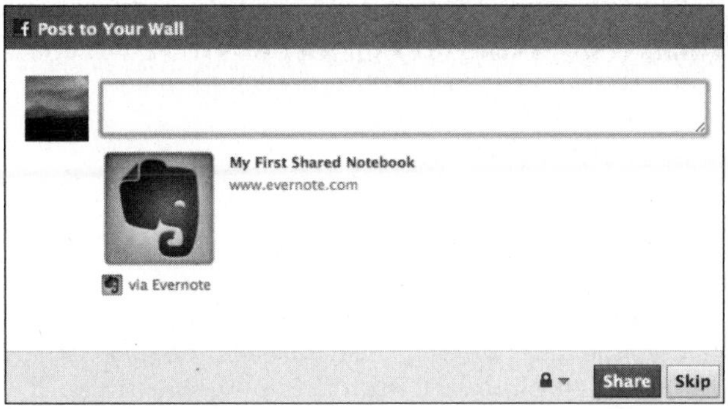

Figure 10-14:
Adding
text and
posting a
notebook to
Facebook.

8. **Enter text to describe the notebook you are sharing,**

9. **Click the down arrow to select your Facebook audience (Public, Friends, Custom, Close friends, Social, and so on) and click Share. Click Cancel to cancel sharing.**

   Your notebook is now available to your Facebook audience.

Publishing in other social media

A web app called Tarpipe can help you publish in several social-media areas at once by automating the publishing and sharing of blogs. The figure shows the four levels and the prices for each level. The basic package is free.

To share on Tarpipe, follow these steps:

1. **Go to www.tarpipe.com, and select a package.**

2. **Select your OpenID (see http://openid.net).**

   You can select your Gmail account, or you can use one of many other IDs

including Yahoo!, Blogger, flikr, mkyspace, Wordpress, and AOL. You will probably not need to create a new OpenID.

This should be enough to get you started. From here, you can select many areas in which to share your notebook, such as 23, delicious, Facebook, friendfeed, identica, jaiku, photobucket, pikeo, plurk, tumblr, twitter, and twitpic (the list changes often).

Pixelpipe (http://pixelpipe.com) is a similar idea to tarpipe. As we go to press, Pixelpipe is closed to new registrations, and a relaunch is promised for 2012.

Making Notes Available to Others on the Internet

An alternative to sharing through Facebook, Twitter, or Gmail, or directly with other Evernote users, is sharing a single note at a specific URL. The most common use of this feature is to publish a list of links on a web page. Use the following steps to create a link on the Internet:

1. **Log in to Evernote Web.**

   You can log in either on the Internet or from your desktop.

2. **Highlight the note you want to share.**

3. **Click the Share button and then choose Link.**

   Alternatively, you can right-click the note and choose Share⇨Copy Shared Note URL to Clipboard from the contextual menu.

   You see a note that acknowledges the sharing (see Figure 10-15).

After you establish a URL for your note, you can share it via e-mail, instant messaging, or any of the social-media methods your heart desires. All you need to do is get the link in one of the following ways:

✔ If you worked off your Evernote Web account, click the Share button and then choose Link. You see a message similar to the one in Figure 10-16.

✔ If you copied the link to the Clipboard, all you have to do is paste it and send. You can still check out the URL created for you when you clicked Share Link by clicking Shared right below the Title of the note you have shared. You see a screen similar to the one shown in Figure 10-17, and you can click Stop Sharing if you no longer want the note to be public.

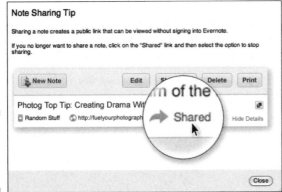

Figure 10-15:
Sharing a note from the Internet.

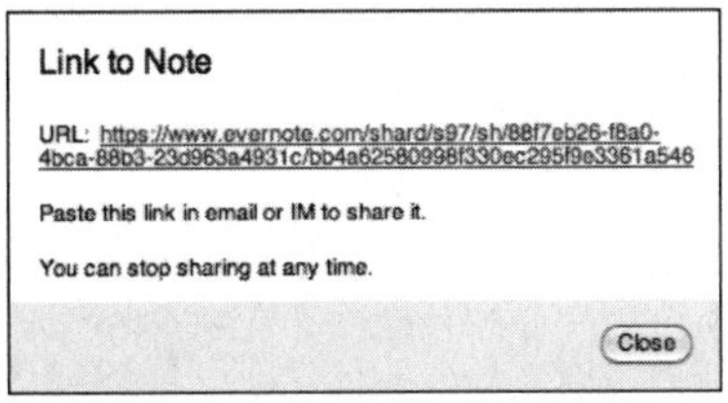

Note Sharing Tip

Sharing a note creates a public link that can be viewed without signing into Evernote.

If you no longer want to share a note, click on the "Shared" link and then select the option to stop sharing.

New Note   Edit   S...   Delete   Print

Photog Top Tip: Creating Drama Wit...   n of the
Random Stuff   http://fuelyourphotograph   Shared   Hide Details

Close

Figure 10-16:
Copying the URL for your note to share it.

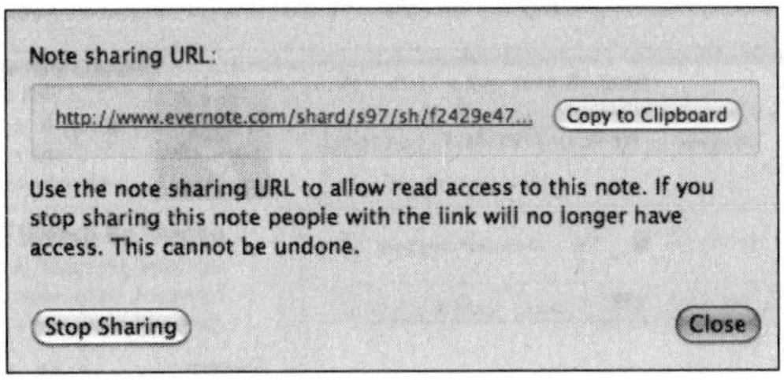

Link to Note

URL: https://www.evernote.com/shard/s97/sh/88f7eb26-f8a0-4bca-88b3-23d963a4931c/bb4a62580998f330ec295f9e3361a546

Paste this link in email or IM to share it.

You can stop sharing at any time.

Close

Figure 10-17:
Copying your URL.

Note sharing URL:

http://www.evernote.com/shard/s97/sh/f2429e47...   Copy to Clipboard

Use the note sharing URL to allow read access to this note. If you stop sharing this note people with the link will no longer have access. This cannot be undone.

Stop Sharing   Close

Creating and Using an RSS Feed

The point of an RSS feed is that you don't need to log in to Evernote to view notes in the RSS feed. By listing a note as an "item" in your RSS file, you can have the page appear in front of those who read information using RSS readers or news aggregators. RSS also enables people to easily add links to your content within their own web pages. As you make changes, additions, and updates, the RSS feed updates to reflect your changes.

Before you can create and use an RSS feed, you need to share your notebook.

After your notebook is ready to be shared, Evernote generates a URL. Here's how you obtain the URL:

1. **Log in to Evernote on your Windows PC or Mac.**

2. **Right-click the notebook you'd like to generate an RSS feed for and choose Share Notebook from the contextual menu.**

   If you haven't set up the folder to share with the world, choose Share with the World and then click Submit.

   After you've shared your notebook, your screen looks like Figure 10-18. Below the title Public URL is the URL to your shared notebook.

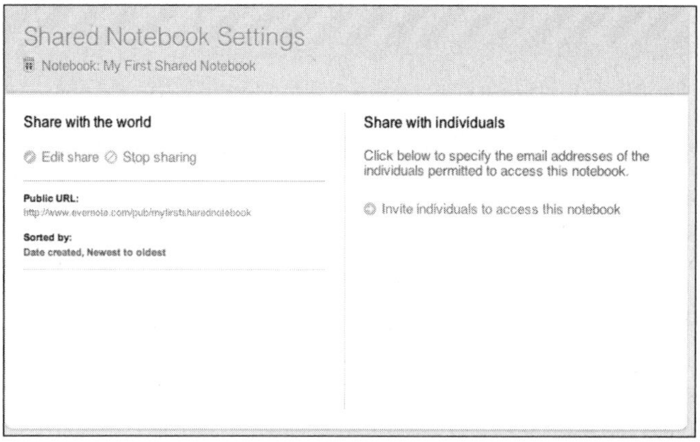

Shared Notebook Settings

Notebook: My First Shared Notebook

Share with the world

⊘ Edit share ⊘ Stop sharing

Public URL:
http://www.evernote.com/pub/myfirstsharednotebook

Sorted by:
Date created, Newest to oldest

Share with individuals

Click below to specify the email addresses of the individuals permitted to access this notebook.

⊙ Invite individuals to access this notebook

Figure 10-18:
URL for
a shared
notebook.

3. **Add /feed to the end of the URL when you enter it online.**

   The notebook is already being shared. In some browsers, the addition creates the RSS feed. In others, you see an RSS icon in the address bar or elsewhere on the screen when the RSS feed is available.

RSS is a method of distributing links to content in that you'd like others to use. No one is able to make changes to the RSS feed. The RSS feed is just a feed — a distribution mechanism for links. It's not a notebook.

You can e-mail this RSS feed to anyone you'd like to visit and view the notebook.

Chapter 11

Exporting, Importing, and Encrypting Notes

· ·

In This Chapter

▶ Importing and exporting notes

▶ Encrypting notes

· ·

*E*vernote has several useful, but perhaps less popular and underutilized features, that actually make the experience more well-rounded, safer, and enjoyable. Importing and exporting notes can be extremely helpful for storing information as an archive. Encrypting notes ensures that your private information is secured.

Exporting Notes

Evernote's three Laws of Data Protection are

✔ Your data is yours.

✔ Your data is protected.

✔ Your data is portable.

There is no data lock in Evernote. Evernote is committed to making it easy for you to get all your data into and out at any time. Evernote desktop software lets you export all your notes and content in human-readable HTML as well as in fully documented machine-readable XML format.

Evernote also offers you a full, free API that lets you access all your data via programs, as discussed in the Appendix. Evernote believes that if you're confident that you can leave at any time, you'll be confident enough to want to stay.

Exporting is a desktop or laptop activity, and it cannot be done from the smaller mobile devices or even from Evernote Web. Exporting lets you back up your notes outside Evernote so that you can retrieve them easily. Exporting is useful if you decide to stop using Evernote, when Evernote's system is down, or when you want to export notes to another application.

Exporting on a PC

You can export a single note, a notebook, or all your notes. The process is the same for each item after you select what you want to export.

To export a note, follow these steps:

1. Highlight the note or notes you want to export.

If you want to export a notebook, highlight the desired notebook. You can also right-click to see a contextual menu of choices.

2. To export a note, choose File➪Export.

To export a notebook, choose Export Notes from *Notebook Name* or from All Notebooks. If you right-clicked, select Export Notes from the contextual menu.

This step archives all your notes from that particular notebook or (in the case of All Notebooks) all your notes.

3. Change the format, if desired, and click Export.

Figure 11-1 shows the Windows version of the dialog box for exporting notes. Figure 11-2 shows the different settings you can choose to export or ignore.

You have four options for saving your archive:

- *.enex* (see the nearby sidebar) archives your information in a single file without links.

- *.html* archives your information as a single web page (.html).

- *.mht* archives your information and separates your notes but keeps them in a single file.

- Export as multiple Web Pages (.html).

Clicking the Options button lets you choose whether or not to export tags. The default is to export them. When exporting as a web archive, or multiple web pages, you have more control over what is exported. Attributes that can be optionally exported include:

- Note title

- Created date

• Updated date

• Author

• Location

• Tags

• Source URL

Unless you have a reason not to, such as a need to import to another program, you might as well export a note with all its attributes.

Figure 11-1:
Windows
export.

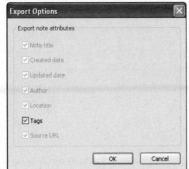

Figure 11-2:
Windows
export
options.

4. **Select a destination for saving the file and give it a name that will be easy for you to remember.**

5. **Click Save.**

   Windows lets you select where you'd like to save your archive file. Then Evernote does the rest and lets you know when the task is complete.

Exploring the .enex and .html file types

Windows and Mac offer the `.html` and `.enex` file types. Saving your archives with an `.html` extension ensures that you can always access the notes, even if you drop your Evernote account. The archive creates a link to attachments, so you don't have to worry about losing them. The price is that you lose the ability to use the optical character recognition and image recognition that makes it so easy to scan your PDFs and pictures, however, so be aware that they won't function quite the same way after they're saved outside Evernote's system.

The `.enex` file type is Evernote XML. It keeps all your information in a single file, and you don't have to follow links to access them. An `.enex` file includes everything in code, however, so unless you know XML, pretty much the only way to use it is to load it into another system.

Windows also has `.mht` and multiple-page `.html` files, which work similarly to `.html` files. Feel free to experiment with the different file types to see which one best serves your needs.

Exporting on a Mac

You can export a single note, a notebook, or all your notes. The process is almost the same as in Windows except what you select when you export.

To export a note, follow these steps:

1. **Highlight the note or notes you want to export.**

   If you want to export a notebook, highlight the desired notebook. You can also Option-click to get a contextual menu.

2. **To export a note, choose Export Notes to Archive, or to export a notebook, choose Export All Notes.**

   This step archives all your notes from that particular notebook or all your notes.

3. **Enter a name you can remember, select a location for it to save, and change the format, if desired.**

   Figure 11-3 shows the Mac version of the dialog box for exporting notes. The default name is My Notes, so if you've exported before, enter a distinct name so that you don't overwrite your older archives. You also need to specify the file type for the export:

- *.enex* archives your information in a single file without links.

- *.html* archives your information as a web page.

- *.mht* archives your information and separates your notes but keeps them in a single file.

- *multipage .html* archives your information as several web pages.

4. **Click Save when you are satisfied with the name, location, and file type.**

   Evernote does the rest and lets you know when the task is complete.

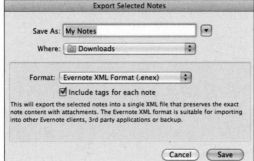

Figure 11-3:
Setting
export
options on
a Mac.

Importing into Evernote

You can re-import any archived `.enex` file that you created into any Evernote desktop client into the same or another account.

To import an `.enex` archive on a PC, follow these steps:

1. **Choose File⇨Import⇨Evernote Export Files.**

   A pop-up window appears.

2. **Browse to the `.enex` file you'd like to import.**

3. **(Optional) Import the tags included in your archive file by selecting or deselecting Import Note Tags.**

4. **Click Open.**

You can import Microsoft OneNote archives the same way. Simply choose File⇨Import⇨Microsoft OneNote in Step 1.

To import an .enex archive on a Mac, follow these steps:

1. **Click File⇨Import Notes for Archive.**

   A pop-up window appears.

2. **Browse to the archived file, and click Open.**

   You can double-click the file to start it. If you'd like to include tags, click the box at the bottom of the pop-up window called Import Tags.

   The import process begins, and the notes are initially placed in a temporary notebook. A dialog box informs you of this temporary location and gives you the chance to add the notes to a synchronized notebook.

Chapter 21, which is intended primarily for developers, offers additional details on the .enex format.

Protecting Information through Encryption

Security and privacy are important concerns when you're working with Evernote, which contains all your valuable information. In addition to the security features of Evernote described in Table 2-1 in Chapter 2, you have the ability to encrypt your own notes, making it easier to protect billing information, bank and credit cards, or your tax information.

The process and the mechanics are very similar on Windows PCs and Macs, so I discuss the subject as a whole and let you know when the steps are different.

Figure 11-4 shows an example note that you may want to encrypt. Here's what you need to do:

1. **Highlight the text to encrypt.**

2. **Right-click the highlighted text, and choose Encrypt Selected Text from the contextual menu.**

   Alternatively, press Ctrl+Shift+X (Windows) or Control+click (Mac) and choose Encrypt Selected text.

   The Note Encryption dialog box appears.

3. **Enter an encryption passphrase, verify it, and click OK (see Figure 11-5).**

Use the hint option if you're like me and at risk of forgetting the pass-phrase. Evernote can't recover your passphrase, so I strongly recommend that you use this feature in case you don't remember your passphrase when you need to get into the note.

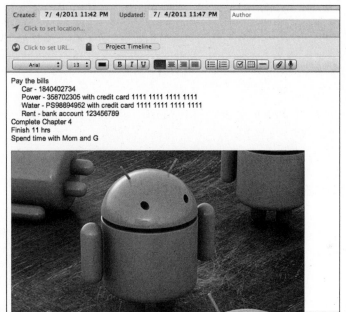

Figure 11-4:
A note
before text
encryption.

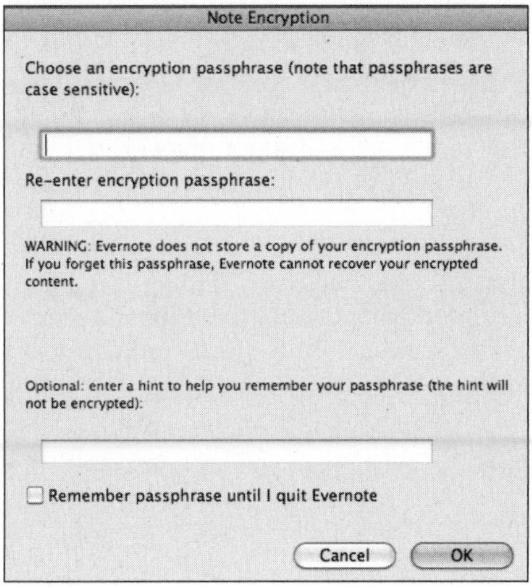

Figure 11-5:
Passphrase
and options.

Your text is now encrypted and looks something like Figure 11-6.

Complete Chapter 4
Finish 11 hrs
Spend time with Mom and G

Figure 11-6:
Successful
encryption.

To see the encrypted text, click the encrypted text and then click Show Encrypted Text. To remove encryption, click on the encrypted selection and click Decrypt Text Permanently. (See Figure 11-7.)

Figure 11-7:
Removing
encryption.

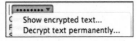

Show encrypted text...
Decrypt text permanently...

Evernote does *not* store your password and can't recover it. If you forget it, you can't access the text if you close out of Evernote. Write down your password!

Use a passphrase that you can remember easily. I like to save passphrases to a spreadsheet, but this method may not be the best one for you. You don't want to save your password as a note because that would defeat the purpose of encrypting it.

PIN lock

Premium subscribers who use Apple (IOS) and Android devices can now lock the Evernote app with a personal identification number (PIN). Whenever you return to the app, you're asked to enter your code. A PIN lock is a great option if you share your phone or tablet with others and want to keep them from accessing your notes. One of the cool things about this feature is that you can still create quick notes via the widget (a mini-App in Android devices that lives on your home screen) even when the app is locked; you just won't be able to view or search your notes until you enter your PIN.

You can set up PIN Lock in the application settings. To change or disable the PIN, return to the PIN Lock screen, and re-enter the PIN. If you mistype your PIN three times, you'll be asked to enter your password.

At this writing, the PIN Lock feature is exclusive to Android and IOS devices; perhaps it will be extended to other platforms in the future.

Chapter 12

Moving from Other Products and Interfacing with Your World

*E*vernote works with many applications, not just many devices and platforms. Trying to figure out the many ways of interfacing with Evernote can be overwhelming. In this chapter, I focus on what you need to do to set up other applications you use to interface with Evernote.

Interfacing with Twitter

Twitter and Evernote are very much in sync with each other. You can share from Twitter to Evernote or from Evernote to Twitter. You can even capture notes from tweets written by people you're following on Twitter.

Before you can have Evernote and Twitter interact, you need to set up accounts in each service. I'm assuming that you've already set up an Evernote account (see Chapter 2) and that you have a Twitter account.

myEN lets you save tweets into your Evernote account. Setup instructions are available at http://twitter.com/myEN.

Follow these steps to interface Evernote with Twitter:

1. **Sign in to your Twitter account at http://twitter.com.**
2. **Click Who to Follow.**
3. **Type myEN in the search box, and click Search.**

4. **Click Follow.**

   myEN reciprocates the follow and sends you a linked direct message (DM).

   If you've protected your Twitter account, you can still access it. All you have to do is accept myEN when it sends the follow request and then send a DM to myEN. This gets you the same DM with the link in the next step.

5. **Click the link that myEN sends you.**

6. **Follow the prompt to link your Evernote account to Twitter.**

   Your Evernote and Twitter accounts are now connected.

Now you're free to tweet away and save to your Evernote account. Simply add @myEN anywhere in a public tweet, or DM MyEN to send new notes directly to your Evernote account. Chapter 6 tells you how to tweet notes, and Chapter 10 tells you how to share your notes via Twitter.

Even if you don't care much for using Twitter, connecting your Evernote account with Twitter is extremely helpful because it enables you to send notes to Evernote as SMS text messages. After you've linked the two accounts, and you have made the connection, use your mobile phone to create a tweet and send it to Twitter with your country-specific Twitter short code (it's 40404 in the United States; to find other codes, go to `http://support.twitter.com/articles/14226`), and the note is saved in Evernote as a note. In less than a minute you should see the text notes sent via Twitter showing up in your Evernote account within a minute, and usually much faster.

Interfacing with E-Mail

One of the greatest things about Evernote is that you can treat it just like a contact, sending e-mails to your notes or attaching information that arrived over e-mail without having to perform half a dozen steps to get it saved to your notebook. It's important to know your address and make sure that your notes are safe.

Your Evernote address isn't one you can select as you do with other email addresses; Evernote chooses it for you. You have to locate it by clicking Settings at the top of the Evernote Web page or go to Tools⇨Account Info to see it and save it in your contacts to be able to e-mail yourself or to forward e-mails to Evernote.

I added my Evernote address to my contact list, and I routinely copy my important outgoing email to it. I also forward incoming email to that address when I want to be sure to save it.

The following sections help you avoid these beginning frustrations by getting down to the specifics.

Adding your Evernote e-mail address to your contacts

Your Evernote address is auto-generated to provide better security. The address contains elements of your name to make it easy enough to remember, plus a few random numbers to ensure that it won't be duplicated. In other words, Evernote's auto-generated address appends a number that is truly random and doesn't indicate how many others have your name.

The location where you can find your Evernote e-mail address varies for each platform and device. Use the following information to locate your Evernote-generated e-mail address and then add it to your contacts:

✔ **Online:** Log in, and click Settings in the top-right corner of the screen. The e-mail information is located on the Account Summary tab, below the Emailing to Evernote section.

You can do something else cool here. Evernote strives to protect you from spam. If your account starts to receive spam, you can click the Reset Incoming Email button. Evernote generates a new e-mail for you. Don't forget to put the new address in your contacts list.

✔ **Windows:** Open Evernote, and choose Tools⇨Account Info. You can also upgrade your account, get a reminder about your password, see how much you've used Evernote, and check out how much more you can do before you reach your limit. This command is good to use when you need to see basic information in one place.

✔ **Mac:** Open Evernote, and choose Evernote⇨Account Info. You can also upgrade your account, get a reminder about your password, see how much you've used Evernote, and check out how much more you can do before you reach your limit. This command is good to use when you need to see basic information in one place.

Adding your address to contacts from a mobile device

Mobile devices have very easy one-click solutions for saving your Evernote e-mail address to contacts. The following sections cover individual devices.

Adding your address to iPhone, iPod touch, or iPad

On an iPhone, iPod touch, or iPad, follow these steps to add your e-mail account:

1. **Open the Evernote app.**

2. **Tap Settings.**

3. **Scroll down to Evernote Email Address under Emailing to Evernote. You see your email address for Evernote.**

4. **Tap the arrow to the right of the address.**

5. **Tap Reveal in Contacts.**

    The Reveal in Contacts button adds your Evernote e-mail address to your contact list. Now you don't have to worry about your e-mails winding up in your junk mail.

Adding your address to Android devices

On an Android device, follow these steps to add your e-mail account:

1. **Press the Settings button at the bottom of your phone (not on your screen).**

2. **In the menu that appears, tap Settings.**

3. **Scroll down to Account Info.**

    Below this heading, you see the entry Evernote Email Address. The address listed below this area is your autogenerated e-mail address.

4. **Tap the address.**

5. **Tap Add to Contacts.**

6. **Choose whether you want to save it to your phone or your Google account.**

    Note: You must have a Gmail account for the latter option to work.

7. **Enter contact information on your account.**

    Yes, it seems like mostly a formality, but it's worth the minute or two to enter a minimal amount of information so that you don't lose information to your junk box.

8. Tap Save.

   Now whenever you e-mail from your Android device, you can avoid having to hunt for your notes in your trash can.

Adding your address to a BlackBerry

On a BlackBerry device, follow these steps to add your e-mail account:

1. **Navigate to `http://evernote.com` from your BlackBerry browser.**

2. **Log in with your username and password.**

3. **Scroll to the bottom of the page and tap Settings.**

4. **Scroll down to Incoming Mail Address.**

5. **Highlight the address and copy it to the clipboard.**

6. **Go to Contacts and tap New Contact.**

7. **Paste in the email address you copied in step 5.**

8. **Press the BlackBerry key and select Save to save the address in your contacts.**

Delivering Your RSS Feeds to Evernote

At this writing, the easiest, most efficient, guaranteed way of getting RSS feeds into Evernote is e-mailing them. If you need to save only the web address and page, that task is relatively simple to accomplish. Here's a free way to do it:

1. **Highlight the URL, and copy it to the clipboard.**

2. **Navigate to `www.feedmyinbox.com`.**

3. **Paste the copied RSS URL into the Website or Feed URL field.**

4. **Paste your Evernote e-mail address into the Your Email Address field.**

5. **Click Submit.**

Feed My Inbox is a free service for up to five websites (with a few restrictions). After you add the feeds, all new feeds are sent to Evernote as notes. To direct more feeds to Evernote or to remove the restrictions, choose one of the paid plans, which at this writing range from $5 per month for up to 25 feeds to $16 per month for an unlimited number of feeds.

Notes created from feeds (whether or not you use Feed My Inbox) go against your monthly upload allowance (1GB per month for Premium subscribers and 60MB per month for free accounts). Also, you're limited to 250 e-mails per day in an Evernote Premium account and 50 e-mails per day in a free account. Therefore, you should use the RSS once-a-day feed option, if it's available.

If the daily option isn't available, you can use a site such as `http://habilis.net/dailyfeed` to generate a daily feed from any website. These will appear as new notes in your default notebook. Halibis is a simple way of saving a page so that you can come back to it and catch up on the latest news.

All notes will be delivered to your default notebook.

You can also send notes from several apps from mobile devices, such as from the iNews app (available from the App Store), to Evernote. Finally, you can use Google Reader (`www.google.com/reader`) to direct your subscribed RSS feeds directly to Evernote (see the next section).

Using Google Reader with Evernote

Google and Evernote are a great combination. I love it when Google and Evernote play nice because that makes saving things so much easier. The first step in using Google Reader is getting a Gmail account, which Google Reader requires. After you have a Gmail account, you can get moving on saving information to Evernote.

Creating a Gmail account is pretty quick and easy. If you don't already have one, go to `http://mail.google.com/mail/signup`. Google gives you a sign-up option and then walks you through the necessary steps.

To save info that Google Reader collects into Evernote, follow these steps:

1. **Log in to Google.**

2. **Choose Account Settings⇨Reader Settings.**

3. **Select Send To.**

4. **Select Create Custom Link.**

   The Create Custom Link feature has many uses outside Evernote, but these steps concentrate on adding the Evernote-specific information so that you can save to Evernote. Feel free to come back to these first four steps as often as you like to hook up Reader with other programs, too.

   Evernote isn't one of the default programs offered by Reader, so you have to go technical to add your Evernote account (see Figure 12-1).

   If you're interested in coding, Google tells you everything you need to know about the different coding types to access a custom linked app. Spend a little time getting familiar with the descriptions in Figure 12-2 if you want an explanation of the elements of the URL.

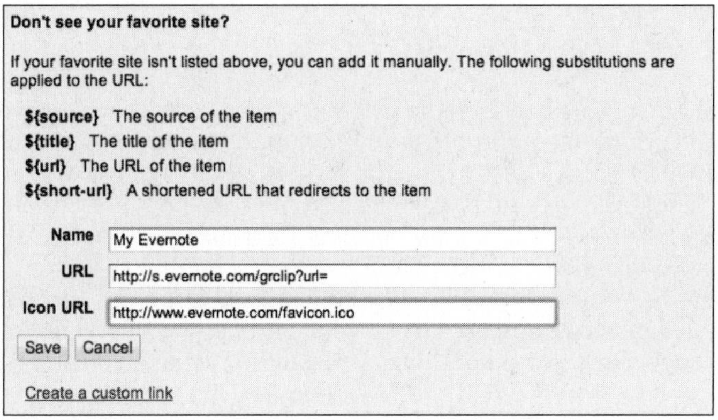

Figure 12-1:
Adding
Evernote
to Google
Reader.

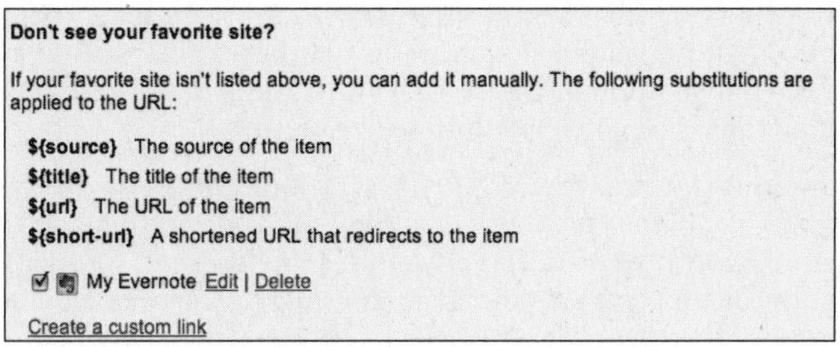

Figure 12-2:
The key
to the
substitutions
in the URL.

5. **Give your site a name.**

   I've named mine My Evernote, as shown in Figure 12-1.

6. **Add the URL `http://s.evernote.com/grclip?url=`.**

7. **Add the Icon URL `http://www.evernote.com/favicon.ico`.**

8. **Click Save.**

   The Evernote icon appears at the bottom of Google Reader, as shown in Figure 12-3. Whenever you're subscribed to an RSS feed, you can send the articles to Evernote. Check out the bottom of one of your articles. The Evernote icon lets you send to your default Evernote notebook.

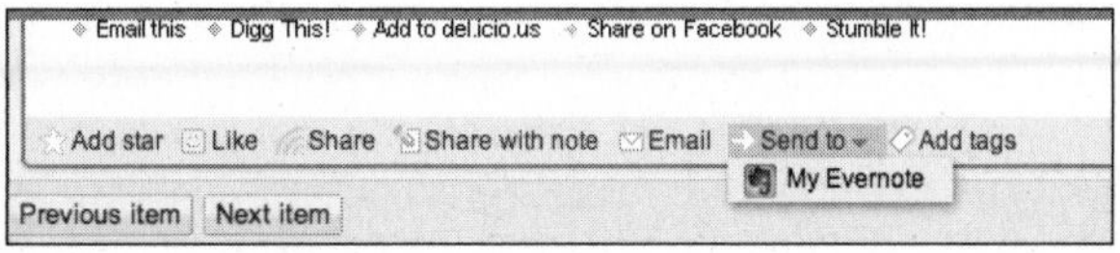

Figure 12-3:
Google
Reader after
you add
Evernote.

Blogging with Evernote

If you're one of the many people who has a blog, wouldn't it be fantastic if you could coordinate your blogs with Evernote to save duplicating your work? Evernote has already thought of bloggers and gives you just that option. Those of you who have multiple blogs can now use Evernote as a centralized work location to draft your blog posts and coordinate your various blogging endeavors.

You're welcome to set up and track your blogs any way you like, of course, but here are some very cool things you can do to make your blogging life easier:

- ✔ **Set up a `Blogging` notebook, and create a template.** I recommend setting up a template from which you can start building blog posts. See Figure 12-4 for a simple example of a template. You're welcome to begin with the information in Figure 12-4 and update it as you become more familiar with the types of items you want here.

- ✔ **Create new notes as you come up with new ideas.** If you have multiple blogs, it may be easiest to have a template tag and then tags for each of your blogging sites. You can always set up different notebooks for each blog source, but working between multiple notebooks may become a bit confusing as you try to remember what you were saying for which blog. Tags are slightly easier to track because you can deal with all the blogs within a single folder instead of having to give up and find something in All Notes because you accidentally dropped it in the wrong folder.

- ✔ **Save research to your `Blogging` folder.** This folder doesn't have to be just for writing. For most bloggers, a good bit of research goes into blogging. Even if you don't do research because you blog about yourself, you probably have pictures and websites that you regularly include in your blogs.

- ✔ **Create a new note from the template when you're ready to start preparing a blog.** You've saved your ideas. You've modified your template as you realize what you need. That should be everything you need to start populating your blog.

- ✔ **Load your blog post into your blogging site.** Any text that you have developed in Evernote is just a simple copy/paste away from posting.

- ✔ **Set up a time and date for the blog to post.** This makes it so that you can post first thing in the morning without even having to wake up to do it.

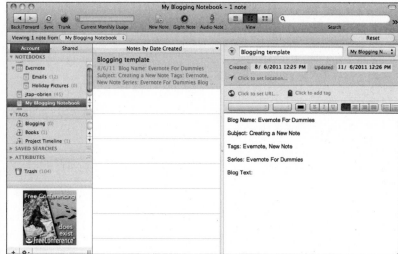

Figure 12-4:
Evernote
blogging
template.

You soon find that blogging takes far less time than it did in the past because you've used Evernote to get organized.

Chapter 13

Troubleshooting Problems

· ·

In This Chapter

▶ Dealing with common issues

▶ Taking advantage of Evernote's many resources for troubleshooting

· ·

A s with most software, it may take you a while to get used to all of Evernote's many features. You are bound to encounter unanticipated issues and may need help finding answers quickly. Besides, Evernote is software, and software bugs are common.

The good news is that Evernote has established several areas on its website to assist you with troubleshooting. In this chapter, I offer you solutions to common problems and also let you know where you can find additional help.

Finding Solutions to Common Problems

Although a section on fixing problems could take up a book all on its own, I focus on what I consider to be the top ten issues not covered elsewhere in this book and suggest solutions for them. For more complicated problems, check out the other sections in this chapter.

This section is meant to handle generic questions, so I don't cover issues specific to any one platform or device. Instead, I discuss problems that you may encounter as a newbie or that may recur.

My confirmation code never arrived

After you have signed up, and after you complete the registration process, a confirmation code is sent to the e-mail address you provided while signing up for your Evernote account.

If this e-mail gets lost or isn't delivered, try the following things to recover your confirmation code:

- Check your e-mail program's spam or junk folder. This is far and away the most common place for confirmation e-mail messages to end up (aside from the Inbox).

- If you can't find the e-mail in your spam folder, visit the Password Reset page (www.evernote.com/User.action#password) and enter the e-mail address you used when registering for your account. The confirmation e-mail will be re-sent to you.

- If nothing else works, contact Evernote support (www.evernote.com/about/contact/support/) for assistance.

Evernote won't open

When Evernote won't open, a rare occurrence, you face a very frustrating issue. You really have only one way to fix it: Uninstall Evernote, reboot your system, and reinstall the app. (You can try simply rebooting before uninstalling, but I haven't see that alleviate the situation.)

If you sync as often as you should — you should sync your notes more often than once a day — you won't lose anything by uninstalling Evernote. If you have unsynced notes, however, this drastic remedy causes you to lose the notes you wrote that have not been synced. Unfortunately, for some problems, you have no other remedy.

I forgot my password

You use Evernote to help you remember everything, but what happens when you forget your password? It's like you can't get into the safe where you're storing all your jewels right before the guests arrive for the party!

If you forget your password, follow these steps:

1. **Open Evernote on your desktop or laptop.**

2. **Click Sign In.**

3. **Click Forgot Password below the login information boxes.**

4. **Enter either the username or e-mail address associated with your Evernote account.**

Evernote e-mails you instructions on resetting your password (see Figure 13-1). If you haven't added Evernote to your safe contact list, make sure to keep an eye on your junk-mail folder.

```
We have received a request to change the password for
your Evernote account: jtap-obrien

If you made this request, and would like to change your password,
please click on the link below.

http://www.evernote.com/ResetPassword.action?
username=vsrichie&sig=06d4c9aec3ec53f7db66db4595d1e723&expire=21889566

This link will work for 2 hours or until you reset your password.

If you did not ask to change your password, then another
user probably submitted this request by mistake. In this
case, you can ignore this email and no changes will be made
to your account.

- The Evernote team
```

Figure 13-1:
Follow the instructions to reset your password.

This link works for only two hours, so you need to quickly use it to reset your password.

Changing your password affects your login on every device you use with Evernote. If you change your password, you need to reset it on your iPhone, iPad, Android, Windows phone . . . you get the idea.

My password doesn't work

If you just changed your password, and you're trying to access your account from a phone or other mobile device, make sure to enter your new password.

Everything is synced, even the password.

If you haven't changed your password recently, and your password is rejected, check to make sure that you don't have caps lock on. Otherwise, see the preceding section for instructions on resetting your password.

The server is acting up

Occasionally, something happens that makes your account on the Evernote servers inaccessible. You can go to the Evernote website at `www.evernote.com/about/contact/support` (see Figure 13-2) for help. The first item on the support site is the server status, which gives you an easy way to find out when the server is having trouble.

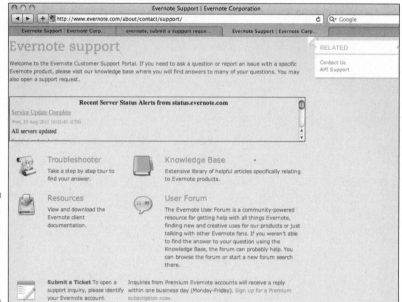

Figure 13-2:
Evernote's
main
trouble-
shooting
page.

You don't have to be logged in to an Evernote account to get the answers
you need.

In Figure 13-2, the most recent posting in the Recent Server Status Alerts box
was August 10, 2011. So if you were trying to create notes and to sync notes
and notebooks between 17:53 and 18:05 on that day, you may have experi-
enced some issues. If you find that something like upgrades or interruptions
have occurred while you were creating or syncing notes, make sure that you
resave your changes. Evernote tries to minimize downtime, but server out-
ages can happen from time to time.

The alert box shows only the five or six most recent status updates, so if
you have reason to suspect that something is wrong, check here as early as
possible.

My notes are out of sync

Suppose that you created a new note on your phone earlier today. Now
you're on your computer and want to update the note. The problem is that
you don't see the note.

Odds are that your settings should be adjusted so that Evernote syncs more frequently. Syncing is different by platform and device, so for full details, you need to check out Chapter 9. For a more immediate fix, try these steps:

1. **Click the Sync button in the top of the screen (the exact location depends on the version of Evernote you are using).**

   When the Sync arrows quit spinning, the sync is complete. If you still don't see the note, go to the next step.

2. **Open Evernote and make sure that you saved the note.**

   A saved note displays on your notes screen as part of the list of notes in your notebook. If you didn't save the note, it may still be open. If you didn't save and the note isn't open, you've probably lost your work in that note.

I can't display all my notes

You know you have a lot more notes than you see below All Notebooks. Where did they go?

Check out the search box to see whether you've recently run a search, which hides the notes that don't meet the filter criteria. If the search bar looks more like Figure 13-3 with text after All Notebooks, you have a search running and should delete it. (Click the X after the search item or items.)

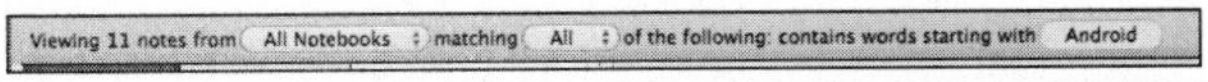

Figure 13-3:
You have a search running.

Viewing 11 notes from (All Notebooks ÷) matching (All ÷) of the following: contains words starting with   Android

If the bar below the menu looks like Figure 13-4, you may want to make sure that your computer is synced (see the preceding section).

Figure 13-4:
No searches appear to be running.

Viewing **42** notes from (All Notebooks ÷)

My searches aren't working

Are you having problems with your searches? You probably have one of two problems:

TIP

✔ You're looking in just one notebook (the wrong one or not All Notebooks). Check out your notebooks on the left side of the Evernote screen. In Figure 13-5, for example, the In and Around the Kitchen notebook is selected, which is not where you should search for information for a blog. Make sure that you select the appropriate notebook or choose All Notebooks before starting a search.

Clicking All Notes rules out this possibility.

✔ You already have a filter running that is further reducing your notes (see the preceding section).Compare your Evernote bar to Figure 13-3, earlier in this chapter. The more searches you have running, the more text you have after All Notebooks (or whatever notebook you're running the search on). So if you ran a search on Android, but there is text in this area that includes Android, To Do, and iPhone, click the x beside the two searches you don't want.

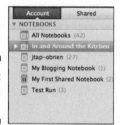

Figure 13-5:
Wrong
notebook!

TIP

Remember to clear your search box when you're done. If you don't, what you type is appended to the search you've entered. (Honestly, this one trips me up time and again.)

No one but the creator can update shared notebooks

You've shared a notebook with friends or colleagues, or they've shared one with you, but only the creator can update the notebook. The problem is that the person doing the sharing isn't a Premium subscriber.

Notebook modification by multiple users works only for Premium subscribers and the individual must be granted editing rights. Everyone else can share so that others can read the shared notes. Other users can even clip information from a shared note and create their own notes to share (which you should attempt cautiously, lest the note soon mushrooms into so many versions that you'll never be able to track it), but access remains read-only.

I have a problem after installing a new release

This issue is an ongoing one, as Evernote releases updates frequently. No matter how much beta testing occurs, releases always fix some problems while creating some unexpected issues. For applications such as Evernote that cross over to so many platforms and devices, odds are even greater that issues will occur with a new release.

If you encounter problems following a new release of Evernote or even an update to your platform/device, the best place to start looking for answers is the user forum (see the next section). You'll likely find either a solution or a known issue on the subject.

Finding Answers on the User Forum

The user forum is a good source for answers. Users visit the forum to ask specific questions and get answers. Most answers are provided by other users, although Evernote does monitor the forum. Odds are that with more than 20 million users and counting, you aren't the first to encounter the problem. Think of the User Forum as a form of crowd-sourcing for finding answers.

Here's how to access and search the user forum:

1. **Go to `www.support.evernote.com`.**

2. **Scroll down and click User Forum.**

   Figure 13-6 shows a screen shot from a day at the forum. To access a more specific subject without having to comb through the discussions, go to the next step.

3. **Enter a subject in the search box in the top-right corner of the forum page, and click Search.**

   The notes matching your search criteria are displayed.

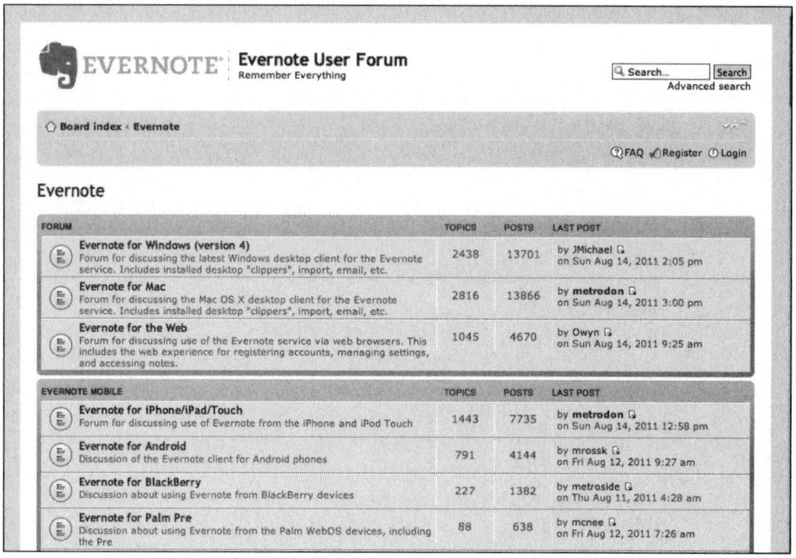

Figure 13-6:
The main
page of the
user forum.

Suppose that you're having trouble with your icon after downloading the
newest version of Evernote. Here's what you'd do:

1. **Type** My icon disappeared **in the search box and then click Search.**

   Figure 13-7 shows an example of results for this search topic. You may
   need to narrow down your search so that you aren't plowing through a
   bunch of posts to get your answer. But you should start by looking at
   previous posts before asking your own questions.

Figure 13-7:
Searching
the forum
for icon
issues.

2. **Scroll through the questions and answers.**

    Your issue probably isn't new, so a diligent search should help you narrow down your possible solutions. You can also do a more detailed "advanced" search (see Figure 13-8) if you'd like to further narrow your search options. Click the wheel to the right of the search box. A Search form opens and you can make the search as restrictive as you like, limiting results by specific phrase, tags, author, date range, product, and other search criteria.

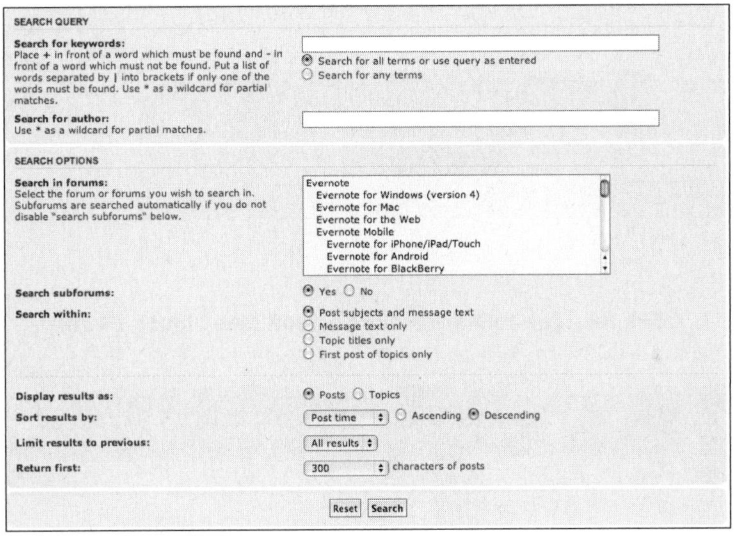

Figure 13-8:
Advanced
search
options on
the user
forum.

Using the Evernote FAQs

Personally, I find that the frequently asked questions (FAQs) are often the best place to begin troubleshooting. The vast majority of the time, you can find answers to basic questions on Evernote's Questions and Answers web page by following these steps:

1. **Go to www.evernote.com/about/support/qa.php.**

2. **Search through the ready-made questions.**

    The most likely questions/issues are collected at the beginning in the General Evernote Issues section. Three other sections cover the most frequently used platforms: Windows, Mac OS X, and iPhone. If you don't see your question in one of these sections, go to the next step.

3. **Scroll down to Evernote Knowledge Base (see Figure 13-9) and type in your question. Click the magnifying glass icon to the right of the search box.**

   A shared Evernote notebook then opens in a new tab. It's the perfect place to find answers to your questions, but it may take a little looking to find what you want.

   It's easiest to link your account to the shared note so that you can access the area without having to log in, as I show you how to do in the next step.

Figure 13-9:
Accessing the Evernote Knowledge Base.

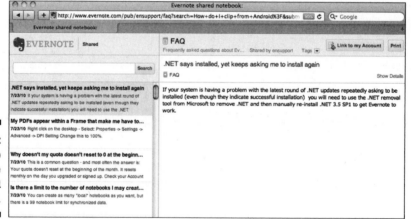

4. **Click the Link to My Account button (see Figure 13-10).**

Figure 13-10:
Linking to the Evernote FAQ notebook.

If you aren't already logged in to your account, you need to do so now. Figure 13-11 shows the Evernote FAQ notebook being linked to an account. (Refer to Chapter 10 for sharing if you would like to learn more about the Shared tab.)

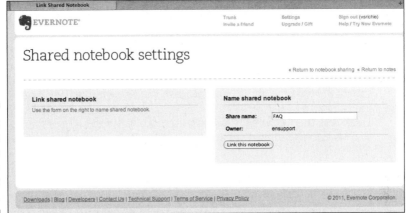

5. **Go to your Evernote account, click the Shared tab, and click FAQ below ensupport (see Figure 13-12).**

It may take a while to download all the FAQs. When the Sync symbol stops rotating, your newest notebook is ready for you to use.

From here, you can use the Evernote FAQ just like any other notebook. Refer to Chapter 8 for guidelines on running the best searches.

Figure 13-12:
Syncing
Evernote
FAQ notes
to your
shared area.

Accessing the Evernote Knowledge Base

The Evernote Knowledge Base gives you general information on many topics. It's the best place to start when you want to do specific troubleshooting. The advantage of searching the Knowledge Base is that you may get the problem solved in real time and the answers in the Knowledge Base are authoritative.

To access the Knowledge Base, go to `www.evernote.com/about/contact/support`, and click Knowledge Base.

The topics are divided by account and device type (see Figure 13-13). If you have questions about your account, the first link is for you. If you're looking to answer a device-specific question, start with the menu on the right side of the screen (see Figure 13-13). Each area provides detailed information in a long list of possible questions. Browse through them to see whether your question is answered before submitting a support request. Take note that there's a Web Clipper category, so if you have a Web Clipper question, start with the link for that before moving to something device-specific.

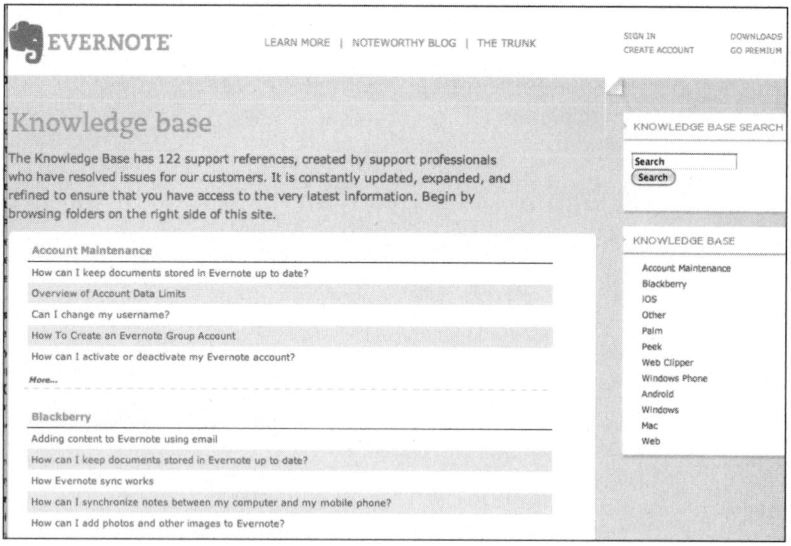

Figure 13-13:
Knowledge
Base
sections.

Submitting a Support Request

Evernote has set up a user-friendly way of requesting help to solve your problems quickly when you can't locate an answer in the user form or Evernote Knowledge Base. To submit a support request, follow these steps:

1. **Go to www.support.evernote.com.**

2. **Scroll down to Submit a Ticket, and fill in the required information.**

3. **Click Submit.**

The Evernote staff replies to you as quickly as possible. If you're a Premium subscriber, you can rest assured that you'll get a response within one business day. (Sorry — you shouldn't expect an answer if you're having issues right after church on Sunday.)

Make sure that your response didn't arrive in your junk-mail folder, especially if you keep rather strict filters on your inbox. After you receive an answer, if you find that it was delivered to junk mail, make sure to add the address to your safe list.

Getting Insight with a Podcast

Evernote even has a podcast to help those who need more detailed instructions. The podcast isn't the place to go for troubleshooting specific issues, but it provides valuable lessons on working with Evernote that can make your life easier. The first podcast posted in March 2009. Evernote posts a new podcast about once a month.

To check out posted podcasts, go to blog.evernote.com/category/podcast . This URL takes you to the most recent podcast. Scroll down to see the last ten posted podcasts. At the bottom of the page is the Previous Posts button; click it to see older posts.

Evernote has a template for most of its podcasts. Figure 13-14 is the first podcast; Figure 13-15 is one from the summer of 2011. You can see some very basic changes in the way the podcasts were presented, but no major changes make it difficult to go back to earlier versions. Check out the podcast area to see whether Evernote has covered territory in which you're interested.

Figure 13-14:
The first
Evernote
podcast.

Figure 13-15:
A more
recent
Evernote
podcast.

Chat with Evernote

Premium users can go to the Evernote Web and click on Chat with Evernote.
A Live Chat window opens.

1. **Under Department, click on the pull-down menu and enter the Evernote Product you're using.**

   Also enter your full name, e-mail address, and your question.

2. **Click Start Chat.**

   A live person will try to address your question.

Part IV
Just For You — Device-Specific Features

The 5th Wave   By Rich Tennant

"Well, here's what happened—I forgot
to put it on my 'To Do' list."

In this part . . .

With this part, you go beyond the basics of Evernote and expand on the specific features as they are applicable to a range of platforms and devices: Windows, Mac OS X, tablets, smartphones, and web browsers.

Chapter 14 is about working with Evernote on traditional desktops and laptops using the Windows or Mac operating systems.

Chapter 15 covers using Evernote on a sampling of different tablets (Android tablets or iPads) and smartphones (iPhones, Android phones, or BlackBerry devices). In Chapter 16 you find out how to access Evernote on the web using any Internet browsers so that you can stay connected to your notes even when you're on the go.

Chapter 14

Computers: Windows and Mac

● ●

In This Chapter

▶ Pointing out the differences for Window devices

▶ Using new features for PDFs using Windows devices

▶ Taking advantage of extra features for Macs

● ●

*F*ortunately, this chapter got shorter and shorter as work on the book progressed, as Evernote discovered that some device-specific features are generally useful and implemented those features across all platforms. Nearly all Evernote features are available cross-platform. Still, some differences in the experience remain, and this chapter is where I discuss them.

Discovering Windows-Only Features

Evernote supports many devices. Some support, however, is unique to Windows. One such feature is `ENScript.exe`, a command-line interface. You can use `ENScript.exe` to create new Evernote commands and applications that look and feel like stand-alone applications. You can kick them off by double-clicking and launching `ENScript.exe` as you would any other application on your desktop. (Read Chapter 20 for more information about using `ENScript.exe`.)

Creating a shortcut

Create a shortcut to the `ENScript.exe` utility in your Evernote installation folder.

As a security measure, Windows 7 doesn't allow users to create files in the Program Files folder. It wants you to use the Downloads folder in your user profile: (`C:\Users\<username>`).

To create a shortcut to ENScript.exe in Windows 7, use the following steps:

1. **Navigate to the location or folder where you want to create the shortcut.**

2. **Right-click an empty location of the folder or screen, and choose New⇨Shortcut from the contextual menu.**

   The Create Shortcut wizard appears (see Figure 14-1).

3. **Type or browse to the location of ENscript.exe and then click Next.**

   On my computer, ENscript.exe is located in C:\Program Files (x86)\Evernote\Evernote).

4. **In the next window, name your shortcut (see Figure 14-2).**

   I named my shortcut Recent Notes.

5. **Click Finish.**

   The shortcut is created where you specified.

6. **Right-click the shortcut, and choose Properties from the contextual menu.**

   The Properties window opens.

7. **Click the Shortcut tab, if it isn't already open.**

8. **Click Change Icon to assign your shortcut a custom icon.**

   Ignore the message The file . . . ENScript.exe contains no icons.

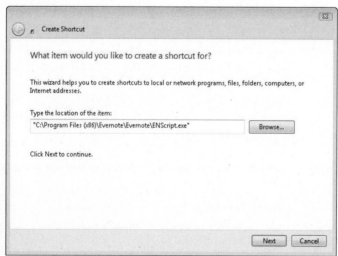

Figure 14-1:
The Create
Shortcut
wizard.

Figure 14-2:
Name your
new
shortcut.

9. **Click OK.**

The Change Icon window opens, showing some available icons (see Figure 14-3).

Figure 14-3:
Assign an
icon to the
shortcut.

10. **Browse to Evernote.exe and select an Evernote-developed custom icon, or select your own icon.**

11. **Click OK to accept the icon.**

The icon appears in the Properties window.

12. **Click OK again to update the properties.**

The shortcut has been created, sits where you put it, and sports the icon you selected.

If you think you'll use the script often, you can pin it to the taskbar. Simply right-click it and choose Pin to Taskbar from the contextual menu. Then you can execute it any time by clicking the icon in the taskbar. If your version of Windows doesn't support right-clicking to pin to the taskbar, hold down the Shift key and right-click again.

Getting the script into the shortcut

After you cause ENScript.exe to execute, you need to edit the target in the shortcut you created to add your query after the filename. This makes it into a stand-alone executable that loads ENScript.exe and executes your script. Here's an example of a simple query you can store in this fashion that lists all the notes created in the notebook *Evernote For Dummies:*

```
"C:\Program Files (x86)\Evernote\Evernote\ENScript.exe" showNotes /q
              "notebook:\"Evernote for Dummies\""
```

The syntax of command-line commands isn't very forgiving. Make sure that you have your quotes placed correctly around the path to ENScript.exe if there's a space in the path. Also, you need to use quotes for the search string and for the notebook name, if your notebook name has a space in it, as in the preceding example.

A collection of ENScript.exe scripts that you can install is available at www. howtogeek.com/howto/26100/make-evernote-more-approachable-with-custom-windows-7-taskbar-integration.

Webcam Notes

If Evernote detects an installed webcam, then New Webcam Note (Ctrl+Shift+W) becomes a New Note option. Choosing this option lets you preview a picture. When you are happy with the photo, click Take Snapshot. Otherwise, click Cancel. The picture is taken. You can then click Retake Snapshot, Save to Evernote, or Cancel.

Save to Evernote creates a new note with the title Webcam Note and the snapshot. You can then edit the note like you would any other.

New PDF functionality

The latest release of Evernote for Windows includes several very useful features related to PDFs that are not available as the book goes to press on any other Evernote platform.

✔ If you have a scanned document or a digital PDF in Evernote then search results are highlighted in yellow right inside the PDF. You can also use CTRL+F to search inside a specific note. To do this, click and drag the middle section of the Evernote for Windows toolbar, then drop the file.

✔ Search results are now highlighted inside of PDFs, and you can drag PDFs out of Evernote and into other apps, or on to your desktop.

✔ You can now copy text and paste it into other programs right from the note pane.

The EvernoteExperience on the Mac

Evernote has strived to accomplish two seemingly contradictory goals: make Evernote for Mac OS X a natural Mac application (one that is intuitive to Mac users and takes full advantage of the Mac's capabilities) while also minimizing the learning curve for those who, like me, use Evernote on the Windows Desktop and on mobile devices. I think it has accomplished this difficult jujitsu with aplomb.

However, there are some important differences that are specific to the Mac version of Evernote, which I describe in this section.

AppleScripting

AppleScript, Apple's scripting language, is an easy-to-use and powerful way to extend your use of Evernote. It's built into OS X, is supported by Evernote's Open Scripting architecture, and is easier to work with than ENscript for Windows. Read Chapter 20 to find out more about AppleScript.

Sharing notebooks in Mac OS X

Sharing notebooks on a Mac is really easy, and similar to the way it works in Windows. The best part is that you don't have to do it online. You can share your notebooks and view other people's notebooks right from your Evernote on your Mac. Here's how:

1. **Open Evernote on your desktop or laptop.**

   Did you ever notice the two tabs on the left where you can see your notebooks, tags, and other information? The Account tab is your normal tab for your account information. The Shared tab is for shared notebooks (see Figure 14-4).

Figure 14-4:
The Shared
Notebook
tab houses
shared
notebooks.

2. **Click the Shared tab.**

   To start with, the area is empty, but you can change that very quickly. When you share notebooks, those notebooks appear here. The Shared tab is also where you can view notebooks shared by others — one location where you can check everything that's shared.

3. **Create a new notebook.**

   If you don't know how to create a notebook, check out Chapter 3 for instructions. For this example, I named my notebook My First Shared Notebook.

4. **Click Manage Sharing.**

   You see something that looks like Figure 14-5. The notebooks available on the right are contingent upon the notebooks you're sharing and those you're set to view.

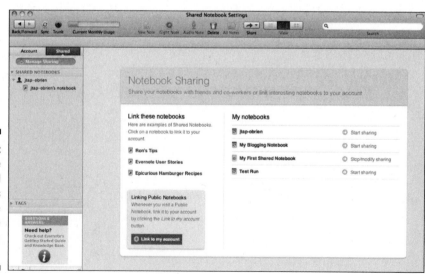

Figure 14-5:
You see
the shared
notebooks
in the
Manage
Sharing
window.

5. Click Start Sharing.

Check out Chapter 10 for the differences between sharing with the world and selective sharing. After you make a choice, your notebook on the main screen looks like Figure 14-5.

Connecting to shared notebooks

In addition to sharing your own notebooks, you may want to access notebooks that other people have shared. Use the following steps to start syncing with a shared notebook:

1. Click the name of the shared notebook that you'd like to link to.

Any notebooks you linked when you receive a linking invitation appear below Shared Notebooks (see Figure 14-6).

Figure 14-6:
Evernote
shared
notebooks.

2. Click the name of a shared notebook to see options you can customize for the notebook.

Figure 14-7 shows the pop-up window that appears.

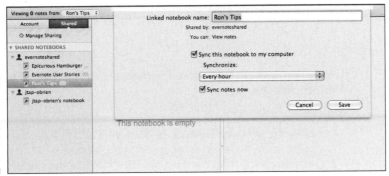

Figure 14-7:
Sync
options
for shared
notebooks.

3. **Feel free to make changes if you'd like to adjust the settings.**

4. **Click Save.**

   After you add a notebook, your Mac automatically starts syncing. Watch as the notes start piling up. When it's done, you see something that looks like Figure 14-8.

Figure 14-8:
Synced
notes from
a shared
notebook.

If you're a Premium subscriber, you can enjoy even more special treatment. When you share notebooks, you can give write access as well as read-only access, making the note sharing a lot more user-friendly because you can get others' opinions right in your notebook instead of having them e-mail responses to your notebook and notes.

Linking to a shared notebook

What's so special about links? Well, using a link is the same thing as sharing, but you can add a link more quickly.

To add a link, use the following steps:

1. **From your desktop version of Evernote, click the Shared tab, and click Manage Sharing.**

   You have two choices:

   • **Link the account from an invitation.** The advantage of this choice is tracking. If you're on a project, you can see what day you began working on it. You can also see how early in the planning process you got involved so that you can narrow down when you started calling to make appointments.

- **Visit a publicly shared notebook.** Choose this option when you're less likely to need tracking.

2. **Click the Link to My Account button (see Figure 14-9).**

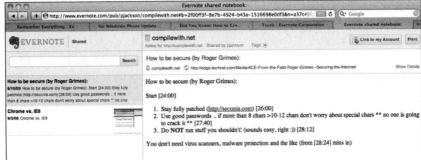

Figure 14-9: Link to your account.

If you get an invitation, click the e-mail link and then click Link to My Account for the same results. It's brilliant and fast.

Working with notebook stacks on a Mac

Notebook stacks is an interesting term, but what does it mean and how does it work? Notebook stacks are just as easy as organizing your bookshelf.

If you have several blogging projects that you want to keep together, for example, you can use Evernote to organize your notebooks. You can place them in alphabetical order so that your blogs are spread out all over the notebook screen. Or if you like to experiment in the kitchen, it's really annoying to have different recipes mixed between to-do lists and bills. Notebook stacks take care of this problem by enabling you to drop related notebooks in a stack.

Stacking is as easy as dragging and dropping or Command+clicking the notebook and choosing Add to Stack.

Use the following steps to group multiple notebooks:

1. **From your desktop version of Evernote, click one notebook and drag it to another.**

    The order in which you drag the notebooks really doesn't matter. Evernote puts them in alphabetical order in a new notebook called `Notebook Stack` (see Figure 14-10).

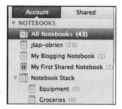

2. **Right-click** Notebook Stack, **choose Rename Stack from the contextual menu, and give the notebook an appropriate name.**

   Now you can start creating new notes to go into the notebooks.

3. **To create a new notebook within the stack when you have a new category of notes, right-click the notebook stack, choose New Notebook in** *<notebook stack name>* **from the contextual menu, and enter a name.**

Using audio notes on a Mac

Audio notes are available on Windows too (see the information about webcam notes discussed earlier in this chapter), but creating them is really intuitive on the Mac. I find them to be a fantastic tool for creating lists or quickly capturing ideas when you don't have time to type them. No matter how fast you type, you'll almost always be able to speak your notes faster than you can type them.

The process is relatively simple. As with most Apple innovations, creating audio notes is very user-friendly and intuitive.

1. **In your desktop version of Evernote, click the Audio Note icon, select your notebook, and click OK.**

2. **Click the Record button when you're ready to start recording your first voice note.**

   If you have trouble, get interrupted, or realize that you just aren't ready to start recording yet, you have the choice to cancel. You don't have to delete what you've done. Evernote leaves the note with a recording file just waiting for you to be ready. (Check out Step 5 if you want to restart from here.)

3. **Click Save when you're done with the initial recording.**

4. **Click Play to determine whether you want to keep your audio note or record it again.**

Evernote makes it easy for you to check out what you've recorded. I strongly recommend that you do so because if you mumble through some of it or speak too softly, you may not remember what you were trying to say two weeks later. Should you decide that you need to redo your note, go to Step 5.

5. **Click the Record Audio icon on the note bar just above the notes to record a new note or to rerecord a note that wasn't quite what you wanted.**

If you want to add notes or text, you can do that, too. Just click in the note area and begin typing. Best of all, you can add the text on any device you use, not just desktop computers or laptops.

Taking advantage of iSight notes

iSight notes are entirely unique to Macs because Macs have a built-in camera. This feature makes note-taking infinitely easier because you don't have to scan or do a whole host of things to get information into a note. Simply take a picture, and Evernote does the rest.

The process of creating a note by using iSight notes is relatively simple. Use the following steps:

1. **Open a notebook to which you have write access.**

2. **In your desktop version of Evernote, click the iSight Note icon along the top menu or choose File⇨New iSight Note.**

   Whichever way you open iSight, the next few steps are the same. You may need to be a little patient while your Mac boots up the pictures.

   This option isn't available on the Evernote website because no other platform supports iSight, although webcam notes is supported on Windows computers with a webcam installed.

3. **After the camera opens, point it at the object that you'd like to photo-graph, and click Take Photo Snapshot.**

   You can retake the picture as many times as you please until you're happy with the results. You can even take a couple shots for the same note if you want to compare the pictures to make sure that the text is as easy to read as possible for Evernote.

4. **When you're satisfied with the picture, click Add to Evernote to save it to your default notebook.**

   You can now go in and check out what you and Evernote have created.

Differences between Notes on Your Desktop and Notes in the Evernote Cloud

In Evernote, the mobile devices communicate directly with the Evernote servers. Limitations of bandwidth and memory mean that certain great features for Windows and Mac aren't available on mobile devices. Mobile devices do have at least one very useful compensating advantage, however, which is the geotagging feature.

Here are a few differences between desktops and mobile devices that you should be aware of:

✔ You can't initiate a notebook share from some mobile devices; for these, you have to initiate a share from a desktop, laptop, or mobile device that supports iOS or Android and then you can access the shared notebook from any device.

✔ You can't create web clips in mobile browsers.

✔ Not all formatting that's visible or editable on a desktop or laptop computer is visible or editable on mobile devices. If a feature isn't visible on your mobile device, it isn't available.

✔ Drag and drop isn't available in mobile.

✔ Unlike mobile devices, desktop and laptop computers don't capture location information (geotagging) when you create notes.

Chapter 15

Working with Evernote on Tablets and Smartphones

In This Chapter

▶ Getting familiar with Evernote on iPhone, iPod touch, and iPad

▶ Working with Evernote on Android tablets

▶ Getting the most out of Evernote on BlackBerry devices

Smartphones and tablets, including iPads and Android tablets, hold an ever-more-prominent place in computing. Many people use only these devices. I still use a desktop and a PC too, but I rarely walk around with anything but a tablet and a smartphone. Fortunately, Evernote has embraced all devices and supports tablets and smartphones well.

Using Evernote on iPhone and iPod

Evernote's extraordinary connection to Apple products makes using Evernote on iPhone and iPod nearly an addiction — especially with the new iPhone 4S. Siri (the personal assistant) is darn well like having your own private secretary for the price of the latest and coolest toy. The future has never been so close at hand.

Siri, which is built into the iPhone 4S, is (according to Apple), "an intelligent personal assistant that helps you get things done just by asking." It lets you speak to do things such as sending messages, scheduling meetings, and placing phone calls. Siri understands ordinary, natural speech, and it asks you questions when it needs more information to complete a task. You start using it by holding down the Home key.

Quickly previewing your notes

Snippets view is arguably one the easiest views to use in Evernote, and the most popular. (Check out Chapter 7 for descriptions of the different views.) It makes working in Evernote easier because you can see everything you need in one easy-to-access location. Check out the opening text of all your notes at one time, for example. If the note is a picture, you can see enough in the view to know what the note contains without having to open it. You can see all your notes from the unified home screen, so you don't have to open notes one at a time to tell what's what.

Better yet, Snippets view is now the default view of Evernote, so you don't have to do anything to set it up for your notes. Evernote versions from 4.0 on offer users a unified home screen and Snippets view to view photos and drawings on their mobile Apple devices. For images, the Evernote app places the picture to the right of the title so that you get all the information you need in one location that you can easily scroll. Figure 15-1 shows how many notes you can fit on a screen and how much information you can get at a single glance.

Unsure how to add a title to a picture you've taken? Check out Chapter 7 to see how to take a picture and add text. Or scroll through your existing Camera Roll and save the picture to Evernote.

Figure 15-1:
Snippets
view on
iPhone or
iPod touch.

Using the note screen

The note information panel is crisp and clear, with the title, notebook, and source links right up top. Just as you can in the search panel, you can open the note information panel to access the details. Navigating the note info panel and tagging notes by using your keyboard is fast and efficient.

Adding notes manually

To create a note by using the sleek new note screen, follow these steps:

1. **Tap the + icon in the Evernote app.**

   The Untitled Note screen opens; available actions display at the bottom of the screen (see Figure 15-2).

Figure 15-2:
iPhone
Untitled
Note
screen.

2. **(Optional) To add a tag, tap Tags; enter a tag or select as many exist-ing tags as you like; then tap Done.**

   A new screen pops up when you tap Tags, allowing you to create a new tag in the top box or select an existing tag (see Figure 15-3).

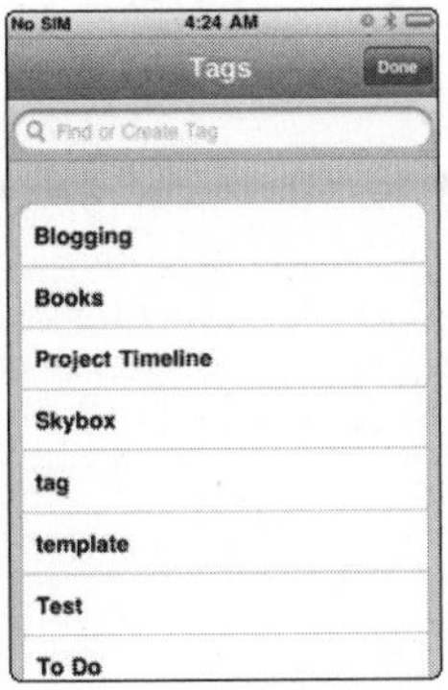

Figure 15-3:
View your
existing
tags.

3. **(Optional) Repeat Step 2 to add other functions.**

   Simply tap the icon for the function you'd like to perform. Tap Location to add a location, for example. At the bottom of the Untitled Note screen work the same way and are user-friendly.

4. **Tap the Untitled Note section, and give the note a title.**

5. **Tap the Tap to Edit Body Text section when you're ready to start adding text.**

   The onscreen keyboard appears (see Figure 15-4. If you want to change the basic information, just tap the keyboard icon to hide it, and then you can make easy updates.

6. **Tap Save.**

   You've created a new note with just a few taps and some light keyboard work. Awesome.

Figure 15-4: Start typing your new note.

Adding notes with Siri

Sure, everyone wants a personal assistant, but who can afford one? Well, if you own an iPhone 4S, you have an assistant built right in. All you have to do is make sure that you save your Evernote email address to your contacts.

When you set up a note with Siri, you don't have to deal with a Save button or tapping. If you're on the go and want to keep the process mostly hands-free, Siri is absolutely the best way to get things done, knowing that what you've done will be there for you later. After you start using Evernote on Siri, you'll have no idea how you were able to survive without Siri.

Here's how to create a new note by using Siri:

1. **Launch Siri.**

   To use Siri, you have to tap the microphone at the bottom of the screen before you start talking.

2. **Tell Siri, "Send e-mail to Evernote."**

   You can say whatever you like, of course, but Siri definitely understands this command.

3. **Dictate your note.**

When you stop talking, Siri sends off the note. Expect to find the new note in your default notebook.

Selecting multiple camera roll images

Who wants to add one photo at a time to a note? It takes forever, especially if you've had your phone for years; no one has that kind of time. Well, you don't actually have to add one photo at a time. Evernote enables you to select up to ten pictures at a time. (You can add only ten pictures to a note anyway, so you don't need the ability to select more).

Here's how you can select multiple photos and add them to a new note:

1. **Tap the + icon.**

   Make sure that you enter any information related to the photos, especially the title and tags you want to associate with the note.

2. **Tap the Paper Clip icon and then tap the Camera Roll.**

   All the photos you have on your camera appear.

3. **Tap the arrow in the bottom-left corner of your screen.**

   This step lets your device know that you may want to add multiple pictures. Two options appear at the bottom: Single Note and Multiple Notes.

4. **Start tapping pictures.**

   As soon as you tap a photo, the Single Note option lights up. If you tap a second photo, Multiple Notes lights up. All the photos you've tapped have a red check mark so you can easily see whether you've inadvertently added an unwanted picture.

5. **Tap Multiple Notes.**

   Your phone saves all the images to their own note with the title and other information you entered in Step 1.

Browsing by notebook and tag

Being able to see all your notebooks at one time is a positive boon for getting work done. Ditto for checking out all your tags in one location.

Here's how you can check out your notebooks and tags:

1. **Open the Evernote app.**

2. **Tap Notebooks for a quick view of all your existing notebooks.**

TIP

From this view, you can check out your favorite notebooks, view the contents of each notebook, or check out what's in the trash.

Tapping Edit in the top-right corner enables you to change the notebook's name.

3. **Tap Tags to check out all your existing tags.**

You're not creating tags in this step — just checking them out — but you can edit them and see what notes each tag applies to.

4. **Tap Edit.**

If you want to change a tag universally, editing the tag is the easiest method.

5. **Tap the right arrow to open the title of the tag.**

6. **Change the tag name.**

7. **Tap Save.**

It takes about 30 seconds to do all this (unless you decided to rename all your tags, in which case you'd probably want to use a computer).

Remembering with Resource view

Resource view is designed to help you remember things. Here's how to open it:

1. **Tap All Notes in the Evernote app.**

2. **Tap the box in the top-right corner.**

Resource view opens, as shown in Figure 15-5. This view tells you everything you need to know about each note, including what pictures are attached to every note, all the attachments for each note, and even the locations where the notes were made.

Figure 15-5:
View your
resources —
pictures,
attach-
ments, and
locations.

You can also use this function in a specific notebook instead of using All Notes. Narrow your search considerably if you already know where you saved your note.

Searching

The problem with taking notes using paper and pen is finding them later. Searching your notes with the Search feature is so ridiculously easy that you'll never want to use a paper note again. Figure 15-1, earlier in this chapter, shows the Search feature in the lower far-right corner of the screen as soon as you open the Evernote app. Simply tap it and start searching. Figure 15-6 shows the Search screen.

Figure 15-6:
The Search
screen.

Unsure how to work with searches? Check out Chapter 8.

Sharing notebooks

Chapter 10 provides the bulk of the information you need about notebook sharing. This feature is useful because you can check out all the notebooks other people have shared, just as you can any other notebook you create. And, of course, if you're the one doing the sharing and you're a Premium subscriber, you can see what updates others have been allowed to make to your notebook.

Here's what to do to share a notebook from an iPhone:

1. **Tap Notebooks to go to the Notebooks screen.**

2. **Tap the Edit button in the top-right corner.**

3. **Tap the notebook you would like to share.**

4. **Tap Share This Notebook.**

Evernote is updated and enhanced often, but unlike Chrome, which updates itself automatically, you need to check periodically for updates to Evernote. Tap Help/Check for updates to be sure that you have the latest release.

Working with Evernote on an iPad

When iPad first arrived, many people questioned its usefulness and wondered whether it would be a player in the market. Well, when it comes to using Evernote, iPad is absolutely one of the best things ever. Bigger than a phone and smaller than a laptop, iPad is portable without sacrificing many computer functions.

The following sections describe a couple of extremely helpful features that make having an iPad for use with Evernote much more enjoyable.

Adding a Snapshot to a note

Being able to take a picture with an iPad is an outstanding feature of the tablet. When Evernote gave photos additional functionality, saving entertaining memories to Evernote as something more permanent became much easier. And it isn't just for fun. With many businesses providing their employees iPads for work, getting pictures of the whiteboard or presentations really does increase productivity, especially when you know that the presenter either won't send around the slides or won't send them around for weeks.

 Taking a snapshot is simple. Press the Home button and also press and release the On/Off/Sleep/Wake button at the top of the iPad. The iPad makes a picture shutter noise and the picture is taken. Check out Chapter 7 to see how to capture a picture as a note.

Marrying PhatPad for iPad with Evernote

PhatPad (available in the App Store) is just plain exciting when combined with Evernote on your iPad. PhatPad is an app that enables you to write with something even better than a permanent marker. More than just another note-taking app, PhatPad turns your iPad into an advanced brainstorming tool. You can draw, write, and type your ideas and then instantly share them via Evernote, e-mail, Wi-Fi, or Dropbox. PhatPad captures scribbles using smooth-flowing digital ink technology. Its handwriting-recognition engine enables you to convert your hand-written notes into text and your rough drawings into smooth geometrical shapes.

If you're the type of person who finds writing is easier than typing, PhatPad is perfect for you. If you doodle ideas on scraps of paper and constantly lose those little pieces of ingenuity, PhatPad is an infinite improvement.

Using PhatPad, you can write directly on an iPad (using a stylus or your finger, not a pencil) and have it all recorded for future reference. Now you start to see where Evernote comes in. Doodle your note into permanent existence in the guise of a note. I found PhatPad to be very intuitive and did not require a substantial learning curve.

PhatPad works with the Evernote handwriting-recognition system so that your handwriting can be correctly translated for searches. The process works similarly to a scan.

If you want to check out another drawing app, Skitch, Evernote's free drawing app, is available for the iPad and is discussed in Chapter 19. It is available in the App Store.

Using Evernote on an Android Device

Apple products aren't the only mobile devices that get special treatment from Evernote. The Android platform has proved its worth and is a phenomenal asset for every Evernote user who has an Android device.

Perhaps the most convenient feature of Evernote for Android devices is its ease of sharing notes with other Android apps and social media. Also, unless you have deliberately turned GPS off, Evernote records the GPS location of each note, and you can tap on the Map pin (to the right of the search box) to see you all notes created near a geographical area.

Collaborating via mobile devices

If you enjoy the benefits of being a Premium subscriber, you can share your notebooks with others and allow them to have the same editing privileges as though you were sharing from a desktop computer.

You can access a notebook shared by a Premium subscriber even if you aren't one yourself.

To access a shared notebook, follow these steps:

1. **Open the Evernote app.**

2. **Tap the Shared icon.**

   An area opens to show all notebooks that you're sharing.

3. **Tap the shared notebook you'd like to work on.**

   The notebook opens.

4. **Tap Sync if you want the notebook to sync at the same time as Evernote.**

Gaining offline access

Offline access is also possible for Premium subscribers on an Android device. Whenever you open a notebook from your Evernote app, Evernote asks you whether you'd like to open the notebook offline.

Offline access is outstanding because you no longer have to rely on a signal to work on your notebooks. Maybe you can't call people, but you don't have an excuse for putting off writing that list that you have been meaning to do or researching your notes for information you know is there. When you are back online, your notes are synchronized automatically.

Quick Notes and Auto-titles

Android devices are designed to be used on the go. There are times when you need to remember something on the go — a fast snapshot or a quick voice memo. But how do you find those notes later? Evernote for Android creates a title based on the content of the note, and the time that the note was created, making it much easier to find it later. An example auto-title is `Snapshot @ San Francisco, California`. Of course, you can always re-title notes later, as you prefer.

Save anytime

If you tap the Save button in the note, a version is saved to your device's memory. There is no need to exit the note. When you're finished, tap Done and the note syncs. This feature is especially useful if you compose lengthy notes on your Android phone or tablet.

Sharing on social media

Evernote does many things well. One feature I use a lot and that Evernote does very well, is making sure that you can always share your notes through social media on your Android device. Whether you want to update Facebook, write a tweet, or send an e-mail, it's all possible with a few taps on your Android screen. The good news is that you don't have to be a Premium subscriber to share notes to social media.

If you're a typical Evernote user, you more than likely have a Facebook or Twitter account (or both). And what better way to get everything into one location than to post to Facebook from your Android device? (Refer to Chapter 6 to connect your Facebook and Evernote accounts.) Of course, you can also e-mail your note.

Here's how:

1. **Open the Evernote app.**

2. **Tap and hold the note you'd like to post.**

   A new menu appears, with an option to post to Facebook.

3. **Tap Share.**

   A new menu appears. The options in this menu enable you to send an e-mail or even text with a couple of extra steps.

4. **To post a note to Facebook, tap Post to Facebook; to share a note over Twitter, tap Twitter; to e-mail your note, tap Email; to text the note, tap Share.**

   If you post to Facebook or Twitter, you have the opportunity to add text and then tap the Share button.

   If you opt to e-mail the note, tapping Email and entering the recipient's address completes the process. You can also add some text if you like. Tap Send when you are ready for the note to be delivered.

   If you are texting the note, simply select the contact you would like to send the note to and tap send.

Searching notebooks when you're on the go

One of the best universal features of Evernote and one that is especially easy on the Android devices is searching on the go. You can even narrow down the number of notes you have to comb through if you know in which notebook to search. Of course, you can always run a search from All Notes (which searches all notebooks) if you aren't sure where to begin your search; the same steps apply from the All Notes screen.

Here's how to search a single notebook:

1. **Open the Evernote app.**

2. **Tap the notebook you want to search.**

3. **Tap the magnifying glass in the top-right corner.**

   A new screen opens.

4. **Type the text that you'd like to search for.**

   The notes that contain the text appear below the search box.

5. **Scroll through the notes to find the one you need.**

Editing saved searches

You can not only run searches on your Android device, but also modify your saved searches. Although you can't create new saved searches on your Android phone (yet), after you've created a saved search on a desktop or laptop computer, you can execute it on your Android phone.

To modify a saved search, follow these steps:

1. **Tap the magnifying glass on the main Evernote screen on your Android device.**

   You can also open your saved searches. (See the previous section if you want to run a new search.)

2. **Tap and hold the saved search you'd like to modify.**

   You're asked whether you'd like to edit the query before searching.

3. **Tap the text to edit the search.**

   The search information appears in the search box at the top of the screen.

4. **Modify the search as needed.**

5. **Tap the magnifying glass to execute the search.**

6. **Select the note you're looking for in the search results.**

Taking advantage of maps and GPS support

One interesting feature of smartphones and tablets is the capability to track your location with GPS coordinates. Evernote uses the phone's ability to add location information to your notes. The location tag for a note gives you one more thing to search on and allows for easy retrieval of notes by location. This feature is incredibly handy when, for example, you're decorating and visiting many stores and want to locate that adorable table you found on Route 4 in Paramus, but whose name escapes you.

You need to have the GPS feature enabled to use this ability. To enable the GPS function, follow these steps:

1. **In the Evernote app, press the Android Menu button on the device.**

   This is a physical button just below the screen.

2. **Tap Settings.**

   A window opens, displaying your saved settings.

3. **Scroll down to Use GPS Satellites, and make sure that its check box is selected.**

After you enable GPS on your Android device, you can use it with your notes. To take advantage of GPS, follow these steps:

1. **Tap the magnifying glass on the main Evernote page on your Android phone.**

2. **Tap the pinpoint bubble in the top-left corner of the screen.**

   A map of all your notes appears, with GPS information recorded.

3. **When viewing a single note, press the Menu button on your device and select Note Info. Then, tap the Location button to plot the note's location on a map.**

   On the location screen, there are a few things you can do, so just play around until you feel comfortable with the feature.

 You can also set up future locations on your phone to make trip planning much easier. Press the Menu button and choose Map. From the map, tap Set Location, and drop a pin on the map location where you plan to go. Repeat Steps 1 to 3 of the preceding list for each location where you want to go and want to track on your phone.

Each pin on the map can have notes added to it so that you know what you were interested in seeing. (You may change your plans after you get to the location.) You can even enter opening and closing times to the note so that you have all the information you need in one place.

Locking Evernote via PIN lock

PIN lock is another reason to be a Premium subscriber; it enables you to lock Evernote, preventing people without the PIN from accessing your notes. If you don't want the hassle of always locking your phone just to lock Evernote information, now you can lock just this app. Here's how to set up PIN lock:

PIN lock is also available on iOS devices.

1. **In the Evernote app, tap the Android option.**

   A little menu appears at the bottom of the phone.

2. **Tap Settings.**

   Another window opens, displaying your saved settings.

3. **Tap Setup PIN Lock.**

   This step opens a screen where you can enable, change, or disable your PIN information.

You get three attempts to enter your password before you're locked out and have to reenter your Evernote password information from the Settings menu to access Evernote on your phone.

Editing styled notes

Being able to work with styled fonts, including check boxes and bulleted lists, is a fantastic way of tracking information and putting emphasis on key phrases.

The formatting bar contains all the icons that you need to style your notes. As you would expect, you can use bold, italic, or underline, or you can set up bulleted lists. You can even create a list with check boxes on your Android device by following these steps:

1. **Start a new note.**

2. **Scroll the style menu until you reach the check-box icon.**

3. **Tap the check-box icon.**

   Your phone automatically makes every new row part of a checklist.

Tap Backspace if you want to end the checklist and start a row of regular text.

Creating a notebook

Creating a notebook isn't limited to your desktop or laptop computer; you can also create a notebook on your Android device.

Follow these steps to create a notebook on your Android device:

1. **In the Evernote app, tap the Notebooks icon.**

2. **Press the Android Menu button.**

This button appears just below the screen.

3. **Tap New Notebook in the menu that appears.**

   A window appears where you can give the notebook a name.

4. **Name the new notebook, and tap OK.**

   You can't leave the notebook nameless; you do have to enter a name before Evernote creates the notebook.

   After a few seconds, your new notebook appears in alphabetical order with your other notebooks.

Working with Evernote on a BlackBerry

Nowadays, working with Evernote on a BlackBerry is very similar to using it on an iPhone. That's good news. Early versions of Evernote for the BlackBerry were — and I can't be delicate —unusable. For one thing, notes took forever to load, find, and upload. Fortunately, all those issues have been fixed.

Before you do anything else, make sure that you have the latest version of Evernote installed by navigating to `http://appworld.blackberry.com/webstore/content/1700`.

You can download the app from BlackBerry App World on your BlackBerry or your desktop computer, which may be faster. (It was for me, even with a Wi-Fi connection to the BlackBerry.) If you choose the computer route, you may be prompted to install an add-on the first time you use the app. After you've downloaded the app to your computer, the next time you sync your BlackBerry with it, the app is installed on your BlackBerry.

Releases beginning with version 3.3 support offline notes. Sync and loading are much faster. Evernote for BlackBerry lets you create new notes with text, audio, and photos. These notes are pinned to the top of your note list in a pending state until you get on a network, at which point they sync into your account. You can even edit the pending notes, if you need to.

Whenever you create or view a note, it's stored locally on your device. You don't need a network connection to view the note later. If the note has an attached file, such as a PDF, you need to view the file while you have a network connection before it becomes available offline.

Now you can save to a note, and retrieve from a note, any file stored on the device or on an SD card (as long as it falls within the size restrictions). Also, support for SD cards (where Evernote for BlackBerry stores the local copy of your notes) has been improved so that space is used more efficiently and retrieval is faster.

The basic Evernote functions supported are

- View headers (All Notes)
- Create a note (Text Note)
- Take a photo and add it as a note (Snapshot)
- Record (Audio Note)
- Create a new note and upload any file (Upload File)
- Search anything in Evernote (Search)

Improvements to Evernote for BlackBerry include the following useful features:

- The home screen has been revamped to make it easier to see which items are selected. The screen has better colors, an easy-to-see grid, and clear text labels.

- You can filter the Notes screen to show your notes by notebook. This improvement is great for quick browsing. To switch between notebooks, tap the green bar along the top of the list, and choose a notebook. All the notes filter instantly.

- When you're appending text to complex notes, you can see the content of the note just below the text that you're adding so that you can easily reference the content of your note in what you're appending.

- Synchronization is significantly faster, and text throughout the app is easier to read.

- The newly redesigned List view shows many more notes on a single screen than in the past.

For me, the most useful features are the ease of creating a note without carrying around a larger device and snapping pictures throughout the day and then saving them as notes. I also love having access to my entire collection of Evernote notebooks and notes on the device I use most all day long.

Chapter 16

Using Evernote on the Web

*J*ust like hardware and operating-system platforms, different browsers have various capabilities. In this chapter, I go over things that are universal about using Evernote across all the browsers. Then I present some of the differences that make each working with each browser unique.

Working with Evernote Web

Using Evernote on the web provides the most consistent way of working with the application. Although you can accomplish most of the tasks in this section in other versions of Evernote, doing them through Evernote Web means that you never have to sync because you've made your changes directly on the server.

The screen captures in this section are from Google Chrome, but Evernote's features generally work the same way in all browsers, with slight differences in appearance.

Attaching files

Attaching files to notes is a very handy feature. If you have files that you saved on your desktop and want to open them on a laptop or on one of your mobile devices, attaching them to notes is a quick way to do it, and drag-and-drop makes it simple to attach and dash.

To attach files to notes in Evernote, follow these steps:

1. **Log in to Evernote.**

2. **Create a new note or open the note to which you want to attach the file.**

3. **Do one of the following:**

     • Drag the file into the note.

     • Click the paper-clip icon.

   The easiest way to attach a file in Chrome is to simply drag it into the note. (On my machine, I have to drag s-l-o-w-l-y for this method to work reliably, even with a fast Internet connection.) You can also click the old familiar paper-clip icon to attach the file. Figure 16-1 shows the dialog box that appears when you click that icon, allowing you to browse to the file location.

   You can attach multiple files — up to ten — to a single note. For information on dragging and dropping multiple files, see "Selecting multiple notes and notebooks" later in this chapter.

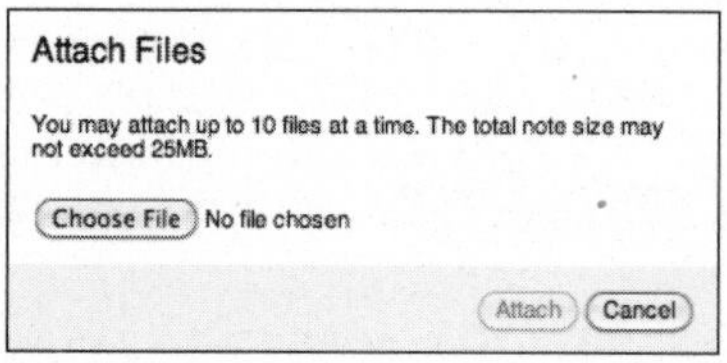

Figure 16-1:
The Attach
Files dialog
box.

> **Attach Files**
>
> You may attach up to 10 files at a time. The total note size may not exceed 25MB.
>
> (Choose File) No file chosen
>
> (Attach) (Cancel)

Stacking notebooks

Stacks are the ultimate way to organize multiple notebooks into a single notebook. You can think of a stack as being a visual binder for multiple notebooks.

Suppose that you use a stack for a notebook for vacations. You aren't sure where you want to go, so you create two notebooks: one for a trip to Florida to check out the beaches, and one for a trip to London. What you need for these trips is very different, so you want separate notebooks to keep the information specific to each trip separate.

Here's how to create stacks for multiple notebooks:

1. **Log in to Evernote online.**

2. **Create a new notebook for each item you'd like to organize.**

If you're trying to decide between a vacation in Florida or in London, for example, create two notebooks: one called Florida and one called London.

3. **Click one folder and drag it on top of the other to create a notebook stack.**

   In the example, you'd drag the London notebook to the Florida notebook, or vice versa. (The order really doesn't matter.) When you do, Evernote creates a stack and assigns the default name Notebook Stack.

4. **Give the notebook stack a more informative name.**

   For the trips example, you might name the stack Vacation.

After you create your stack, you can create new notes to go into any of the notebooks in a stack. Or, if you decide to add another notebook — perhaps you have another vacation that you're thinking about — simply click the Notebook header and then click New Notebook, name the new notebook, click Save, and drag the new notebook into the notebook stack.

Catching a glimpse with Snippets view

Snippets view gives you the basic information about each note in the view panel. This view isn't cluttered with pictures or other items, giving you a glimpse idea of what's in each note. It's very easy to switch between List and Snippets views.

Snippets view is the default mode for online viewing. Just in case you've changed your view, though, here's how you change back to Snippets view:

1. **Log in to Evernote online.**

2. **Click the drop-down arrow next to View Options, and select Snippets (see Figure 16-2).**

   Now you can enjoy a more detailed view of your note.

Figure 16-2:
Choosing
Snippets
view for
Evernote
online.

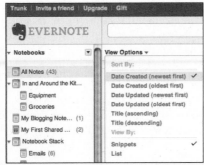

Saving searches online

Saving Evernote searches online is simple and fast. You can build up a useful personal collection of searches to make your work more efficient.

To initiate and save a search:

1. **Log in to Evernote online.**

2. **Highlight the notebook in which you want to search.**

   It's a good idea to run searches on All Notes, just in case you dragged and dropped or saved something in the a location other than where you intended. You can select a more specific notebook if you're sure where you're going.

3. **Click inside the Search box.**

   From here, you can also select the notebook to be searched if you decide to go with something different from the one you highlighted.

4. **Start typing your search terms.**

   Evernote starts suggesting tags that match what you type. You can type any search term you like, however, and you can search in tags, notebooks, mobile notes, and files.

   Evernote pulls up the rest of the criteria for you and executes the search.

5. **To save a search, click File⇨Save Search.**

   When the dialog box opens, give the search a name, and click OK. To repeat a search that you ran previously, check out the list of recently run searches at the bottom of the list of notebooks, under Saved Searches (in new versions of Evernote) or click in the Search Box and then click the search you want to run (on older versions of Evernote).

Filters

When you click in the search box, you can filter notes according to various criteria. Click in the search box and then click Add Filters. Filter options include the following:

- ✔ **Match** defaults to All filters, but you can also click the Any Filter radio button to select notes matching any of the criteria.

- ✔ **Contains** opens a series of check boxes that enables you to restrict the search to notes containing the criteria you check, including Images, Encrypted Text, Attachments, Audio, PDF, or Ink.

✔ **Source** opens a series of filters including Emailed to Evernote, Web Page, Another Application, Evernote Hello, Clipped from email, Mobile, and Evernote Food (a free iPhone app to preserve memorable food experiences. See `www.evernote.com/food/` to download).

Evernote Hello is a free iPhone App for creating a browsable history of people you meet and experiences you share with them. Go to `www.evernote.com/hello/` to download it.

✔ **To-do** lets you filter notes as Finished or Unfinished.

✔ **Created** enables you to filter notes by the time frame in which you created them.

✔ **Modified** works like Created but filters based on the date you modified notes rather than the day you created them.

Would you like to try using all the search- filters? Absolutely give it a shot. Before executing a search, restrict the search using filters as much as you like, and see what you get. Using a series of filters may not be too useful when you start using Evernote because you won't have many notes, but as you accumulate more notes, this method may be your best bet for quickly getting at what you are looking for and filtering out what isn't relevant.

Selecting multiple notes and notebooks

You don't have to click and drag one note at a time. You can move multiple notes, or even notebooks, at the same time. Here's how:

1. **Log in to Evernote online.**

2. **Highlight the notes you want to move.**

   To select more than one note, hold down the Ctrl (Windows) or Command (Mac) key and then click all the notes you want to move.

3. **Drag and drop the notes into the appropriate notebook.**

Sharing notes and notebooks

Sharing from the Internet is the same as sharing from any of the other platforms or devices. The following sections take a quick look at note sharing and notebook sharing.

Note sharing

Sharing a note link creates a public link to a note that someone can view without signing in to Evernote. You can also share a link using Facebook, Twitter, or e-mail.

1. **Log in to Evernote online.**

2. **Highlight the note you want to share.**

3. **Click Share.**

   To share on a PC, click on the down-arrow to the right of Share on the Evernote menu bar to open a small window where you can choose the share destination. Evernote remembers your last selection as the default. On a Mac, click Share on the Note menu.

   The first time you do this step, a pop-up window like Figure 16-3 appears showing the shared public link (a URL). Click Copy to Clipboard to copy the link to the clipboard. If you want to stop sharing, Click on Shared to the right of the note, and then Stop Sharing. Click the Stop Sharing button to stop sharing your note publicly.

   The shared link URLs are long. I click Copy to Clipboard and then use a URL shortener, such as goo.gl (Google's URL shortener), and then paste in the shortened URL because it's much easier to share.

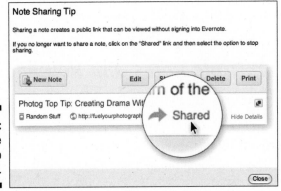

Figure 16-3:
Initial Note
Sharing Tip
window.

Figure 16-4 shows you the options for posting.

Figure 16-4:
Sharing
options
online.

4. **Choose what you want to do.**

   You have three options:

   - To post to Facebook, click the Facebook option (refer to Figure 16-4), add a message, and click Share. If you haven't set up your account to post to Facebook, Chapter 10 provides detailed instructions to get you connected.

   - To e-mail the note, click the Email option (refer to Figure 16-4). In the resulting window (see Figure 16-5), fill in the requested information, and click the Send button.

   - To post a URL, click the Link option (refer to Figure 16-4), copy the displayed link and paste it where you want to share it. You can do as you like with this link — e-mail or text it to friends, post it on your website — anything you can do with a hypertext link.

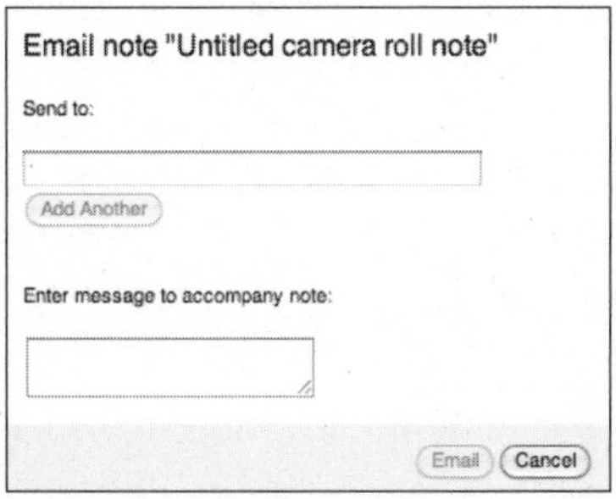

Figure 16-5:
Emailing a
note.

Email note "Untitled camera roll note"

Send to:

[   ]

(Add Another)

Enter message to accompany note:

[   ]

(Email) (Cancel)

Notebook sharing

You can also share an entire notebook. You can make the link public (Share with the World) or only with invited individuals whose e-mail addresses you provide.

The uses of public links or notebooks are as varied as the uses for Evernote. Here are a few ideas to stimulate your imagination:

- Share a notebook of your favorite recipes, movies, or songs with your friends
- Maintain a list of "known bugs and workarounds" for your project
- Publish an updated project plan to your colleagues

To share a notebook, follow these steps:

1. **Log in to Evernote online.**

2. **Highlight the notebook you want to share.**

3. **Choose Share➪Share Notebooks.**

    When you share this way (rather than right-clicking on the notebook to be shared in the desktop application, and clicking Share Notebook) you get more sharing options and can share multiple notebooks instead of one at a time.

4. **Click Start Sharing next to the notebook you'd like to share.**

    Clicking Share Notebooks opens the Notebook sharing screen. Click Start Sharing to the right of the notebook name to begin sharing it. The Shared Notebook setting screen opens. It has two panels. The left side enables you to share your shared notebook with the world. A settings screen opens with a proposed public URL consisting of `https://www.evernote.com/pub/[your user name]/[notebook name]`. You can modify the name of your notebook if you want something more descriptive. Feel free to add a description to give people basic information about the notebook. Set the notebook to sort by date created or date updated, or by newest to oldest or oldest to newest.

    You can also share a notebook with individuals by entering the individuals' e-mail addresses. Each named recipient receives a unique link for accessing the shared notebook. Only invitees can access a non-public notebook.

    If you're a Premium subscriber, you can use the Modify This Notebook option to enable others to edit your notes.

    Optionally, you can require those with modification rights to log on as Evernote users (may be done with a free account). You can also send an optional message with your invitation.

    You can share your notebook on Facebook. All you have to do is check the check box in the bottom-left corner of the screen.

5. **Click Save.**

    You've shared your notebook.

If you decide that you don't want to share the notebook anymore, return to Share Notebooks and click Stop/Modify Sharing to change the sharing options for the notebook or to stop sharing it entirely.

Filtering

Filters limit the notes returned from a search. Adding filters gives you a fast, efficient way to get to your notes without having to spend a lot of time looking for them. Filtering is easier and less time-consuming than searching for files in Windows Explorer because you know that All Notes covers everything instead of having to guess the location or running a find on files and folders that certainly won't have what you need. And you can't even compare filtering with trying to find hard copy. Even if you're super-organized on paper, it takes longer than you need to find information than it does if you scan your notes into Evernote and then search for them using a filter. Filtering is one of the primary benefits of Evernote.

To filter, follow these steps:

1. **Log in to Evernote online.**

2. **Highlight the notebook that you want to filter.**

3. **Click the Search box and then choose Add Filters from the drop-down menu (see Figure 16-6).**

   The resulting window (see Figure 16-7) shows you the options for each category. As you can see in the figure, these options give you full control of the output.

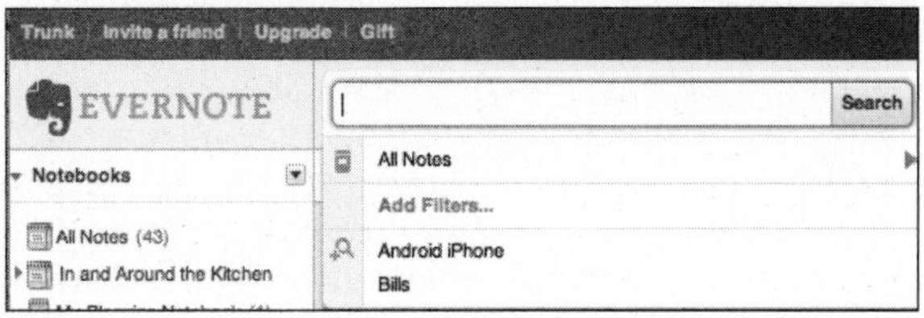

Figure 16-6:
Choose Add Filters.

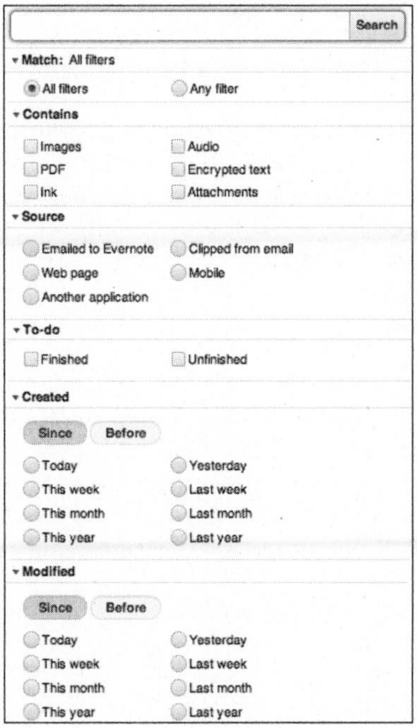

Figure 16-7:
Online filter options.

If you want to narrow the search to one note but don't remember the notebook it's in or the note's title, you can zero in on it through a filter. If you captured a web page last year, for example, and all you can remember about it is that it was a year or so ago, and a common phrase or subject, you can add a date filter to filter out more recent notes from the search, which greatly reduces how much hunting you have to do.

Reviewing note history

Note history is a really cool feature that's reserved for Premium subscribers only. If you want to view or recover a previous version of a note, you can do that in just a couple of clicks. Note history is great if you accidentally erase something.

Evernote takes several daily snapshots of Premium subscribers' information. The server determines whether changes have been made to notes before Evernote takes the snapshot. Talk about service! The only thing to remember is that your notes aren't stored following every change — just when the server checks in your notes. (When you work from the web browser, the notes are always saved when you click away from the note, and that triggers the snapshot to be created. You can't see an entire snapshot, but clicking Note History for any note enables you to see the note as it was captured during each snapshot.)

Your note history doesn't count against your capacity quota, because it's stored on the Evernote server.

You access your note history from your web browser. In Evernote online, click the down arrow to the right of the note to show additional details and then click Note History to retrieve the history from the online version. In the resulting window, you're invited to import the note history. You see the history of changes to the note, and you can click any one of them to view or export. If you do, you see a new notebook created called Imported Notes, and you can see the earlier versions.

Any note you delete is also deleted from your note history (but it goes to the trash), so make sure that you really want to erase notes in the trash completely before you empty your Evernote trash. The trash is at the bottom of your list of notes. You can click Restore Note to restore any note to the notebook from which it was deleted or Erase Note to permanently expunge it from Evernote and consign it to the great, big bit bucket of irretrievable deletions.

To access your note history, follow these steps:

1. **Log in to Evernote.**

2. **Click the note with the history you want to check.**

3. **Click Note Attributes.**

4. **Click View Note History.**

   From the Note History screen, you can review the history of the note in all its forms, going all the way back to when it was created. This feature is perfect if you want to add information that you deleted (intentionally or not) without losing your other updates.

   You can also export the note so that you can import it again as a different note.

To Export or Import notes, click Import or Export on the File menu. For more details on importing and exporting, see Chapter 10.

 One of the best uses for note history is when you've shared a note and allowed write access to it, and you want to go back and see how it changed. By using note history, you can see what's been done and when, making project tracking about as simple as you could want.

Google Chrome

Google Chrome is the first browser to get Evernote updates automatically. It's fast, streamlined (compact), and secure. It provides native support for drag-and-drop and for HTML5, the newest version of HTML that, among other features, allows for the display of presentations and video without plug-ins, offline storage, and real-time communication.

Google Chrome also has the easiest, most open development tool set of any web browser, making it the platform of choice for software developers. For these reasons, new Evernote features are first implemented in Chrome. For more information, see `http://google.com/chrome/intl/en/more/index.html`.

Persistent sign-in

If you're using Google Chrome for something like Evernote, which you're likely to use daily, you won't want to have to sign in all the time (Evernote also supports this feature on other browsers.)

 The first time you open Evernote in Google Chrome on a computer, the browser asks whether you want to save your password (see Figure 16-8). If you click Save Password, you'll never have to sign in again (desktop versions only) or for one week (other versions) unless you force a logout.

Figure 16-8:
Save-
password
prompt.

Figure 16-8:
Save-
password
prompt.

You'll be asked for your password the first time you open Evernote in Google Chrome on any computer, but as soon as you click Save Password, you're good to go, and you can work on multiple computers without the annoyance of logging on every time (Mac or PC) or for a week (online versions).

Don't save your password on a public computer, because if you do, anyone who uses the computer can access your notes, which may have serious consequences.

Right-click to clip

Hard as it may be to believe, Evernote has made clipping even easier in Google Chrome than when clipping in other browsers. Clipping is as simple as clicking.

To clip, right-click the desired web page and then, from the contextual menu, choose what you'd like to do. You have several choices (see Figure 16-9):

✓ **Clip This Page:** This option, which appears when you don't have text highlighted, stores the entire page for you.

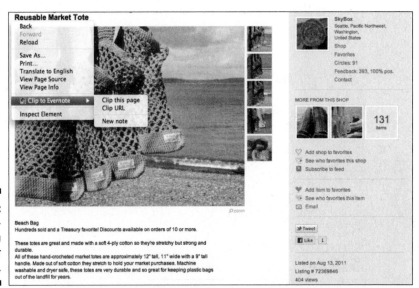

Figure 16-9:
Contextual-
menu
options for
clipping.

✔ **Clip URL:** Choose this option if you want to post the link instead of the content.

✔ **New Note:** Use this option to start a new note in Google Chrome.

✔ **Clip Selection:** Use this option if you want to clip a small portion of the page, whether that portion is text, pictures, or a combination (see Figure 16-10).

✔ **Clip Image:** Use this option if all you want to clip is the image on a page (see Figure 16-11).

Figure 16-10: Choose this option to clip selected information.

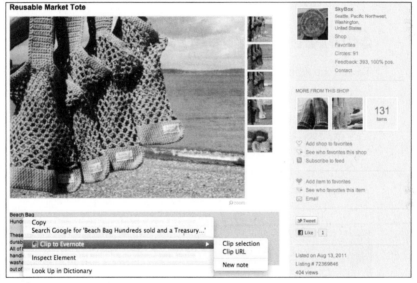

Figure 16-11: Choose Clip Image to clip the selected image.

When you Clip to Evernote a window opens with a title taken from the title of the page you are clipping. (You can modify this title.) Evernote tries to determine the boundaries of an article or image, or you can highlight material yourself. Clip Article is selected option when you highlight information or Evernote identifies an article. You can click the arrow to the right of the Clip to Evernote button to select either Clip URL or Clip Full Page.

In my experience, Evernote does a good, but not perfect, job of detecting the boundaries of an article, so in most cases, creating a note only requires two clicks: one to click the Evernote icon on the browser toolbar and one to save the article into a note in your default notebook.

Snippet and clipping

To see the snippets, you previously clipped, follow these steps:

1. **Click the Evernote icon.**

2. **Click the My Notes tab to see all notes you have clipped or click the URL-specific tab to see notes you have clipped from a particular website.**

   Click the URL-specific tab to see the notes you have collected from a site (see Figure 16-12).

Figure 16-12:
Chrome snippets.

3. **Click the note of interest.**

   The note opens in its own window so that you can examine it more closely.

Eventnote

Evernote lets you handle checklists, bills, projects, and virtually everything except your calendar. Now Eventnote handles calendar tasks. Eventnote is an extension to Google Chrome for Google Calendar that works with most platforms and devices. It's so good at keeping your life in sync that you'll have far fewer excuses for missing another birthday, anniversary, or appointment.

To link Evernote to Google Calendar, follow these steps:

1. **Find Eventnote in the Chrome store (`chrome.google.com/webstore`) by searching on Evernote or from `https://chrome.google.com/webstore/detail/ipogebjapdddlkchpnimcgplonlonkoj`.**

   Click + Add to Chrome to add the extension, and to install the icon on the Chrome browser.

2. **Log in to Evernote.**

3. **After installing, log in to your Evernote account and select the notebook you'd like the events to be posted to.**

4. **Start a new calendar appointment or edit an existing one.**

   You see a Post to Evernote checkbox just under the time and date settings for the event. (See Figure 16-13.)

   Google Calendar gives you confirmation that the event was successfully saved and posted to Evernote

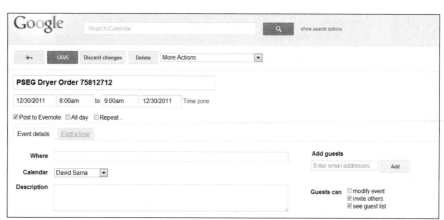

Figure 16-13: Adding a new event to Evernote.

It may take a little while to see the note posted to Evernote

This feature may not work with some versions of Chrome. As the book went to press, when I tried to use the feature I received a message that the extension wasn't compatible with my version of Evernote, even though it worked flawlessly for me.

Mozilla Firefox

In August 2011, Firefox went through some extensive and extremely useful changes, including support for HTML5. The most notable changes for Evernote users include support for web clipping in Firefox that are similar to those in Google Chrome. (You can use information in the preceding section to find out how you can create clippings in Firefox.) That wonderful simultaneous-search feature, that used to be just for Google Chrome is now a fully functional part of Firefox, too.

See Chapter 2 for instructions on installing the Evernote Add-in for Firefox.

You need to enable the option by opening the Firefox browser, clicking Options on the Tools menu then clicking Manage Add-ons. On Evernote Web Clipper, click Options, check Use Simultaneous Search, and then click Save.

Another outstanding Firefox feature is the ability to send notes to either the desktop or online version without having to worry about syncing. After you've clipped the area you want, just clip to Evernote, as described in the preceding section about Chrome, and the note is sent to the destination you choose. If you choose desktop, the note sinks to Evernote's site next time a sync occurs.

You can set sync options in Evernote through Tools ⇨Options⇨Sync. By default, the sync is every 15 minutes, but you can slow it down by clicking a different time interval (every 30 minutes, every hour, or every day). Unless you have a very slow or expensive connection, choose the default of 15 minutes for the most up-to-date results to appear on all your devices.

Internet Explorer

Although its functionality isn't as robust as that of Google Chrome, Internet Explorer has some very cool capabilities. The control you have of clipping in Internet Explorer gives you a better way to create and store information. As with Firefox (see the preceding section), you can send your clipped items to your desktop version of Evernote.

Internet Explorer also enables you to format your text. It even uses the same shortcut keys as Chrome (Ctrl-C and Ctrl-V) to allow for faster copy/paste work. And when you want to add a date stamp to a note, simply press Ctrl - ; (semicolon).

As with many types of software, using shortcut keys can be a way to increase your efficiency when working with Evernote. Check out `www.evernote.com/about/support/3.5_Shortcuts.html` to see a list of the various shortcuts you can use when working with Evernote.

Apple Safari

Evernote for Safari has been updated and is now nearly identical to the Chrome version. Be sure you have the latest version of Evernote to get the most from using it on your Mac devices and high-powered desktop machines.

Safari 5.1 significantly changed the way it supports browser plug-ins, making the Evernote Safari Web Clipper plug-in incompatible with older browsers. As we go to press, a new and improved Web Clipper 3.0.6 was available as a beta version. In my testing, it worked very well. I recommend that you switch to the new extension for the best Evernote experience in Safari. See Chapter 2 for installation instructions.

Part V
Expanding Your Skills

CONVERTS YOUR EVERNOTE VOICE NOTES TO TEXT

Record Your Note

Record voice notes as usual using your favourite Evernote app
on your Smartphone, PC or browser. Or for totally handsfree voice notes, we'll
give you a special phone number to dial and speak your note using ANY phone.

We Convert It

We take your voice note and convert it to text.
You can even tag the notes by saying "TAG WITH" at the end.

Searchable Voice Notes!

Now you can search your voice notes. It's fast and gives you a convenient
way to get useful notes into Evernote quickly and handsfree.
No typing for you!

In this part . . .

"**M**an is Not Alone," said my teacher, the late philosopher Abraham Joshua Heschel, in his book of the same name, and neither is Evernote.

This part is about bringing Evernote into the rest of your world. You can make Evernote immeasurably more powerful by enhancing it with Trunk applications (third-party programs that interface nicely with Evernote and extend its power), with other people's notebooks that leverage your own notes, with social media and with interesting hardware that greatly extends your Evernote experience.

Chapter 17 presents some of my favorite Trunk applications, which enable you to do things such as converting voice notes to searchable, taggable text, interface to the Enterprise world of SAP, saving important, memorable items from social media into Evernote, and much more. Chapter 18 is about enhancing Evernote by importing notes from other people's notebooks, including those from commercial vendors. And Chapter 19 covers information on hardware that can enhance your Evernote experience.

Chapter 17

Enhancing Evernote with Third-Party Applications

In This Chapter

▶ Using the Evernote Trunk ecosystem to enhance your experience

▶ Transcribing your voice notes

▶ Using apps to integrate with social media

With nearly 20 million users and growing, Evernote has attracted a host of third-party developers whose products can greatly enrich your Evernote experience. In fact, anyone can create an Evernote add-on or interface their existing software to work well with Evernote.

The Evernote Trunk offers many Evernote add-ons (there's no actual commerce in the Trunk; you just browse to see what add-ons you can purchase or download elsewhere). There's not enough space in this book to describe all available Trunk applications. The list is continually expanding, so any compilation would be immediately dated. In this chapter, I highlight the add-ons that I think are the most useful. You may just find one that I omitted to be a personal lifesaver; however, so make sure to browse the Evernote Trunk for finds I may have missed.

Introducing the Evernote Trunk

The Evernote Trunk is a pun. Evernote's logo sports an elephant — an animal that is reputed to never forget and is famed for its memory and intelligence. The proboscis, or trunk, is a fusion of the nose and upper lip and is the elephant's most important and versatile appendage. Evernote's Trunk is a site within the Evernote website where you can find applications and hardware that enhance your use of Evernote.

Most vendors of Evernote add-ons choose to list them in the Evernote Trunk (www.evernote.com/about/trunk), where they're grouped in the following six general areas:

- ✔ **New + Notable:** This area is a continually changing list of new and exciting apps. I generally check this area weekly.

- ✔ **Mobile:** Mobile apps are optimized for your mobile devices (smartphones, tablets, and the like). Most apps do one specific thing well. Usually, the interface with Evernote greatly enhances their power.

- ✔ **Desktop + Web:** There are fewer applications for desktop and web than for mobile applications, but some are so useful, you'll wonder how you ever lived without them.

- ✔ **Hardware:** Scanners, tablets, and specialized devices that interface with Evernote are available in this area. Read Chapter 19 for more information about hardware you can use with Evernote.

- ✔ **Gear:** Gear includes learning aids, Evernote wallpaper, T-shirts, and other apparel.

- ✔ **By Evernote:** Applications, extensions, and features built by Evernote.

Unlike Evernote itself, which works well on many platforms, many Trunk applications work only on a specific platform. Make sure that the app you want works with your devices.

Converting Voice Notes to Searchable, Taggable Text

With Evernote, no matter what device you're using, you can easily record your thoughts and save them as a voice note. But how do you retrieve those thoughts when you want to hear them again? You need a way to turn the recorded voice into machine-readable text that can be indexed.

Third-party vendors have developed several approaches, described in the following sections.

Voice2Note (Any cell phone, Android devices, and BlackBerry devices)

Voice2Note by Dial2Do (www.voice2note.dial2do.com) enables you to do exactly what the name suggests: turn a voice recording into a note. This service for Evernote users automatically converts any new audio notes in your Evernote account to searchable, taggable text (see Figure 17-1).

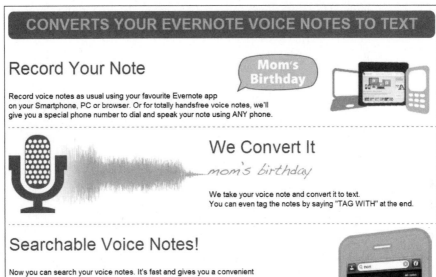

Figure 17-1:
How
Voice2Note
works.

After you've registered for the service, you can create voice notes by using any of Evernote's clients or simply call Voice2Note at (650) 963-5782 to record your note from any phone — mobile or landline — as long as you've registered the number and have Caller ID enabled. Either way, Voice2Note transcribes the first 30 seconds of your note and inserts the text into your note, where Evernote indexes it automatically.

When you call the Voice2Note number, you can record for up to 30 seconds. If you record through an app, you can record your audio note for as long as the app allows. Voice2Note always transcribes only the first 30 seconds of your audio note, however, so it's most useful if you first dictate a summary of key points and then the message. In my experience, that amount of time is usually enough to find the note when you do a search.

You can even tag the notes by saying "Tag with" at the end.

Use Voice2Note to capture great ideas that come to mind, keep track of tasks that you need to get done, and save bits of information that you want to remember, all without typing a word.

You can register for the service on the Voice2Note website. Free and paid options are available. Currently, Basic is free, and a Pro version is offered for monthly or annual subscription. I suggest that you try the free basic plan before you pay for a Pro subscription. The Pro subscription extends recording time from 20 to 30 seconds; adds sending SMS by voice; sending, listening to, and replying to email by voice; listening to and posting tweets by voice;

and, most importantly for Evernote users, posting audio notes to Evernote by voice. You don't receive a refund for payments that have already been made, so unless you're sure that you'll like and use the app, opt for the monthly payment plan.

As of this book's printing, Voice2Note understands only English. Only the U.S. number is available, but you can access it worldwide, and it's been available whenever I've used it.

Quicktate (a dial-in transcription service)

Quicktate (www.quicktate.com) is a general transcription service. You can create audio files by dictating notes into your Evernote app, uploading LiveScribe files, or calling (888) 222-NOTE. Quicktate accurately converts your audio to simple, searchable text and automatically submits the transcript to Evernote.

Quicktate is not a machine-translation service. It strives to achieve high-transcription accuracy by using trained human typists (who are under strict confidentiality agreements) to ensure that your transcription jobs are secure and accurate. Pricing is by the word, based on content. General transcription charged by the word, with special transcription services, such as legal and medical, being more costly than other services. (The average page contains about 250 words, and Quicktate transcriptions typically cost $3 to $5 per page.)

Quicktate may be especially cost-effective for dictating short notes, as there is no per-note charge — only a per-word charge.

Because Quicktate uses humans to transcribe, you don't need any special training to use it. Conference calls, interviews, and phone meetings are just a few examples of the types of calls you can record; have Quicktate transcribe into text; and then submit to Evernote, where the notes can be fully indexed and retrieved.

With Quicktate, you can automatically record all or just some calls, or even manually record just the calls you want, or any other recorded speech you'd like transcribed.

Total Recall (Android devices)

Total Recall (available from the Android Market) is a call recorder and dictating utility for Android mobile devices. You can automatically or manually record all or just some of your calls. You can send your recordings via e-mail or upload them to your Evernote account and use Total Recall's convenient Home-screen widget to record by tapping a single button.

A hardware add-on for non-Android devices

Total Recall Bluetooth Mobile Call Recorder (TRB) is a related hardware device for non-Android devices that claims to be the world's first call recorder unit for all mobile phones. This means you can use it to record calls on your iPhone, BlackBerry, or any mobile phone with Bluetooth. TRB acts like your Bluetooth headset and is just as easy to connect, but it offers you the critical ability of recording your calls easily with high-quality audio. The TRB unit is small, attractive, and very easy to use. You can find out how to get a TRB unit at `www.killer mobile.com/new!-bluetooth-based-mobile-call-recorder.html`.

To send audio to your Evernote account, tap the recording that you want on the Records tab, tap More, and choose Upload to Evernote. After the note is in Evernote, you can use either Voice2Note or Quicktate (see the two preceding sections) to transcribe it, if you want.

Filling In, Signing, Stamping, and Saving PDFs with Nitro (Windows)

Nitro PDF Reader (`www.nitroreader.com`) is a Windows application that bills itself as "The PDF reader, reimagined." It includes an Evernote plug-in. Nitro PDF Reader has a button that lets you stamp a PDF form with a scan of your signature. You can create PDFs of files in more than 300 formats; comment, review, and collaborate; fill, sign, and save PDF forms; stamp signatures; extract text and images; and type text directly on the page. Then, when you're done, you can save PDF files to your Evernote account by choosing File⇨Send to Evernote option from the File menu or from context menus that enable you to select and save specific text and images directly into your Evernote account.

Nitro Pro provides additional features, such as performing optical character recognition.

Scanning and Managing Business Cards

If you network a lot and meet many people, you may have a hard time managing all the business cards you collect. No more! Using one of several third-party apps, you can scan and manage all those business cards you receive.

Business Card Manager (iPhone)

Business Card Manager (www.sourcenext.com/app_en/116430) is an application that enables you to use your iPhone to store and manage photos of business cards that you've taken with the iPhone's camera.

Business Card Manager describes itself as the world's first Evernote-supported business card management application because it integrates bidirectional synchronization with Evernote. It can import photos of business cards from your Evernote account and also save new card images back to Evernote. You can use the Auto-Sync feature to synchronize the data in your business card list with a specified Evernote notebook. After synchronization, Evernote scans the business card so that you can search for it. To exchange business with someone else who has Business Card Manager installed, simply make the motion to exchange cards (by holding out your iPhones to each other). You can then exchange your business cards with your partner, digitally through Bluetooth.

ScanBizCards (iPhone, iPad, Android devices)

ScanBizCards (www.scanbizcards.com) scans business cards or other images. Snap a photo of a business card with your iPhone, iPad, or Android device; ScanBizCards automatically extracts contact information and adds it to your address book. Then you can save the photo and resulting contact information to your Evernote account. You can also import photos directly from your Evernote account and save the extracted contact information back into the original note.

ScanBizCards is fully integrated with Evernote. Tap My Cards, and look for the large Evernote button at the end of the list of folders. Tapping that button prompts you to provide your Evernote credentials (username and password). Then you can search for photos of business cards in your Evernote account and import the image(s) you want, scan them, and optionally store the contact info scanned by ScanBizCards back into the Evernote record. You can also export any scanned card into Evernote, not just those imported from Evernote.

CamScanner (iPhone, iPod touch, iPad)

CamScanner (www.intsig.com/home/us/iphone-/53-camscanner) turns your iPhone, iPod touch, or iPad into a portable scanner. Simply snap a photo of a paper document, receipt, note, whiteboard, or business card. CamScanner automatically crops and enhances the image, making the text easily readable. Then you can save the document as a PDF or export it directly to your Evernote account.

DocScanner (iPhone, iPad, Mac, Android devices)

DocScanner (www.docscannerapp.com) enables you to scan documents on the road. Take a picture of your document, and DocScanner automatically removes shadows, fixes edges, and sharpens the image to make text and images clearer. DocScanner can automatically save documents as PDFs and send them to your Evernote account, where text is recognized and made searchable.

Genius Scan (iPhone and Windows Phone)

Genius Scan (www.thegrizzlylabs.com) is an application for the iPhone or Windows Phone that instantly turns your iPhone into a fast, streamlined pocket scanner. Genius Scan enables you to scan documents on the go by photographing them, converting them to a PDF, and then sending them anywhere by e-mail or exporting them as notes into your Evernote account or sending them to Box.net, Dropbox, or Google Docs. You can also print your documents to an AirPrint-compatible printer. The basic application is free, but the "export" features require Genis Scan+, available in the App Store or the Windows Phone Marketplace.

Saving RSS Feeds to Evernote

In Chapter 12, I discuss interfacing Evernote with social applications and RSS feeds. The tools that I describe in this section make it easier to save RSS feeds to Evernote. Google Reader is discussed in Chapter 12 in the "Using Google reader with Evernote" section.

Reeder for iPhone (iPhone, iPod touch, iPad, and Mac)

Reeder (http://reederapp.com) is an inexpensive Google reader developed by noted developer Silvio Rizzi for the iPhone, iPod touch, iPad, and Mac that is available from the App Store. It supports gestures such as slide, pinch and zoom, swiping, and tapping. I find it to be a timesaver for scanning on many news feeds and honing in on those you actually want to read.

Gruml (Mac)

Gruml (www.grumlapp.com) enables you to view and manage your Google Reader feed subscriptions in Mac OS X. You can read your newsfeeds, manage them in folders, tag them, and much more — all in sync with your Google Reader account.

After you install the Gruml app, click a button when you find an article that you want to remember. You can save articles to Evernote or to your favorite social services. (Digg, Diigo, Delicious, Facebook, Instapaper, MySpace, ping. fm, Posterous, ReadItLater, Reddit, StumbleUpOn, and Tumblr are all supported by Gruml.) You can also use Gruml to send articles directly to your own blog if you use one of these blog editing tools: BlogThing, ecto, MarsEdit, and Xjournal.

Feeddler RSS Reader Pro (iPhone, iPod Touch, and iPad)

Feeddler RSS Reader Pro (www.chebinliu.com/projects/iphone/feeddler-rss-reader) is a fast and highly customizable Google Reader client available from the App Store for your iPhone and iPad that enables you to save articles, web pages, and images to Evernote without leaving the app. Feeddler also filters ads and irrelevant content on web pages, creating notes that contain only articles and images.

Feeddler lets you do the following tasks:

✔ Save RSS or any web page to Evernote

✔ Save any image to Evernote

✔ Sync with a Google Reader account

✔ Sort articles by newest first or oldest first

✔ Cache up to 100 RSS articles for each feed for offline reading

✔ Star/unstar, like/unlike, share/unshare, and mark unread any RSS story, even when offline (syncs when starting app with Internet connection)

✔ Mark all items as read for any RSS subscription, or only loaded items as read

✔ View only feeds/folders with unread items

✔ Share with Facebook and in-app email

✔ Copy and paste titles, links, or full articles

A paid version is available if you require advanced features such as interfacing with Twitter, Instapaper, and Read It Later or batch-syncing all feeds or unread items.

iNews (iPhone)

iNews (`www.ptgdi.com/gdiplus/iNews.html`) is a mobile RSS reader available in the App Store that is similar to Feeddler. It brings you news from a variety of sources or syncs with your Google Reader account. iNews lets you mark (star) feed posts and share them to a variety of services, including Evernote. If you see an item you like, send it to Evernote, and all the text, links, and images are available to you from anywhere.

Sharing with Social Media

Social media uses web-based and mobile technologies to turn what otherwise might be one-way communication into an interactive dialogue. If you want an academic definition of social media, Professors Andreas Kaplan and Michael Haenlein (ESCP) say it's a "group of Internet-based applications that build on the ideological and technological foundations of Web 2.0, and that allow the creation and exchange of user-generated content." (Kaplan, Andreas M. and Michael Haenlein (2010). "Users of the world, unite! The challenges and opportunities of Social Media". *Business Horizons* 53 (1): 59–68.)

Evernote and social media fit as a glove fits a hand.

Seesmic (Windows, Mac, iPhone, iPad, Android devices, Windows Phone)

Seesmic (`https://seesmic.com`) is a popular way to view and update your social streams using your phone, computer, and the web.

Now that Seesmic for iPhone and Android have integrated Evernote, you can stop worrying about forgetting all the interesting things that pop up in your Twitter and Facebook streams. Whenever you see something that you'd like to remember, simply send it to Evernote, and you'll have it forever.

After you have Seesmic installed, you can use it to send information from one of the social networks that integrates with Seesmic to Evernote. A new note is created containing the message with a link to the original content. Because you're in Evernote, you can edit the note and add some additional thoughts, change the tags, move it to a different notebook, and then save it forever. For example, to send a tweet using Seesmic, simply tap and hold on the tweet, choose Share, and then select Evernote.

Sending tweets automatically to Evernote is only supported on the mobile devices (iPhone, iPad, Android devices, Windows Phone) and not on the desktop versions of Seesmic.

TweetAgora (iPhone, iPod touch, and iPad)

TweetAgora (`www.tweetagora.com`) is a Twitter client developed by noted Twitter developer Mark Pavidis that solves three problems: too much information, not enough information, and not enough time. It lets you filter tweets and home in on whatever you need. It is available from the iPhone App Store and requires iOS 4.0 or later.

TweetAgora is a fully featured Twitter client with advanced filtering capabilities. It enables you to filter tweets by keyword; mute people and conversations; and hide Foursquare, Gowalla, and Formspring updates. When you're reading the tweets that matter to you, you can easily save them to your Evernote account with the tap of a button.

Mailplane (Mac)

Mailplane (www.mailplaneapp.com) enables you to send Google Mail messages and attachments you want to remember from Mailplane to Evernote with just one click. With Mailplane, you can automatically convert a message or an attachment to a new Evernote note with an embedded URL that takes you right back to that message in Gmail.

You can create notes linking to a Mailplane conversation and import attachments to Evernote. Mailplane 2.4 added an Evernote-specific button in the top toolbar that enables you to capture a conversation, archive it in Evernote, and have the app automatically include a link to the email message you previously selected in Mailplane. This feature saves a full copy of the message as a new note, so can enter a title and tags, as well as edit text from the message. A new option in Mailplane's download manager enables you to quickly send email attachments to Evernote without first saving them in the OS X Finder.

Use Evernote with Mailplane to organize projects, store important e-mails and documents, and always find exactly what you're looking for in your Gmail inbox.

Creating Meeting Notes, Brainstorming, and Time Tracking

Good meetings have a purpose and can generate great ideas. You want to record what was said so that you can refer to the great ideas that came up. This section describes some tools that help you use Evernote so that your time spent at meetings can be as productive as possible.

TimeBridge (Windows, iPhone, Mac, web)

TimeBridge (www.timebridge.com) connects to your calendar, and the calendars of your co-workers, to figure out when everyone is free for a meeting. Instead of having to work around everyone's schedules, use TimeBridge to discover when a meeting would fit in and schedule it. TimeBridge uses the Evernote API to allow meeting participants to easily save all the notes from a given meeting directly into their Evernote accounts. You can also share your meeting notes by creating a Shared Notebook or by emailing the notes to colleagues.

During the meeting, members can take notes and then sync them to their Evernote accounts, where they can share them via shared notebooks or just access and search them from anywhere.

PhatPad (iPad, Android devices, Windows)

PhatPad (www.phatware.com/index.php?q=product/details/phat pad) turns your iPad, Android tablet, or Windows computer into a powerful brainstorming tool. PhatPad's digital ink technology and handwriting recognition engine enable users to scribble handwritten notes and drawings and convert them to digital text or geometrical shapes. Make your PhatPad drawings and handwritten and typed writings searchable by syncing them with your Evernote account.

Curio Standard and Professional (Mac)

Curio (www.zengobi.com/products/curio) enables you to take notes, manage tasks, make photo collages, sketch, create index cards, tables and "mind maps." In other words, it is designed to promote visual thinking. Curio's freeform interface and tools, facilitate intuitively gathering, associating, and recalling your ideas, while at the same time managing the notes, tasks, and documents associated with your project.

With Curio's Evernote integration, you have immediate access to all your Evernote notebooks from within the Curio environment. All your Evernote items appear within the Curio sidebar, where they can easily be dragged into your Curio workspace.

Curio includes the Evernote shelf so you can easily see the items you've been collecting in your Evernote notebooks. Then you can drag-and-drop notes from the shelf, directly into your Curio idea spaces.

This is very useful if you've collected notes with the Evernote web clipping tools or via Evernote's mobile clients. All of those notes are then instantly available directly within Curio without having to launch the Evernote Mac client application.

When you drag a note from the Evernote shelf into Curio, it is copied into the Curio idea space. Additionally, all tags associated with the note and all text scanned from an image by Evernote are also transferred into Curio via the shelf, so you can then search for those items locally via Curio's Search shelf.

Evernote and Curio complement each other well. Evernote is excellent for collecting information and ideas, and Curio is suited for manipulating those ideas.

Managing Your Expenses

Expensify (`www.expensify.com`) is a web-based expense management tool for individuals and businesses. The tool makes it easy to import your expenses, scan receipts, and create reports so you can be reimbursed. Organizing and managing your expenses is easy with the combination of Expensify and Evernote. Simply add receipt images to the Expensify notebook in your Evernote account. They're automatically copied into Expensify, which you use to create and submit expense reports. When a report has been approved, you can export it directly to Evernote as a searchable PDF for future reference.

Expensify is free for individuals and $5 per submitter per month for companies.

Using Evernote in Collaborative Decision Making

SAP is a long-established leader in enterprise application software and is used primarily in larger companies. SAP's interface with Evernote is recognition that Evernote has made inroads into the enterprise world. SAP StreamWork (`www.sapstreamwork.com`) is a collaborative decision-making application. Like Evernote, it's operated as a software-as-a-service (SaaS) application and has a free version and a premium edition. An in-house Linux-based enterprise edition is also available.

StreamWork enables you to unite people, information, and business methods (procedures) to support swift and informed decision making. StreamWork is a single, cohesive, and usually enterprise-wide environment where you can strategize, brainstorm, collect feedback, analyze, build consensus, and, after decisions have been made, drive toward successful outcomes. You can use Evernote to support decision-making by taking notes, recording audio memos, clipping web pages, and snapping photos — all of which you can do on the go from all Evernote devices. You can then easily share them in StreamWork.

The advantage of a product like StreamWork is that it helps improve the quality and timeliness of decisions, provides transparency across the organization, and creates an institutional memory so that successful decisions are captured and easily repeatable.

Used properly, I think of Streamwork as Evernote on steroids because it helps integrate Evernote with the rest of an organization's decision processes.

As an old enterprise-software guy, I love it when the great divide between personal-use software and big corporate systems is bridged. Ideally, many other enterprise vendors will also interface their systems with Evernote.

A list of partners (consulting firms as well as value-added suppliers of specialized software) that extend StreamWork, including document-sharing tools, issue-tracking software, and other decision support systems, is available at `sapstreamwork.com/partners`.

Associating Objects with Notes

Touchanote (`www.touchanote.com`) is an Android app that lets you associate real-life objects with your Evernote notes. Assign Near Field Communication (NFC) tags to your Evernote notes; then open a note by touching its tag on an NFC-enabled mobile phone.

NFC is a contactless technology that made the mobile wallet possible and is supported by companies such as Google, Nokia, PayPal, Microsoft, MasterCard, Visa, and American Express.

You can order tags from the Touchanote website. At this writing, ten tags cost $10, including shipping and handling.

Touchanote won the grand prize in the 2011 Evernote Developer Competition. See `blog.evernote.com/2011/07/26/evernote-developer-competition-finalists/` for more information about the competition.

Using Scanning Services

You can use several scanning services to get all your important documents into Evernote. The following sections describe two popular services: OfficeDrop (a combination of software and a service) and Shoeboxed.

OfficeDrop (Windows, Mac, iPad, Android devices)

OfficeDrop (www.officedrop.com) is a scanner software for a digital filing system in the cloud. ScanDrop is software that connects your scanner with your online account and makes it easy to get your paper documents into Evernote. Optionally, you can simply mail documents into OfficeDrop using the prepaid envelopes that they provide and let them do the work. They scan your documents into text-searchable PDFs that you can download anytime from the web or from OfficeDrop's desktop software. There are a variety of plans, and if you have a scanner, you can mix and match, scanning some stuff yourself and sending the rest to OfficeDrop. Home and small-business users who own a scanner might find this option cost-effective.

The ScanDrop scanner software doesn't just manage the scanning part, it is also an easy way to get your paper into leading online cloud storage services, such as Google Docs or OfficeDrop in addition to Evernote. Just press Scan, then Upload and your paper is now available in your online account! You can even select the folder or notebook you'd like your document to upload into, add labels and tags, delete pages, and more. You can also scan to your PC's hard drive, and Mac users can also scan to Dropbox and Gmail.

Shoeboxed

Shoeboxed (www.shoeboxed.com/evernote/) is a service. It gives you a way to scan all your business cards, receipts, handouts, and paper of any kind. Shoeboxed sends you a prepaid envelope; you put all your papers in it and mail it back. After Shoeboxed receives the envelope, the staff scans everything, organizes it, and makes it available online.

If you connect Shoeboxed to your Evernote account, you can set it to automatically scan things into your account, such as business cards and receipts.

Shoeboxed is convenient for folks like me that never quite get around to doing the necessary back-office stuff we all should do. It lets you turn piles of receipts and business cards into expense reports, accounting entries, and contact lists. You let Shoeboxed scan and extract the data from your paper clutter. You can access your organized documents online and export data to accounting, CRM, and e-mail marketing tools. For me, that's the good part. Essentially, it "reads" my credit card bills, bank statements and the like and performs optical character recognition so that I can easily process it from there.

Chapter 18

Enhancing Evernote with Shared Public Notebooks

*I*f you've already read Chapter 10, you know that Evernote allows anyone to share any note, either publicly or with specific individuals. One aspect of the sharing process is importing notebooks, which you can do from the Evernote Trunk.

In this chapter, I tell you how to import notebooks. I also provide capsule reviews of the some of the best shared notebooks that I was able to find and give you a feel for what you can do with Evernote.

Because the public notebooks have long names, I have used a URL shortener. Also, in my own public notebook, `bit.ly/EvernoteForDummies`, I provide clickable links to all notebooks in this chapter.

Adding a Public Notebook

Anyone can make a notebook public, publish the link, and share it with the world.

Of course, adding a public notebook to your Evernote account doesn't affect your monthly upload allowance because your limit is only related to notes you upload to the Evernote servers.

If the publisher declared the notebook "read only" and you link it to your account then notes in the Shared notebook are read-only and aren't editable by you. You can, however, copy a note into your own notebook.

To copy a note in Windows, do the following:

1. **Right-click on the note.**

2. **Choose the notebook you would like the note copied to.**

   The note is copied and the copy is editable. That makes each note a starting point for your own notes.

To import a notebook from Evernote Trunk, use the following steps:

1. **Navigate to `www.evernote.com/about/trunk`, and click the Notebooks tab.**

2. **Browse the available public notebooks.**

3. **To add a notebook, click it.**

   The notebook's detail page appears, where you see a list of one or more notebooks. (Some notebooks are provided in packs.)

4. **Click Add Notebook for each notebook you want to add.**

5. **Click Add to Evernote.**

   A message appears, saying `You have just chosen to add: <Name of notebook>`.

6. **Click Add.**

   The notebook is added to your account.

7. **Click Go to Your Notes to see the notebook, or click Continue Browsing to add other notebooks.**

If you find one or more public notebooks uninteresting, simply click the down arrow to the right of the notebook name in the list of notebooks and then click Delete.

Finding Useful Public Notebooks

In this section, I provide links to some public notebooks you may find interesting or useful.

Evernote CEO Phil Libin's Japanese Food Notebook

Phil Libin, Evernote's CEO, travels often to Japan. You can link to Phil's Japan Food notebook, which includes menus and dishes from his favorite restaurants, from `www.evernote.com/pub/chef/thethingsiate`.

EverBUNDLE

EverBUNDLE is an eclectic collection of interesting shared notebooks aggregated by Lindsey Holmes. It is available at `bitly.com/bundles/lindseycholmes/4`. It is primarily devoted to Black history and empowerment.

Recipe Collection

Drew K, an IT industry veteran who goes by the pseudonym Binary Blogger, has shared an eclectic recipe collection at `www.evernote.com/pub/joenobody1877/recipes`. I've tried some of the recipes, including his recipe for Jalapeno Popper Dip and Bean Dip and Crescent Pizza Pockets (I skipped the pepperoni), and I liked them. I hope you will, too.

Things to Read

Andy Zweibel, a music education major who has written extensively on how to take advantage of Evernote, has made his reading list public as a shared notebook at `www.evernote.com/pub/azweibel/thingstoread`. Many of the notes relate to music education.

Colleen Young's Useful Links

Colleen Young has shared a notebook for using Evernote in teaching. It's not only chock full of her own "How to" notes, it also includes tips by Michael Hyatt, Ian McKenzie, and others who have shared their knowledge of Evernote. Link to it at `bit.ly/zY7WGc`. Colleen has also shared information and resources for using QR codes, a technology that makes the real world clickable like a website. You can link to her QR code notebook at `www.evernote.com/pub/colleenyoung/qrcodes`. Finally, she has a great notebook of math video links at `www.evernote.com/pub/colleenyoung/videos`.

Emergency Medicine

Dr. Michelle Lin, MD practices emergency medicine at San Francisco General Hospital and has an academic niche in technology and how it can transform the landscape of medical education. Her fascinating public notebook, at `www.evernote.com/pub/michelleclin/paucisverbis`, is updated weekly with what she calls PV cards (Paucis Verbis — Latin for "in a few words") about medical issues faced in the emergency room.

Entrepreneurship Class Notes

A notebook for an undergraduate class on entrepreneurship (Introduction to Entrepreneurship - Business 181) from San Jose State University was shared as `bit.ly/yLi7y0`. It offers an insight into the characteristics of entrepreneurs, the approaches they use to create, identify and evaluate opportunities for new ventures, and the skills that are needed to start and manage new ventures and develop a preliminary business plan.

Biblical Studies

Brian Davidson, a PhD candidate at Southern Baptist Theological Seminary, has a notebook of 2011 Biblical Studies Carnivals that he has shared at `bit.ly/zV37PK`. For example, searching on the term "Exodus," the second book of the Bible, yielded four relevant hits, including a discussion by John Hobbins on divine and human agency in the book of Exodus.

The Evernote FAQ

A very useful notebook is the Evernote Faq, reachable at `bit.ly/xbyjOw`, that answers many "How can I" type questions about Evernote. It's one I have personally linked to, and I search it when I am stuck for answers.

Ron's Evernote Tips

Ron's Evernote Tips (`http://evernote.tumblr.com`) by Ron Toledo, now an Evernote employee, is a collection of tips from various sources, including Evernote and Evernote users, to improve your Evernote experience and show you some new and interesting ways to use Evernote. Add these tips to your Evernote account today to start building your own collection.

At the present time, there are three Tips packs, and it's best to add them all:

- ✔ **Pack 1** (`www.evernote.com/about/trunk/content/ronstips/ronstips-1?lang=en&layout=default`)

- ✔ **Pack 2** (`www.evernote.com/about/trunk/content/ronstips/ronstips-2?lang=en&layout=default`)

- ✔ **Pack 3** (`www.evernote.com/about/trunk/content/ronstips/ronstips-3?lang=en&layout=default`)

After you've signed in to the Evernote web client, you can add each pack by clicking Add to Evernote.

TEC Shared Notebook

The TEC shared notebook (`http://elephantchannel.net`) contains all the notes for the Elephant Channel, maintained by Pierre Journel. It is an unofficial notebook of Evernote blogs and podcasts and discusses all things related to Evernote as a product and how to use it.

Among the notes are

- ✔ A master list of use cases for things you can do with Evernote

- ✔ Tutorials

- ✔ Analysis and commentary about Evernote from industry "mavens"

- ✔ Advice and quotes from Evernote's CEO

Chapter 19

Interfacing with Digital Cameras, Scanners, and Smartpens

· ·

In This Chapter

▶ Working with digital cameras

▶ Using scanners

▶ Getting the most out of smartpens

· ·

*E*vernote does amazing things for you with a laptop, desktop, or smartphone. Add some specialized hardware, and you can really turbocharge your Evernote experience.

This chapter gives you an inside look at some of the available possibilities for extending the power of Evernote with hardware. Not all supported hardware supported by Evernote is listed in the Evernote Trunk (www.evernote.com/about/trunk) under the hardware tab. The Noteworthy Blog (http://blog.evernote.com) usually carries announcements of new supported devices that Evernote has seen.

Getting Images to Evernote with the Eye-Fi Camera Interface

The digital cameras in your iPad, smartphone, desktop, or laptop usually take pretty good pictures. After you have pictures, getting them into Evernote is easy (see Chapter 3).

But for really important occasions, pretty good pictures are not enough. For great pictures, you need to use a high-quality digital camera. What do you do to get those photos into Evernote? Making those high-quality images findable anywhere can be a challenge.

Until now, you needed to perform many steps: store the images on a memory card; get them into a computer (usually by inserting the memory card into a computer); and upload them to the Internet for further processing, storage, or posting to social media.

I have found that Eye-Fi X2 cards, however, make backing up and sharing photos right from your camera as easy to work with as the lower-resolution cameras built into smartphones. This wireless memory card is unique in that it works in your camera and connects your camera to an in-range Wi-Fi network. Hot spots, such as those provided in public places such as coffee shots and hotels, are also supported.

No Wi-Fi in range? No problem. The really unusual thing about the Eye-Fi X2 is that it creates its own. Whether you're at the beach, on top of Mount Olympus (in Issaquah, WA), or visiting the Golden Gate Bridge, you can use Direct Mode on your Eye-Fi X2 card to directly transfer photos and videos from your camera to your iPhone, iPad, or Android device.

Evernote does all the work of organizing and backing up photos for you. After you take a photo, Eye-Fi wirelessly sends the photo to its own servers and from there to Evernote, where Evernote processes it and makes the text searchable. Then, you can find those photos anytime using Evernote on your computer or mobile device. (Read more about Eye-Fi in Chapter 6.)

Eye-Fi really gives any digital camera the convenience of a cellphone camera.

Getting the Most Out of Scanners

An Evernote-supported scanner is the hardware I use most when I'm sitting at my desk. (As a writer, that's a good part of my day.) I scan in all my paper: business cards, bank statements, bills, pay stubs, receipts, lab tests, handwritten notes, whatever. My paper all gets scanned directly into Evernote, where it becomes searchable and findable on all my devices, wherever I happen to be.

In Chapter 6, I discuss interfacing scanners with Evernote. In this section, I cover specific features of the most popular Evernote-supported scanners. The leading scanner makers have all made sure that their Evernote support is up to snuff. Even when they haven't, Evernote's TWAIN support (see the sidebar) ropes in nearly all scanners, even when the vendor didn't specifically have Evernote in mind.

Never the TWAIN shall meet . . .

TWAIN is a standard software protocol and applications programming interface (API) that regulates communication between software applications and imaging devices. Today, nearly every vendor provides TWAIN support. The name is not an acronym; it's derived from Rudyard Kipling's "The Ballad of East and West" ("OH, East is East, and West is West, and never the twain shall meet . . ."), a choice reflecting the difficulty of connecting scanners and personal computers. TWAIN is spelled in capital letters to make it more distinctive. See `www.twain.org` for more information about the TWAIN standard.

Canon imageFormula

The Canon imageFormula P-150 is a powerful yet compact personal and portable duplex scanner that can scan up to 15 pages per minute and comes with settings optimized for Evernote. After you have installed the software that comes with the scanner, just press the scan button on the scanner, and your document is scanned directly into Evernote.

The imageFormula DR-C125 is a newer, slightly larger, and faster scanner suitable for desktops or even mobile carts. It comes bundled with the new Canon CaptureOnTouch software, which can route scanned images to Evernote and other cloud services. Images are scanned in PDF/A format, which Evernote servers can read and index.

Fujitsu ScanSnap

The Fujitsu ScanSnap one-button color scanner converts paper documents into electronic files. ScanSnap features an auto document feeder (ADF) that digitizes both sides of a document in a single pass in color, making it ideal for an office or home office environment. Now, after you've installed the supplied software, pushing the scan button on the ScanSnap can make your scanned documents instantly available to Evernote and searchable on virtually any computer and mobile device you use.

ScanSnap has a few models, ranging from the tiny ScanSnap S1100 Color Mobile Scanner, the somewhat larger S1300, and the speedy desktop S1500 (which is my personal workhorse), which lets you insert up to 50 pages at a time into the automatic document feeder and scan 20 pages per minute.

Lexmark SmartSolution

Lexmark International's web-connected inkjet printers with touchscreen interface printers include the Lexmark Genesis S615, Interact S605, and Pinnacle Pro901 and Pro915. These multifunction devices can print, scan, fax, copy, and support one-touch scanning into Evernote without requiring you to turn on your computer.

Visioneer OneTouch (Visioneer and Xerox)

The Visioneer OneTouch scanning utility for Visioneer and Xerox scanners enables you to send scans directly to Evernote's cloud-based service with just one touch, just like the other scanners described above, but with an extra feature. It works even if the computer you're using doesn't have Evernote for Windows installed.

Ricoh App2Me

Ricoh's App2Me solution is a little different from the Fujitsu, Canon, Lexmark, and Visioneer solutions, in that it enables you to create personalized workflows that you can use on any App2Me-enabled Multi-Function Product (MFP). Simply download the widget to your desktop and enter your Evernote account information, and your personal Scan to Evernote widget is ready to use on all your App2Me-enabled MFPs.

HoverCam

The HoverCam combines a document scanner and a document camera. It enables you to take a high-resolution image scan in less than a second. Using the HoverCam Flex software, you can send your scans to your Evernote account with a single click.

Sending and Receiving Faxes

Although most messages today are electronic, facsimile (fax) is alive and well. Strictly speaking, e-fax solutions are software products linked to cloud-based services.

In an e-fax solution, the vendor gives you a unique incoming fax number. Faxes sent to that number are actually delivered to you as e-mail, so they can be set up to be delivered to your Evernote e-mail address as well. Usually, incoming faxes can be delivered to multiple addresses. Mine go to my main e-mail inbox as well as to my Evernote e-mail address.

Outgoing faxes are sent out as e-mails, often with files attached. You can register your Evernote e-mail address as an acceptable input source for an e-fax account, which means you can find any note in Evernote, right-click on the note, click Share, and then click Send to E-Mail. In the window that opens, type *your fax number @ your efax provider* as an e-mail address. The note is faxed right out to its destination. It's not only simple, but it provides for a much cleaner fax because it's electronic all the way.

The e-fax solutions listed in Table 19-1 work pretty much alike. I used eFax. com for many years, but in the past few years, I've switched to RingCentral, which I find to be less expensive based on my usage pattern.

Table 19-1	Popular E-Fax Solutions	
Vendor	*Monthly Cost*	*Pages Per Month*
fax.com (also does business as eFax.com)	$9.95	300
myfax.com	$10	100 (send) and 200 (receive)
	$20	200 each
	$40	400 each
Rapidfax.com	$9.95	300
RingCentral.com	From $7.95	500
	$49.99	2,500
send2fax.com	$8.95	150
	$12.95	350

Most services have a free or at least a no-commitment test period. Here's the rub: You often can't keep your existing fax number and move it (*port it,* in telephone lingo) to an e-fax service. eFax.com does allow you to port or connect your existing number to its service. See www.efax.com/efax-signup/number-porting. RingCentral also allows this service, in accordance with FCC rules, as detailed at www.ringcentral.com/legal/policies/porting.html.

If the company supplies the number to you, the company owns that number. There's usually no way for you to take it with you if you change services. The moral of the story is that you shouldn't publish the number until you're sure you're happy with the service.

Working with Smartpens and Tablets

Let's be honest: In a room with many people, the tap, tap, tap of your keyboard can be a distraction to others. Smartpens and tablets provide a way to capture your thoughts or the spoken word electronically without keying. Everything you capture with a smartpen or tablet can be moved to Evernote for searching, editing, and forwarding.

Livescribe smartpens

Livescribe makes a family of smartpens that record what you hear and write, so you'll never miss a word. The Livescribe comes with a built-in microphone, speaker, memory storage (up to 8GB depending on the model), a USB connector to transfer the recording, and, most importantly, a note recorder that records your scribbles as you write. You can play back lectures or meetings with a simple tap on your notes. After the recorded information makes it to your computer, you can also share to Evernote, Facebook, OneNote, Google Docs, and e-mail.

Sharing your notes and audio sessions with your Evernote account is easy using Livescribe Desktop, but it requires a little conversion. During the export of audio, each Livescribe Desktop AAC audio file is converted to a WAV format for Evernote import. Save, search, and organize your notes and recordings on your Mac or PC for fast, easy access to what's important.

You can easily send notes and audio as an interactive digital document, called a *pencast,* to people and destinations of your choice — all by writing (scribbling) on your paper. (The actions — for example, sending a message to an e-mail address you wrote down — only take place once you have transferred what you record to a computer that supports Livescribe. Pencasts allow you to hear, see, and relive notes exactly as they were captured.

You can also use Livescribe Connect, a web-based service, to easily send pencasts to Evernote as well as to people and destinations of your choice — all originating from your paper or Livescribe Desktop.

Wacom Bamboo pen tablet

Wacom pen tablets were introduced in 1984. Early models were very expensive, and were mostly used in high-end design shops. Today, these pen tablets have come down in price and enable you to create digital ink notes and annotate images in Evernote. In many ways, I find them similar to Livescribe, which I described in the preceding section. If you use Evernote for Windows, you can create ink notes right inside Evernote. On both Windows and Mac, you can use Wacom pen tablets to annotate images in your favorite image editor and then bring those annotated images into Evernote.

Getting Creative with Whiteboards

An historical note: When Abraham Lincoln and I were growing up (I was in elementary school in the mid-'60s), teachers used blackboards and chalk in classrooms. The ubiquitous whiteboard was invented by Martin Heit, a photographer and Korean War veteran. It was erasable and chalk-free. Whiteboards began to appear in classrooms in the 1960s (my school was not an early adopter of this technology) and by the 1990s, whiteboards had been widely adopted.

As people figured out great ideas using whiteboards, the need to capture those memorable thoughts grew. Whiteboard sessions are meant to be collaborative, so it feels counterproductive when the team spends as much time feverishly re-creating the whiteboard sketches in their notebooks as participating in the creative discussions. The advent of the digital camera did much to encourage memory retention of solutions crafted on whiteboards, by capturing the whiteboard images as snapshots. Evernote does much more. Evernote's image recognition technology processes all those snapshots and makes the hand-written text searchable, so you can find all those great ideas.

I frequently use the FaceTime camera built-in to my Apple Macbook Air laptop to capture whiteboard drawings as notes in Evernote. This requires no special equipment.

This section covers a few whiteboard products you can use with Evernote.

Panasonic Panaboard

Education institutions love the Panasonic line of pricey but interactive whiteboards. The Panaboard lets you display the contents of a computer screen directly onto the board. It enables three people to write simultaneously on the board and is sensitive to finger touch and electronic pen. With Panaboard, you get built-in speakers, two USB hubs to connect to a printer and document camera, and an optional wireless kit. You can use Wi-Fi to transfer the digital images to Evernote.

IdeaPaint

IdeaPaint is a special kind of paint that can turn anything into a dry-erase writing surface. After a productive brainstorming session with IdeaPaint, snap a photo of your notes with your digital camera or smartphone. Bring the image into Evernote to make all the text searchable so that you can find your great ideas whenever you want from any device you use. Use Evernote's sharing features to share those images with your class, team, or colleagues.

Skitch (Mac, iPad, Android)

Skitch (www.skitch.com), now owned by Evernote, is free and is being fully integrated into Evernote. At this writing, versions for the Mac, Android, and iOS platforms are available. Windows support has been broadly hinted at.

Skitch greatly eases what you do with interactive whiteboards. You can annotate, edit, and crop sketches, and then, share your creation publicly or only to whom you have chosen. Under the covers, it has a vector engine, so the lines and shapes you draw are smooth.

Happily, the only thing missing by using Skitch instead of interactive whiteboards is the cost. Skitch is free. With a smartphone and a Skitch-supported device, you can now do the work of interactive whiteboards costing $2,500.

With Skitch for Mac and iOS , you can

- ✓ **Screenshot anything:** Click the Snap button (Mac) or press both the Power and Home buttons at the same time (iOS 5) to capture a shot of a document, a webpage, something that inspires you, or just about anything else, and save it to Evernote.

- ✓ **Drag files into Evernote:** Hold down the Drag Me tab and pull the file into Evernote.

- ✓ **Rotate Images (Android):** Rotate arrows, text, and shapes by simply tapping on the object, pressing with two fingers, and rotating. You can also rotate multiple objects at once by tapping on them individually to select them and then doing the two-finger rotate. Save the result as a note in Evernote.

- ✓ **Save files in different formats:** Select your preferred file format from a pull-down menu next to the Drag Me tab (Mac) or tap on the elephant icon (iOS 5) to save in Evernote.

- ✓ **Resize and crop an image:** Tools let you change an image's size (shrink or stretch) and to crop out part of an image. Tap the Crop toolbar icon and select the portion of the image you'd like to keep as a note in Evernote.

At this time, you can create a new note in Skitch, but you can't yet annotate notes already in Evernote.

To share your creations, you can drag the annotated image into email or shared Evernote notebooks, or you can sign into Skitch with your Evernote ID and share via the Skitch site.

Part VI

Adding Professional Power

In this part . . .

Previous parts discussed *using* Evernote, and using it right out of its virtual box. This part discusses ways to leverage the power of Evernote by taking advantage of its scripting capabilities and how to take "social" to a new level by participating in or starting an Evernote Meetup.

Read Chapter 20 to find out how you can use scripting to create "mashups" with other applications that let you do things in a few minutes that might take months to program yourself. The chapter covers Mac scripting and Windows scripting, and although the syntax of the two is a little different, the result is the same, as they both are directing the Evernote Application Programming Interface (API) to perform easy-to-learn magic tricks that will amaze and astonish your friends.

Chapter 21 shows you how to meet — in person or through social media — other Evernote users to exchange tips and to enhance your Evernote experience.

Chapter 20

Saving Time with Evernote's Open Scripting

Open Scripting Architecture (OSA) is an optional way to leverage the power of the applications on your computer to perform new tricks. When you write a script, you're creating a recipe. The computer is the faithful cook who follows your recipe precisely. The ingredients are the applications on your computer. Create a recipe for a wholesome and tasty bread. Repeat ten times. Produce 10 tasty loaves, all prepared precisely in accordance with your recipe.

In this chapter, I give you a taste of how Evernote works with OSA on the Mac and with Evernote's proprietary scripting language for the Windows platform. I encourage you to overcome the fear factor and to get your imagination working so that you can create recipes that will make you more productive, and also dazzle and amaze your friends.

Getting the Inside Scoop on Scripting

Scripting is a form of programming that lets you control what happens more precisely than by just selecting menu commands. Scripting is useful because it makes things much easier by giving you much greater control. Even more exciting, after you have a script that does what you want, you can run it over and over (*execute* it, in technicalese), and with a little more work, you can make it do the same thing to lots of different data.

A simple script may just run a set of commands, saving you from the tedium of doing the same thing repetitively. The real power comes from introducing a little logic to control the flow of commands. Techies call this *conditional logic,* and it sounds scary, but conditional logic is just a way of stating and controlling the rules for what you want to happen.

OSA, which stands for Open Scripting Language, is scripting on steroids. It means that you use somebody else's scripting logic but can also define your own. Your new logic fits in so smoothly and naturally that it's as though your logic were part of the original design.

The beauty and power of OSA are that you don't need to do it all yourself, and you aren't limited to prewritten logic in any one application. You stand on many tall shoulders. You can harness the functions of many applications in your computer, including Evernote, and get them all to dance to your flute in a beautifully choreographed dance symphony. The functionality of many programs is at your beck and call.

Scripting languages are like loyal and subservient valets. They do exactly, and unquestioningly, what you tell them to. They don't "think" independently, and if you tell them to do foolish things, they aren't going to come back and challenge you. Therefore, always test a script thoroughly on a practice notebook.

Being Efficient with Mac Scripting

Mac scripting has always been the most user-friendly software around for extending what you can do with computers and for automating repetitious tasks. Mac scripting is what makes it so easy to interact with the components of the Mac.

Scripting languages are like loyal and subservient valets. They do exactly, and unquestioningly, what you tell them to. They don't "think" independently, and if you tell them to do foolish things, they aren't going to come back and challenge you. Therefore, always test a script thoroughly on a practice notebook.

AppleScript is a language for writing scripts that lets you directly control applications and also many parts of the Mac OS. Conveniently, it is built right in to the Mac OS, so you need not do anything to start using it. Like most modern operating systems, Mac OS is event-driven and it responds to messages. Scriptable applications are those that make their functionality and data available in response to messages, what Apple calls *Apple events*. "What Is Scripting Anyway?" from Tom Trinko's book *AppleScript For Dummies*, 2nd Edition, "What Is Scripting, Anyway?" is a good, basic introduction to

AppleScripting. You can find it at the Dummies.com website (www.dummies.com/how-to/content/what-is-scripting-anyway.html).

In addition to AppleScript being used by us (end-users), developers use AppleScript to aid them in rapid prototyping and automated testing.

Think of AppleScript as a language, and the AppleScript Editor as a tool to edit scripts written in the AppleScript language.

AppleScript

AppleScript is the scripting language for the Mac. You can use the AppleScript Editor to modify or create your own scripts. All the examples in AppleScript Help were done with the AppleScript Editor.

You can create scripts in three ways:

- ✔ Start a new script, turn on the recorder, and just do your thing. Your actions are recorded as a script. After you save the script, if you play it back, it repeats your actions.
- ✔ Type the script directly in AppleScript.
- ✔ Record a script and then edit it in AppleScript (often, to generalize it).

All programs that support AppleScript make their major functions available to be controlled by AppleScript. Making functions available for controlling by scripts is called *exposing* the functionality because the functions are visible in the AppleScript dictionary, and you can use AppleScript commands to command them to perform their tricks. (When you open the Script Editor, you can open the dictionary using the Open Dictionary item in the File menu of Script Editor. In other words, they agree to respond to AppleScript commands in ways that are defined in the AppleScript dictionary entry for that application. As with all dictionary entries, if you want to know the meaning of the commands, you can look them up.

When you open the dictionary, you get a listing of the available applications that have dictionaries. If Evernote is installed, choose Evernote and click Open to view the dictionary entries.

For more information about AppleScript, I recommend *AppleScript For Dummies,* 2nd Edition, by Tom Trinko, or, for a more in-depth treatment, *AppleScript (Developer Reference),* by Mark Conway Munro (both from John Wiley & Sons, Inc.). In addition, AppleScript documentation is available at http://developer.apple.com/documentation/AppleScript/Conceptual/AppleScriptLangGuide/index.html.

Evernote support for AppleScript

With the ease of Evernote and its use of the best features of each platform or device, the interaction with AppleScript is natural, robust, and simple to use. Evernote exposes a wide range of Evernote's functions, including notebooks, tags, notes, and some of its properties, to AppleScript.

For example, you can use AppleScript to open a notebook, create a note, perform a search, and accomplish other Evernote tasks. One really useful thing you can do is to create a search, as complicated as you like, and have the search executed whenever you want on your most up-to-date notebooks. So if you clip and save news about your company or set up an RSS feed to send updates directly to Evernote, you can save the search and run a script anytime to see the accumulated notes.

This book provides general information about controlling Evernote's functionality through AppleScript. The Evernote dictionary entries for AppleScript assume that you already know Evernote's basic concepts. Don't try to use scripting until you have created and used notes in the Evernote application.

To get information on specific functionality, follow these steps:

1. **Choose Applications⇨Utilities⇨ AppleScript Editor.**
2. **Choose File⇨Open Dictionary.**
3. **Select Evernote.**

Creating notes from AppleScript

You can create notes from AppleScript in several ways. Here's one way:

1. **In the AppleScript Editor, enter the following lines to create a new notebook called MyAppleScriptNotebook:**

```
-- create notebook AppleScriptNotebook1
tell application "Evernote"
if (not (notebook named "AppleScriptNotebook1" exists)) then
-- NOTE also check out the "create notebook" command
make notebook with properties {name:"AppleScriptNotebook1"}
end if
```

Except for specific titles, such as in AppleScriptNotebook1, you virtually never have to type caps. You do need to pay close attention to the punctuation.

2. **To create a new HTML note in the notebook MyAppleScript Notebook, type the following:**

```
tell application "Evernote"
create note title "Note 2" with html "<strong> Here is my new HTML note</
        strong>"
Notebook "MyAppleScriptNotebook"
end tell
```

Here is a sample AppleScript to illustrate how you can replace the contents of a note:

```
set new_Text to text returned of (display dialog "Enter New Text"
     default answer "")
     tell application "Evernote"
set the_Note to selection
set HTML content of item 1 of the_Note to new_Text
 end tell
```

Here is another script for stripping the formatting from a note, and converting it to text.

```
on getTextInNotebook(NbName)
tell application "Evernote"
activate
tell notebook NbName
set totalNotes to (count notes)
set totalWords to 0
set allWords to ""
repeat with n from 1 to totalNotes
set hc to HTML content of note n
set w to (count words of hc)
set totalWords to totalWords + w
log (title of note n) & " - " & w


set allWords to allWords & " " & hc
end repeat
end tell

set totalCharacters to (count characters in allWords)
log totalCharacters

-- eliminate stuff between < and > markers
set c to ""
set i to 0
set allText to ""
repeat while i < totalCharacters
set i to i + 1
set c to character i of allWords
if c = "<" then
repeat until c = ">"
set i to i + 1
set c to character i of allWords
end repeat
else
try
set allText to allText & c
end try
end if
end repeat
```

```
log allText
log "Size of allText - " & (count characters of allText)
end tell

return allText
end getTextInNotebook
```

A useful AppleScript script to export one or more notes from Evernote to Rich Text Format (RTF) is available at `veritrope.com/tech/evernote-rtf-export/`. A whole collection of useful scripts is available at `veritrope.com/tech/evernote-applescript-resources-and-accessories/`.

Visit `http://evernote.com/about/developer/mac.php` for other ways to create notes. You can also get some basics on working with tags and new notebooks. The Evernote dictionary entries in AppleScript show the full set of commands that Evernote responds to.

Compiling and saving scripts

You can save your script as a compiled script that runs when you double-click it in the Finder. To compile and save a script, follow these steps:

1. **Choose File⇨Save to open the Save dialog.**

2. **Choose a location to save your file.**

3. **Choose Script from the File Format pop-up menu.**

4. **Enter a name for the script.**

   `.scptd` is the file extension.

5. **(Optional) To save the script in a form that can't be changed or edited, select the Run Only check box.**

   If you select Run Only, you can't edit the script again. If you want to be able to make changes to the script in the future, save the original script in the standard editable format and then save the run-only version with a different name.

6. **Click Save.**

Scripting in Windows

Windows, unlike Mac, does not have a built-in scripting language, so Evernote provided its own that is based on the command line that has been around since the earliest days of Windows.

Command-line scripting

In Windows, you can drive Evernote by invoking it from the command line. Table 20-1 shows you the commands you can use.

You can't combine individual commands. If Evernote is already running, your command is passed to the existing instance.

Table 20-1	Scripting Commands in Windows
Command	*What It Does*
[filename]	Creates a new note if you pass the full path to a file. If you pass a .txt, .htm, or .html file, the file contents are used as the new note's content. If you pass an .enex file, the Evernote notes that it contains are imported. If you pass a .url file, the hyperlink is used as the new note's content. If you pass any other file type, that file is attached to the new note.
/NewNote	Opens a new window with a new, empty note. This command is equivalent to right-clicking the Evernote icon in the taskbar and choosing New Note from the contextual menu.
/NewInkNote	Opens a new window with a new, empty ink note.
/NewWebCamNote	Opens a new window that enables you to capture a new webcam note.
/Task:ClipScreen	Invokes Evernote's screen-shot clipper, which enables you to take a screen shot of the desired portion of the screen and save it in a new note. This command is equivalent to right-clicking the Evernote icon in the taskbar and choosing Clip Screenshot from the contextual menu.
/Task: PasteClipboard	Creates a new note containing the contents of the clipboard. This command is equivalent to right-clicking the Evernote icon in the taskbar and choosing Paste Clipboard from the contextual menu. If the clipboard contains a .txt, .htm, or .html file, that file is used as the new note's content. If the clipboard contains an .enex file, the Evernote notes that it contains are imported. If the clipboard contains a .url file, the hyperlink is used as the new note's content. If the clipboard contains any other type of file, that file is attached to the new note.
/Task: SyncDatabase	Causes Evernote for Windows to synchronize with the Evernote service. This command is equivalent to right-clicking the Evernote icon in the taskbar and choosing Sync from the contextual menu.

ENScript.exe scripting

When you install Evernote for Windows, one of the programs that is installed is a scripting program called ENScript.exe, which is installed in the same path (directory) as Evernote. Although it's not nearly as convenient as scripting on a Mac with AppleScript, ENScript.exe lets you accomplish the same things to control Evernote, if a little less elegantly.

I initially had some trouble getting ENScript.exe to work because I didn't pay sufficient attention to the following caveat: To invoke one of the executables, you must make sure that Evernote's program directory is in your shell path, or you must give the full path to the executable when you invoke the command.

Table 20-2 lists the main verbs you can use with ENScript.exe.

Table 20-2	ENScript.exe Main Verbs
Main Verb	*What It Does*
createNote	Creates a new note
importNotes	Imports one or more notes from an Evernote Export (.enex) file
showNotes	Sets the current note list to view the results of a query
printNotes	Prints a set of notes
exportNotes	Exports a set of notes to an .enex file
listNotebooks	Lists your existing notebooks
syncDatabase	Synchronizes your Windows desktop with the Evernote service

To create a new notebook with ENScript.exe, for example, assuming that the path is correct, you'd type the following:

```
ENScript.exe createNotebook /n "New Notebook"
```

These commands are documented at http://evernote.com/about/developer/windows.php - enscript.

Chapter 21

Connecting with the Evernote Community

. . . .

. . . .

*E*vernote has about 20 million users, and more than 1 million new users join every month. Evernote has an awesome community, and other users have ideas and techniques that they'd love to share with you. This chapter describes how you can meet other users and exchange ideas with them.

Getting Tips from the User Forum

The Evernote User Forum (`http://discussion.evernote.com`) is the online place for users to meet and help each other.

The forum is organized in major subgroups, such as Evernote Products, Learn & Share, and Other Discussions. Major forums you might be interested in include the following:

- ✔ Evernote for Windows
- ✔ Evernote for Mac
- ✔ Evernote for the Web
- ✔ Evernote Mobile
- ✔ Evernote Food
- ✔ Evernote for Developers

There are also forums in Japanese and Russian, a section on Localization (translating Evernote into languages it doesn't currently support), a section for Skitch users, and a section for general discussion of Evernote.

Anyone can read the posts, but active participation in the forum requires a free registration.

To register, go to http://discussion.evernote.com. You're asked to agree to the terms of use, which essentially request that you not post any abusive, obscene, vulgar, slanderous, hateful, threatening, or sexually suggestive content, or any other material that may violate any laws.

After you've registered for the forums, you can follow a topic and reply to posts in the forum. One hot topic related to using Evernote, for example, is GTD (short for *Getting Things Done)*, the work–life management system developed by David Allen (www.davidco.com/about-gtd). Many people use Evernote as the basis for their own GTD systems, so it's not surprising that GTD is one of the most popular forums, with thousands of page views.

Other popular forums are Get Organized and Increase Your Productivity with Evernote, Large Amount to Get into Evernote, and Wrangling Recipes (the single most popular forum).

You can search for a forum by typing your search terms in the search box in the top-right corner of the main forum page.

The forums are indexed by Google, so when you need to search the forums, you may find it easier to type **Evernote** followed by your query in Google and let Google do the work.

Each topic has its own unique URL. You may want to save topic links in Evernote or share them in e-mails with others who might find them useful.

Being Social with Meetups

Evernote meetups are a great way to meet fellow Evernote users, swap stories, share ideas, have a great time, and build your network. You can locate Evernote gatherings through Meetup (www.meetup.com), which claims to be the world's largest network of groups. More than 2,000 groups get together in local communities each day.

To find a meetup near you or to schedule one yourself, navigate to www.meetup.com/Evernote. When you schedule a meeting, specify the topic, the time, and the venue. If you live in or near a large city, you may find more than one meetup. At this writing, more than 500 Evernote communities exist, and there's no obvious rhyme or reason about which Evernote communities are strongest. Austin, Texas, is home to the largest community, with 218 Evernoters; Stockholm, Sweden, has 43; and New York and Los Angeles have 62 each.

If you plan to hold a meetup, post details on the Evernote User Forum (discussed earlier in this chapter), which gets lots of views.

Keeping Up to Date

Evernote is constantly — and I mean constantly — improving. Each of the versions for the various platforms is being improved on an ongoing basis, and new things happen on a weekly basis. It's also a very substantial product with many possibilities. So more than with most products, you may want to stay up to date on the latest improvements and to stay in touch with other users, who are always finding new and innovative things you can do with Evernote and workarounds to limitations that you might encounter.

The Evernote blog

The Evernote blog, dubbed the Noteworthy Blog (`blog.evernote.com`), provides the latest in what Evernote dubs "noteworthy news." You can visit this blog to get the latest on all things Evernote. Check out tips, news, and cool ways people are making their world more notable. You can subscribe to the feed at `http://blog.evernote.com/feed`.

The Evernote blog includes a series of "Did You Know . . ." posts. To find them, search for *"Did You Know:"* on the home page (remembering to include the quotes in your search term). These posts, generally authored by Evernote staff members, provide in-depth focus on a single topic. Some of the most interesting tips dig into features that aren't necessarily obvious or intuitive, including these:

- ✔ Note Links, and How to Use Them
- ✔ Skitch for Visually Telling a Story
- ✔ How to Access Notes Without an Internet Connection
- ✔ How to Create a Checklist in Evernote
- ✔ How to Clip Web Content

I find two sections of the blog to be the most useful. I subscribe to the blog feed (just click RSS Feed on the right hand side of `http://blog.evernote.com/`) so that I see the latest Evernote news right away.

- **Product updates:** A special section of the Evernote blog is devoted to product updates. You can click the Product Updates tab on the blog home page or access the updates directly at `http://blog.evernote.com/category/product-updates`. Product and corporate news is available on the Our Notes page (`http://blog.evernote.com/category/our-notes`).

- **Podcasts:** Evernote has been offering increasingly sophisticated podcasts over the past few years. The podcasts are available in MP3 format, in iTunes, or as audio feeds. Each podcast usually focuses on a single topic or a related collection of topics. You can access the podcasts from the Podcast page of the Evernote blog (`http://blog.evernote.com/category/podcast`).

The Evernote Ambassador Program

Evernote has appointed *ambassadors* — experts and fellow users who help you get the most out of Evernote. Each ambassador has a Twitter feed and maintains a discussion forum. You can meet the ambassadors at `www.evernote.com/about/community`. Each ambassador specializes in a particular area, such as the following:

- Organization
- Teaching
- Paperless living
- Crafts
- Productivity
- Blogging and public speaking
- Design

The ambassador forums are part of the Evernote Lifestyle section of the discussion forums (`http://discussion.evernote.com/forum/39-evernote-lifestyle`).

Case studies

Another interesting part of the Evernote blog is the case studies, which you can find on the Tips and Stories tab (`blog.evernote.com/category/tips_stories`). (They're also among my favorite parts of the blog.) Try reading the case studies to get ideas about cool things you can do with Evernote. Recent topics include the following:

- How a Private Investigation Company Uses Evernote for Case Management, Field Work, and More

- Evernote for Non-Profits: How Regional Food Bank CEO Dan Flowers Transformed His Workflow, and His Organization

- How Guitar Columnist Pierre Journel Uses Evernote for Podcasting and House Hunting

- How to Cook a Delicious Meal with Evernote

- Student Ryan Kessler Transformed His Workflow, Raised His GPA and Left His Textbooks at Home (Back-to-School Series)

Other online resources

If you haven't found what you're looking for using the resources covered thus far, a couple other tools can help you stay current with Evernote happenings:

- **Social media:** Facebook has an Evernote page (`www.facebook.com/evernote`), and Evernote updates are posted to Twitter (`http://twitter.com`). Sign in to Twitter search on the evernote# hash tag).

- **Webinars and conferences:** Evernote periodically offers free webinars, which are usually geared to developers. Webinars and conferences are prominently announced on the Noteworthy Blog (`http://blog.evernote.com`). You can also subscribe to the Evernote RSS feed (`http://blog.evernote.com/feed`) to ensure that you see new blog posts as they become available.

- **Chat:** Premium subscribers can chat with Evernote staff Monday through Friday between 9:00 am and 5:00 pm, U.S. Pacific Time. Chat is currently only available in English. You can access it by clicking Chat with Evernote on the Support Page (`www.evernote.com/about/contact/support`).

The first Evernote Trunk Conference

In August 2011, Evernote held the first Evernote Trunk Conference. I attended the event, which seemed like a huge success. Videos of the conference have been posted to `bit.ly/ tIaYLN`, so you can have a look at some of the conference activities. Topics included the future of Evernote; an inside look at the Evernote architecture; details on the Evernote application programming interface (API); and a fascinating discussion with Gordon Bell, whose iconoclastic ideas ultimately provided the inspiration for Evernote.

Part VII
The Part of Tens

In this part . . .

In every book in the *For Dummies* series, the Part of Tens provides concrete suggestions for enjoying the subject matter. There are so many fun things to do with Evernote, The Part of Tens could have taken up the whole book, but I managed to limit it to three chapters. Here, I share fun ideas for using Evernote at home, at school, and in business.

Chapter 22 provides a few of the many ways you can use Evernote at home — for tracking personal finances, managing the inventory of household supplies, and (the really fun part) using Evernote for planning a vacation.

Chapter 23 gives you ideas for using Evernote to track classes and school projects and suggests ways you can use Evernote to have a more paperless existence.

Chapter 24 is a turbocharger for business, with ten creative ways to use Evernote for businesses large and small.

Chapter 22

Ten Home Improvements

. . . .

In This Chapter

▶ Tracking personal finances, school information, and more

▶ Managing household supplies

▶ Being prepared for vacation

. . . .

*E*vernote is extremely useful for doing nearly anything necessary for organizing and maintaining your home life. Personal organization is always
a matter of preference. Whether you need ten notebooks to get yourself in
order or just one in which notes are properly tagged and titled, Evernote
can help you do just about anything around the house. Here are ten ideas to
transform your desk from messy to fantastically organized.

Managing a Successful Home Decorating Project

Without a doubt, Evernote makes home decorating simple. If you're planning
to go to as many stores as possible to make sure that you get the best price,
tracking all the prices, styles, and thoughts on each option will be difficult.
With Evernote, all you have to do is create a notebook, take pictures, and
add notes about each item from your phone or tablet. You can compare the
different places you've been and colors you're interested in while you take a
lunch break or at the end of the day. All your information will be neatly organized when you're ready to make your final home-decorating decisions.

Voting Smarter

You may not have thought that Evernote could be a big help on Election Day,
but you can use it to keep yourself organized and aware of everything you
need to know when you head to the polls.

During the weeks or months leading up to the vote, start clipping all your research and news articles into an election notebook. Create a checklist of qualities you want in candidates and how they rate, or post all the latest news on bills and propositions of concern to you. Don't forget to get the statistics and charts that help summarize information.

If you go through everything in your notebook in the days leading up to the election, you can create a list of how you want to vote. When the time comes, you will have all your votes right there on your phone, making the process much quicker.

Monitoring Your Home Finances

Using Evernote for your daily finances is a fantastic way to keep track of everything you do without having the messy counter tops at the end of the day. From all of the receipts you accumulate during vacation to your regular bills, Evernote can help you get organized. It's safe too, as all your notes are safely stored in Evernote's servers.

You can use Evernote to track all your receipts so that you no longer have to worry about entering information from scraps of paper. Simply take a picture of the receipt on your phone. If you're shopping at a place that offers to e-mail the receipt to you, all you have to do is forward the e-mailed receipt to Evernote to be stored in a receipts notebook. At the end of the day, all purchases are in one notebook so that they're easy to follow.

You can also track billing information, but you should use caution in case something happens, such as the theft of your phone or if you lose your tablet. Encryption really helps protect you in case of theft or loss. Check out Chapter 11 to set up encryption.

You can also e-mail sales information (such as coupons or special sales events) to your financial notebook so that you have it on hand when the time comes. This organization is especially helpful if you get information weeks in advance and know you won't remember when the time comes. You can also keep notes on products from research and gift ideas between holidays.

Creating a Memorable Baby Book

On its own, Evernote is a powerful tool for things like cherished memories, but with Lil'Grams (`http://lilgrams.com`), Evernote becomes a way to create a memorable baby book so that you never miss a shot or important first of your baby. Lil'Grams is a website that makes creating and electronically sharing baby albums fast and easy. The website offers numerous packages, starting at $19 a year for 1GB of storage. Check out `http://lilgrams.com/guides/evernote` to set up and link your accounts.

After you link your Lil'Grams and Evernote accounts, all you have to do is let Lil'Grams know which tags and notebooks to associate with your account, and it automatically pulls them into your Lil'Grams account. Then all you have to do is add notes to your Lil'Grams baby book to let people know what's going on in the picture.

You set your own privacy settings and decide who has access. Lil'Grams and Evernote ensure that your information stays secure. Linking the two accounts makes sharing the latest with your baby so much easier than scrapbooking or even emailing. Better still, it's there for when your baby becomes an adult and you finally have time to sit down and enjoy the pictures yourself.

Creating a Notebook for School Information

The amount of information that schools send home with students is staggering. Evernote gives you a couple of ways to keep your student's information easy to access, depending on whether you prefer to scan or take pictures. For any paperwork that comes home, whether in the mail or in your child's backpack, scan it as soon as it arrives, and move it into a school-specific notebook.

I strongly recommend putting any forms or other items that need your signature in a location where they're easy to access or tagging them for easy retrieval.

You can also track events with Evernote and Google Calendar. To keep up with school events, connect your Evernote account with Google Calendar (see Chapter 16), and you'll have all school appointments, notes, and forms in one place.

Creating Your Shopping Lists

If you're like me, you've spent several days diligently writing down what you need at the store on a single piece of paper, only to forget the list when you actually head to the store. Thanks to Evernote, you don't have to worry about forgetting your list, because you can write your list right on your mobile device and take it with you.

If you prefer to continue adding to a physical list so that others can jot down things you need, just remember to take a picture periodically and update the note with the latest additions. This simple technique ensures that you have most, if not all, of your list every time you go to the store.

Maintaining a Home Inventory

A special combination of Evernote and storage totes can make your home, garage, and closets so neat that you look like you're the most organized person in town. Here's what to do:

1. **Pack a storage box with the items you want to keep out of sight but nicely organized.**

2. **Place a label on the outside for tracking.**

3. **Take a picture of the contents.**

   Try to include the exterior label in the picture.

4. **Add text to Evernote detailing what's in the box.**

   Don't forget to note the box's location in your home (a specific closet or the garage, for example).

Now when you need to find items, it's so simple and quick, you'll wonder how you used to find stuff. It's also useful for providing the information to the insurance company. Getting it on file will help you if the unthinkable should happen and you need a list of what you lost.

Keeping a Light Bulb Database

Tracking your light bulb use through a database in Evernote really illuminates the application's abilities. Track how long light bulbs are lasting, which lamps or sockets seem to be defective, or which bulbs seem to work the best for your home. All you have to do is start a note with the types of bulbs you have and which rooms and lamps have which light bulbs. (If you're really strapped for time, just take pictures.) Not only will you be able to save money if you post how often you've changed the bulbs, but you can also see which bulbs work best in different parts of the house when you're at the store shopping for more.

Listing Your Packing Information

Packing for a trip is challenging enough without having to keep track of a paper copy of your packing list. Evernote makes dealing with lists much easier, and even gives you a way of checking things off from your mobile device. So whether you are packing your suitcase or have some last-minute shopping to do, your list is always right there with you.

Create a checklist of things you need to pack, and mark them off as you load them into your suitcase. You can add things to the list over time so that you no longer have to rely on your memory while you dash about to gather everything together.

You can even create a list of all your traveling items with pictures of what is in them and what the cases or bags look like so that you'll know exactly what goes missing if you leave a bag behind or if something gets lost on the way to your destination.

Planning Your Next Vacation

There's much more to vacationing than just packing. With so many places to go and things to do, tracking it all can be overwhelming — or it could be overwhelming if you didn't have Evernote to organize and plan your vacation.

From the start, you can do the research and create comparison notes to help you decide where you (and maybe your family) want to go. After you decide where you want to go, you need to figure out what you want to do. Create a schedule, or clip pages that tell you the opening times for theme parks, hotels, restaurants, or anywhere else you may want to go. Get your many lists set up. Add all your travel plans for planes, trains, and automobiles, with pictures of reservations for good measure.

Before long, you'll want to plan all holidays and vacations with Evernote. If you're the type who plans in detail, you can map out your schedule down to the minute, barring the unexpected. If you prefer to keep your options open, you'll have a way to find out which things of interest are open on any particular day. It's your notebook; have it all your way.

Chapter 23

Ten Best Business Uses

*E*vernote can be useful for every aspect of your life, both personal and business. If you're a small-business owner or an executive, you may never completely separate your business and personal lives. It's beneficial to use Evernote because it can help you organize even the most stressful aspects of your life. Making your business streamlined and more efficient has never been easier. This chapter shows you ten ways you can take a load off your mind by using Evernote, your loyal assistant.

Generating and Capturing Ideas

Inspiration is one of the hardest things to create, let along capture. Waking up in the middle of the night to find a full writing pad or no pencil means that your brilliant ideas may be gone by daybreak. Odds are that you have your smartphone close by. After all, smartphones have become alarms, e-mail conduits, and work ball-and-chains for many people. When you have a middle-of-the-night brainstorm, use Evernote on your mobile device to record the idea.

Why not make your smartphone useful in another positive way? When you see something interesting on the Internet, clip it to an ideas notebook. When inspiration strikes, jot down notes or take pictures, and expand your thoughts later. With Evernote, it's always easy to capture ideas and save them for later.

Doing Your Research

As all business owners know, research isn't just for students; it's also a requirement for every successful business.

If you have a project that involves research, create a new notebook, and start clipping your research into it. If your research leads you to the library or on a field trip, make sure to have your camera or phone fully charged, and take snapshots of the pages, storefronts, or other items you need. If you need information from numerous pages in a book, you can use a scanner to get what you need so that you don't fill up your phone with individual pictures. When the time comes to pull all the research together, you have a single notebook that covers everything.

Saving Material to Read Later

If you find a great article in a magazine while you're at the dentist's office and know you won't have time to read it until later, use your phone to capture the article in a note that you can view when you have more time. If you're surfing the web while you're waiting in a ticket line and come across a breaking-news story that won't be up for long, clip it to Evernote for later perusal. Check out Chapter 7 for how to use your smartphone to take pictures in Evernote or to clip websites. Web clipping is covered in Chapter 2.

No matter where you are or what you're doing, you can capture text to read when you have time. All you need are your mobile device and Evernote.

Planning Your Day More Effectively

You know what they say about the best laid plans of mice and men . . ., but Evernote helps consolidate your lists and activities to maximize your efficiency, barring the unexpected, and to update them when the unexpected happens. Create a list of all your daily activities, from opening a shop to setting up your morning workload. Make sure to put your highest priorities at the top of the list.

If you have a Google Calendar account, you can access it from Evernote, and vice versa using a Google gadget (see Chapter 16).

Calculating Expenses the Easy Way

Depending on your preference, you can scan or take pictures of your notes and receipts and save them in an expenses notebook.

I recommend that you use a notebook stack so that you can keep regular purchases apart from occasional or one-time purchases. See Chapter 16 for details on notebook stacks.

To track bills and expenses separately without having to store them in different notebooks, you can keep a single spreadsheet. At the end of the day, mark expenses as entered so that you won't have to wonder whether you've already recorded them and then flip over to another tab and do the same for bills.

Plenty of apps and other accessories can help you get and stay organized if you want a more advanced method of handling your expenses. The Evernote Trunk (http://evernote.com/about/trunk/) is the best place to start for the most reliable apps that are known to work well with Evernote.

Collaborating and Whiteboarding

Most collaborative sessions end up being more about trying to record everything that's being discussed than they are about generating ideas. At your next collaborative effort, whether it involves storyboarding or whiteboarding, bring Evernote to record ideas.

After you have an idea fully developed on the screen or board, just snap a picture, save it to a new note, erase the board, and keep brainstorming. Just make sure to save the note with each addition you make. You can save up to ten pictures from each session and add other notes if you need more. When you want to review the notes later, Evernote has developed recognition software just for "reading" images, enabling you to run searches on the text in photos. Checkout Chapter 8 to learn more about running searches on images.

Premium subscribers have a distinct advantage because all team members can write in shared notebooks. Having a way of distributing the ideas through a single medium is a vast improvement over e-mail or shared areas that can't be accessed from everywhere. Now you can collaborate without losing focus on what's important, and you won't have to worry about forgetting brilliant ideas that can be so fleeting.

Creating Mood Boards

A storyboarding or whiteboarding session (see the preceding section) helps develop established ideas, and mood boards get everyone thinking along the same lines. Generally used for design projects, *mood boards* are a collage of ideas, illustrations, and colors that help establish the base of the project and the direction. A mood board is the perfect type of project for organization with Evernote.

Mood boards are about visual presentation, but you have to do your research first. Starting with a new notebook, clip images and graphics into the notebook. You can use as many notes as you like. When you feel that you have enough to start putting together the collage, create a new note, and put your collection of notes together in an aesthetically pleasing display. Not sure that the first version works for you? Make a second note, and try again.

Archiving and Retrieving Articles and Blogs

You've probably found websites that you loved or words of wisdom that made you feel better but later couldn't find them. Of course, you never know when websites will just disappear. With Evernote, it doesn't matter whether those pages, blogs, or articles are unceremoniously yanked from Internet existence. By simply clipping them into Evernote as you find them, you create an archive so that you can always retrieve them when you want them.

The best way to make sure that you can find items later is to tag them. (Chapter 8 provides more details on tagging.) Make sure to use a tag that's descriptive but not too specific. (Retrieval requires you to know what you're looking for, but you don't want to make such a specific tag that you can't remember it later.) Tags make it easier to locate your notes from the All Notes or All Notebooks area without having to remember where you saved it.

Planning for Year-End Taxes

As a business owner, you know that the amount of paperwork associated with taxes makes the tax season just about unbearable. Completing taxes is always a chore, but Evernote can help streamline the process.

As you collect tax-related information throughout the year, scan (or photograph) the items into a note and save them to a tax notebook. This step makes sure that all your tax information has a central location instead of being spread over many areas. Add your statements, receipts, applicable charitable donations, and even your basic business information (such as ID and address) to the notebook. Save your tax form from last year in the folder to speed up filling out this year's form. When it's time to pull everything together, you have everything you need in one notebook.

After the painful process is over for the current year, don't forget to save your completed tax information so that it's available for next year.

Scouting Locations

For those entrepreneurs who need to scout out locations, such as wedding planners, photographers, or event coordinators, Evernote provides a quick and easy way to store scouting finds. When you arrive on location, start taking pictures, and save them as a new note into a location notebook. If you have an iPhone or an Android device, you can even geotag (mark the latitude and longitude) your pictures for easier reference later. As you find out more about the site, either from searching online or from asking questions, you can add notes or clip information into the same notebook.

When you feel that you have what you need, you can easily compile information about the locations you found and present it to clients without having to dig through networks or old files. With the right tools, you can even provide the location in Google Maps and include instructions on getting to the different places to make a final decision that much easier.

Chapter 24

Ten School Shortcuts

In This Chapter
▶ Tracking projects and classes
▶ Organizing schedules and shopping

*T*his chapter is for students. Evernote may not be able to help you clean out your locker, but with a little bit of time and effort, it can work marvels on the organization of your book bag and binders, and even help you remember your gym clothes or the campus bus schedule.

Taking Notes in Class

Do you have a teacher who likes to show slideshows or write all over the chalkboard? Nowadays, homework is often posted on the Internet, but some old-school teachers may still expect you to hastily jot down assignments from the board. Fortunately, no matter which method you use, Evernote offers you a couple of ways to record all your notes and assignments in one place.

If you have a laptop and love typing your notes, Evernote gives you a single place to get everything into one application; you don't have to try to remember where you stored the information. Simply type a quick blurb in Evernote, give it a time/date stamp, and then attach whatever file you were working on (such as an Excel grid, graphics programs, or even a web page) to that note. The process takes you an additional 2 minutes and saves you 20 minutes of searching for everything later.

Evernote does an amazing job with scanned handwritten notes, too. Check out Chapter 6 to learn how to scan into Evernote. See the next section for details on how Evernote recognizes your handwriting.

Recognizing and Accessing Your Handwritten Notes

Maybe you don't have a laptop, and your cellphone's battery is dead. Occasionally, you may have to resort to handwritten notes, but Evernote has them covered too.

As always, your scanner or camera phone (so long as you keep it charged) is going to save your bacon and get your notes into Evernote. And you won't lose your ability to search for these notes, because Evernote reads your handwriting and interprets all but the worst chicken scratch handwriting (although for the sake of your own reading, you should probably aim to keep the writing a little clearer). You don't have to worry about someone "borrowing" your notes or having them get drenched in the rain. Now they're backed up and ready to go whenever you need them.

Going Paperless

Binders can be a thing of the past if you get organized in Evernote. On the first day of school, keeping up with all the teachers' handouts used to mean a messy backpack at the end of the day. How on earth are you supposed to track it all, keep up with your new schedule, and get to the next class on time with this increasing mountain of paperwork? Easy. Evernote to the rescue.

Before you even go to class, use a scanner or your camera phone to capture your schedule so that all you need is your phone (make sure the battery is charged) or other mobile device to get around. (See Chapter 19 for more on how to scan notes.)

When you get to class, you can take an extra couple of minutes to take pictures. Are you afraid that you won't have time to take pictures and still dash across campus in the next 15 minutes? Place all your syllabi in your book bag, and scan them in when you get home. Now all you have to do is remember to track when you have due dates.

You can use to-do lists to track what you need to do each week for school. Make sure to enter that information the first evening so that you can make the most of it right from the start of the semester. An Evernote to-do list will help you track each class's important assignments (such as research assignments, midterms, and final) right off the syllabus.

Lugging Textbooks No More!

Back pain has historically been an issue for students — it's almost a rite of passage — but with Evernote, you can work your brain without punishing your back. For large books, either scan the pages into Evernote or use your camera phone to collect pictures of the pages you need to study. The process is fast, easy, and painless.

Managing Your Life

With so many things to track in college, it becomes a real juggling act to keep up with it all, especially over the millions of applications (calendars, e-mail, alarms, Facebook, Twitter, and on and on) required to schedule your day. Although this is excellent practice for what life will be like after college, you may wish for a way to make organization and socializing easier. Enter Evernote. Check out Chapter 16 to see how to connect Google Calendar with Evernote to make keeping track of appointments, study sessions, club meetings, and fun activities effortless. Chapter 6 tells you how to use your apps like Twitter, e-mail, and Facebook, or your Kindle or Nook with Evernote.

You can create different notebooks to track different events, such as sporting events, student governance meetings, and different clubs you want to visit. Store everything in one place and always know what you have going on every day and night of the week.

Remembering Your Numbers

When school starts, tracking all the random numbers thrown at you can be an insurmountable task. Classroom numbers, class times, phone numbers, important dates, and personal information all take a lot of effort to track if you don't have a handy tool like Evernote. With Evernote, though, you can easily store all this information and access details when you need them. Keep up with everything from your student ID to your locker combination to addresses to classroom numbers without having to dig through a packed book bag.

Shopping and Window Shopping

It's Monday, and you've found the perfect school-spirit shirt and hat, but you don't have the money to buy them right now. You get paid Friday and want to come back. The only problem is that you're in a different part of town, and you don't know the name of the place. Take a quick picture of the clothing and the name of the shop, and you're good to go. You can come back any time to pick up your stuff (as long as the store doesn't sell out first).

Another excellent time to use Evernote for shopping is when it's time to buy school textbooks. You can go to the school bookstore to take pictures of the books that you need for class and then access the pictures from home to compare prices on the Internet. If you can find the book online for less money even with shipping, you have no reason to pay more money as long as you can wait until the book arrives. And now you may be able to go back and buy that shirt and hat you were looking at a couple of stores ago!

Making Your PDFs Smarter

Often, you can find books and information you need online as PDF files. In addition, many college libraries offer short stories and short books as PDFs. The files are extremely handy, but the PDFs aren't always the best quality.

If you're a Premium subscriber, you can use Evernote to clean up the PDFs and make them searchable. Then you can use Evernote to run a search to locate keywords.

Organizing Your Research

Researching today is nothing like it was even a decade ago. The Internet has so much information of varying quality that finding reliable sources that won't disappear can lead to long nights. Also, you might still be required to use hard-copy sources, such as newspapers and magazines, for some of your work.

The good news is that Evernote can store all your research, regardless of the source. Clip pertinent information from the Internet, or save entire web pages (see Chapter 4); scan or use your cellphone to take pictures of hard-copy text in the library (see Chapters 7 and 19); and share information for group projects through a shared notebook (see Chapter 10).

Recording Important Lectures

Typing isn't always practical in class, especially if you aren't a terribly efficient typist. With a mobile device, particularly a cellphone, you can make an audio recording of everything that your teacher says and that the class discusses. (See Chapter 7 for how-to information.)

You don't want to be distracted by taking notes; it's better to concentrate on listening and thinking about the discussion. Also, starting and stopping your recorder can be a big distraction. So record the entire discussion so that you can listen the first time through and get reinforced on the lecture or conversation later.

Appendix

Evernote for Developers

*M*ore than 8,000 developers are working on apps and customizations for Evernote, and that number is growing by leaps and bounds. This chapter is geared to developers who want to build Evernote support into their own applications and to those who want to extend Evernote's capabilities.

Before starting to develop applications for Evernote, I suggest you gain some experience using scripting, which is covered in Chapter 20. In the appendix, I assume you are already familiar with the information in Chapter 20.

Getting Started with the Evernote API

Evernote's application programming interface (API) lets your applications access the Evernote service using the same protocols that are used under the covers by Evernote's own client software.

The most powerful way to integrate with Evernote is to develop based on directives sent to the Evernote web service API. The API enables you to access a user's account in the cloud, whether or not that user has an Evernote client installed on the machine (so long as she has an Evernote account and Internet connectivity). With the API, you can create, search, read, update, and delete notes, notebooks, and tags. This eliminates concerns of whether the local version of Evernote has been synchronized.

Another way to develop an app that works with Evernote is to develop for one of Evernote's mobile client applications on a user's desktop PC or mobile device. Use the following links to find out more about the platform that you're interested in developing for:

✔ **Android:** Android apps can work with the Evernote web service API and with intents. See www.evernote.com/about/developer/android. php and www.evernote.com/about/developer/api.

Three of the core components of an Android application — activities, services, and broadcast receivers — are activated through messages, called *intents*.

✔ **iOS (iPhone, iPad, and iPod touch):** The great popularity of iOS devices, the simplicity of development with Objective-C Cocoa, and the quality of Evernote support have made iOS the most popular development platform for Evernote. See www.evernote.com/about/developer/ios.php.

✔ **BlackBerry:** Evernote scripting is not supported for the BlackBerry operating system at this time. Evernote has considered creating a JME code generator for Thrift that would produce Java mobile stubs for the API that would then work on BlackBerry and other JME-based devices.

✔ **Mac:** Evernote for Mac has great support for AppleScript, as discussed in Chapter 20. See www.evernote.com/about/developer/mac.php.

✔ **Windows:** Applications integrate with Evernote for Windows by passing command-line options to the Evernote.exe and ENScript.exe executables. Interface notes are provided at www.evernote.com/about/developer/windows.php.

✔ **Mobile web:** Evernote on a mobile device can integrate with Evernote's mobile web application. Using a mobile web interface, users can search, browse, view, and edit their notes. Find out more about the mobile web application at www.evernote.com/about/developer/mobile_integration.php.

Registering for an API key

To get the Evernote API and all the goodies it provides, you need to request a free API key by completing the online form at evernote.com/about/developer/api/ and click the API Key link.

Client keys use a username and password for authentication and can be used by desktop and mobile client applications that authenticate a single user at a time. This is the type of key you need if your application accesses Evernote as a single user at a time. If you want to develop a server application that is Evernote-aware and that many users can connect to, you need a web service key.

Request a key by completing the form at www.evernote.com/about/developer/api/.

Using dynamic interfaces

You can view the Evernote mobile web application by using plain or dynamic interfaces. The plain interface targets a larger variety of mobile devices and has a simple and flat navigational design. The dynamic interface targets higher-end devices with browsers that support JavaScript and with touch navigation. Evernote attempts to deduce what type of interface to use based on the incoming HTTP requests. A perfect match isn't guaranteed, however.

The web form asks you to provide an Evernote username, your name, the organization's name, your e-mail address, and a brief description of what you're trying to accomplish.

When you receive your key, you can test your application. The test server's host name is `http://sandbox.evernote.com`. Initially, the API key works against `http://sandbox.evernote.com` but not against `www.evernote.com`. Evernote can activate the API key on the production system after you let it know that you're ready to go live. Also, you need to let Evernote know by email if you want to change any detail of the service configuration — organization name, session duration, and so on. Details are provided when you apply for the key, which is supplied without charge.

For web service keys, users authorize your application to access their account for up to 24 hours for a testing period, with full permission to read and modify their accounts. Contact Evernote if you'd like to change the access duration or user permissions.

Keep an eye on the developer forum at `http://discussion.evernote.com/forum/61-evernote-for-developers/` to stay on top of any changes to Evernote that can affect developers.

Authorizing an application for authentication

Evernote users entrust Evernote with important information, so security and authentication are important considerations to ensure the data can't be hacked. For this reason, Evernote needs to know who you are and to ensure that your code is authorized to access the user's information. The account and authentication information for every user is bundled into a logical component called the UserStore. According to Evernote, the user's notebooks and all of the contents (notes, tags, resources, saved searches, and so on) are maintained within the NoteStore component of the Evernote service. The NoteStore is responsible for maintaining the correct data model for each Notebook in a persistent, transactional database.

License agreement

Evernote's web service API is provided under the terms of the Evernote API license agreement, which is available at www.evernote.com/about/developer/api/api_license.php. You need to read and adhere to all the license terms, but perhaps the most important terms are that *the API may not be used to create Applications that offer or promote services that may be damaging to, disparaging of, or otherwise detrimental to Evernote* or its licensors, licensees, affiliates and partners; and the API may not be used for or to create Applications that transfer, display or use Content from Evernote without the Application creating an additional or distinct benefit for Evernote's end users' use of the Service.

In other words, you can use it to create your own applications that have a value-add; you can't use it to build an Evernote clone.

For local (desktop or mobile) client applications, the primary function of the UserStore is to authenticate a user to create an *authentication token*. An authentication token is required for any requests to access private data via the NoteStore API. Evernote states that "Authentication tokens are short-lived, cryptographically protected strings that grant the bearer access to some set of operations within a single user account." This means that you ask for and then get a token, and you are granted access to the NoteStore for a short time.

Here are considerations for choosing UserStore the most-effective method of authentication for your application:

- **Local access:** Local (single-user) applications can take a username and password from an Evernote user. This means that the user's login information isn't transferred to any third parties; it's used only for direct authentication to Evernote's servers (over SSL).

- **OAuth:** OAuth is an open protocol to publish and interact with protected data. It's also a safe, secure way of granting access to secure data. The idea is that if you're storing protected data on your users' behalf, they shouldn't be spreading their passwords around the web to get access to it. OAuth gives your users access to their data while protecting their account credentials. Therefore, web applications that need to access data from multiple Evernote accounts shouldn't retrieve an authentication token via a username and password; instead, they should use the alternate OAuth to receive authorization via the OAuth protocol (http://oauth.net). Evernote has implemented an OAuth service provider that complies with a profile (subset) of the OAuth 1.0 Protocol as defined in RFC 5849, available on the Internet Engineering Task Force (IETF) website at http://tools.ietf.org/html/rfc5849.

✔ **XML:** Evernote uses Extensible Markup Language (XML). XML is a set of rules for encoding documents in machine-readable form. A markup language is a way to annotate (mark up) text to specify things' formatting. XHTML (Extensible Hypertext Markup Language) is a general name for a family of standards-based markup languages that mirror or extend versions of the widely used Hypertext Markup Language (HTML), the language invented by Tim Berners-Lee at CERN, the European Laboratory for Particle Physics in Geneva, Switzerland. The current version of HTML is HTML5, which is still being refined. See `dev.w3.org/html5/html4-differences/#refsHTML` for more information about HTML5.

✔ **EDAM and XML:** Evernote's accessibility is based on an API called the Evernote Data Access and Management (EDAM) protocol. Related, is the Evernote Markup Language (ENML), which is a flavor of XHTML that was designed to provide a secure and portable document representation that could be consistently rendered on various clients and platforms. The service validates the note content against this Document Type definition (DTD) before accepting any call to `NoteStore.createNote()` or `NoteStore.updateNote()`. A DTD defines the legal building blocks of an XML document. You can download Evernote's DTD from `xml.evernote.com/pub/enml2.dtd`.

For more information on ENML, see "Gaining Secure Programmatic Access to Evernote," later in this chapter.)

Gaining Secure Programmatic Access to Evernote

Evernote's API provides secure access for your trusted local or web-based applications, using the same network communications that are used by Evernote's own client software. In the following sections, I discuss secure access to Evernote via programmatic interfaces.

Evernote Data Access and Management (EDAM) protocol

Evernote Data Access and Management (EDAM) allows secure access to account data via standard web protocols. This API is used internally by all of Evernote's own client applications, and Evernote has made this protocol available at no charge for third-party developers to integrate into their applications.

EDAM is designed to support both *thick and thin* applications, which remember their own state even if control is shifted to another application. Thick applications are known as *stateful* and include most desktop clients that maintain a full local copy of user data. *Thin* applications need to access only a small amount of current information at a given time — for example, web services. These cases vary a bit in how they securely authenticate the user, but they use a common set of interfaces after authentication is completed.

Thrift

Thrift is a software framework for development of cross-language services. Thrift was originally developed at Facebook to support its core software infrastructure. It was declared open source in April 2007. It entered the Apache Incubator in May 2008 and is maintained by the not-for-profit Apache Software Foundation that supports about 100 open source projects (`projects.apache.org/indexes/category.html`) including Open Office. Through a collaborative and open development process, Apache projects aim to deliver enterprise-strength, freely available software products that attract large communities of users. The most famous Apache application is Apache HTTP server.

According to the Thrift website, (`http://thrift.apache.org/`), "Thrift is a software framework for scalable cross-language services development. It combines a software stack with a code generation engine to build services that work efficiently and seamlessly between C++, Java, Python, PHP, Ruby, Erlang, Perl, Haskell, C#, Cocoa, JavaScript, Node.js, Smalltalk, and OCaml."

Thrift enables you to define your own data types and service interfaces, called declarations, using a standardized and simple definition file. The Thrift compiler uses that file as input. Then the Thrift compiler generates code that developers can use using the Remote Procedure Call (RPC) protocol to easily build RPC clients and servers that can communicate seamlessly across a wide variety of programming languages.

You can find the Evernote Thrift declarations at `www.evernote.com/about/developer/api/ref`. Essentially, everything you can click in the Evernote client application has a related Thrift declaration that you can call from any of the applications that Thrift calls. For example, `emailNote` is the Thrift call defined by Evernote for e-mailing a note. It does the same thing as right-clicking a note and then choosing Share and Send by Email from the contextual menu in an Evernote desktop client.

A white paper describing Thrift is available at `http://thrift.apache.org/static/thrift-20070401.pdf`.

Thrift didn't originally support Objective-C Cocoa. Evernote extended Thrift by adding support for Objective-C, which is used extensively by Apple.

Keeping up with the Evernote Developer Forum and Techblog

The Developer Forum (`discussion.ever note.com/forum/61-evernote-for-developers/`) is the Evernote developer's private space, where technical development issues of interest to third-party developers can be discussed separately from end-user discussions. On Techblog, developers can find details on the Evernote API and peruse questions posed by developers that have been answered by other developers.

Another resource is Techblog, (`blog.ever note.com/tech/`), which contains a lot of information, on Evernote's inner workings, such as how the Evernote Indexing System works, how the image-recognition component works, and what functionality it provides in relation to the Evernote platform as a whole. In addition, you can find a lot of detail on security and architectural issues.

Evernote developers actively support the Evernote Developer Forum by responding to developed issues and by periodically updating the Evernote Techblog.

API Software Development Kit (SDK)

To get started using the API Software Development Kit (SDK), download it from `www.evernote.com/about/developer/api`. The file contains documentation, Thrift declarations, and many useful sample codes that can help you understand the Evernote API and use it in your programming language of choice.

Exploring Open-Source Projects

If you want to develop an application to support and work with Evernote, it helps to see some examples of applications that other developers have created. Many developers have helpfully contributed their projects and applications that integrate with Evernote as open source projects that you can access to use and modify. You can find out about them at `www.evernote.com/about/developer/projects.php`.

Open-source projects are great ways to find out how to build an application that works with Evernote because you can see what others have done. The following list includes some of the open-source projects and applications that the Evernote developer community has produced:

✔ **Apple Aperture 3 to Evernote (AppleScript):** This simple program posts image thumbnails from Aperture right into Evernote.

✔ **Delicious bookmarks importer (Perl):** This code takes an export file from Delicious and imports the bookmarks into Evernote.

✔ **Emacs Evernote mode (Ruby):** Emacs Evernote mode is a collection of code that offers functions to view and edit Evernote notes directly from Emacs, which is an extensible and customizable open-source text editor.

✔ **en4j (Java):** This code is a Java replacement for Evernote desktop client applications.

✔ **Everboard (PHP):** This is an online idea board that takes its inspiration from a traditional corkboard or wall with lots of photos, images, and sketches all pasted to it to form a collective theme. It is integrated with the Evernote API and enables you to visualize your notebooks in a unique way and to share your inspiration with your collaborators in real time.

✔ **Evernote for ColdFusion (ColdFusion):** This project is a ColdFusion implementation of the Evernote API. ColdFusion is a server-side scripting language.

✔ **Evernote RubyGem (Ruby):** This is a high-level wrapper around Evernote's Thrift-generated ruby code. It bundles Evernote's thrift-generated code and enables you to create some simple wrapper classes for using Evernote in your Ruby applications.

✔ **Journler to Evernote (AppleScript):** This project converts Journler entries to Evernote notes. Journler (www.journler.com) is a popular notebook and entry-based information manager.

✔ **NeverNote (Java):** This open-source clone of Evernote is designed to run on Linux.

✔ **NoteScraper (AppleScript):** This script exports your Kindle notes and highlights to Evernote.

✔ **Palm Desktop memo importer (Python):** This project is a utility program to bring your existing memos or notes from Palm Desktop into Evernote.

✔ **People's Note (C++):** This Windows Mobile note-taking application has full-featured Evernote integration.

✔ **Veritrope (AppleScript):** The Evernote page of this website (http://veritrope.com/tech/evernote-applescript-resources-and-accessories) enables you to share your bits of AppleScript with others or find snippets of code you can reuse in your own AppleScript projects.

To add your project, post your project to the Evernote Developer Forum at discussion.evernote.com/forum/61-evernote-for-developers/. You have to be signed in first.

Index

• K •

Apple & Mac

iPad 2 For Dummies,
3rd Edition
978-1-118-17679-5

iPhone 4S For Dummies,
5th Edition
978-1-118-03671-6

iPod touch For Dummies,
3rd Edition
978-1-118-12960-9

Mac OS X Lion
For Dummies
978-1-118-02205-4

Blogging & Social Media

CityVille For Dummies
978-1-118-08337-6

Facebook For Dummies,
4th Edition
978-1-118-09562-1

Mom Blogging
For Dummies
978-1-118-03843-7

Twitter For Dummies,
2nd Edition
978-0-470-76879-2

WordPress For Dummies,
4th Edition
978-1-118-07342-1

Business

Cash Flow For Dummies
978-1-118-01850-7

Investing For Dummies,
6th Edition
978-0-470-90545-6

Job Searching with Social
Media For Dummies
978-0-470-93072-4

QuickBooks 2012
For Dummies
978-1-118-09120-3

Resumes For Dummies,
6th Edition
978-0-470-87361-8

Starting an Etsy Business
For Dummies
978-0-470-93067-0

Cooking & Entertaining

Cooking Basics
For Dummies, 4th Edition
978-0-470-91388-8

Wine For Dummies,
4th Edition
978-0-470-04579-4

Diet & Nutrition

Kettlebells For Dummies
978-0-470-59929-7

Nutrition For Dummies,
5th Edition
978-0-470-93231-5

Restaurant Calorie Counter
For Dummies,
2nd Edition
978-0-470-64405-8

Digital Photography

Digital SLR Cameras &
Photography For Dummies,
4th Edition
978-1-118-14489-3

Digital SLR Settings
& Shortcuts
For Dummies
978-0-470-91763-3

Photoshop Elements 10
For Dummies
978-1-118-10742-3

Gardening

Gardening Basics
For Dummies
978-0-470-03749-2

Vegetable Gardening
For Dummies,
2nd Edition
978-0-470-49870-5

Green/Sustainable

Raising Chickens
For Dummies
978-0-470-46544-8

Green Cleaning
For Dummies
978-0-470-39106-8

Health

Diabetes For Dummies,
3rd Edition
978-0-470-27086-8

Food Allergies
For Dummies
978-0-470-09584-3

Living Gluten-Free
For Dummies,
2nd Edition
978-0-470-58589-4

Hobbies

Beekeeping
For Dummies,
2nd Edition
978-0-470-43065-1

Chess For Dummies,
3rd Edition
978-1-118-01695-4

Drawing For Dummies,
2nd Edition
978-0-470-61842-4

eBay For Dummies,
7th Edition
978-1-118-09806-6

Knitting For Dummies,
2nd Edition
978-0-470-28747-7

Language &
Foreign Language

English Grammar
For Dummies,
2nd Edition
978-0-470-54664-2

French For Dummies,
2nd Edition
978-1-118-00464-7

German For Dummies,
2nd Edition
978-0-470-90101-4

Spanish Essentials
For Dummies
978-0-470-63751-7

Spanish For Dummies,
2nd Edition
978-0-470-87855-2

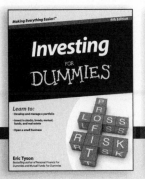

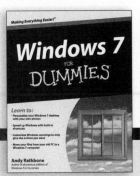

Math & Science

Algebra I For Dummies,
2nd Edition
978-0-470-55964-2

Biology For Dummies,
2nd Edition
978-0-470-59875-7

Chemistry For Dummies,
2nd Edition
978-1-1180-0730-3

Geometry For Dummies,
2nd Edition
978-0-470-08946-0

Pre-Algebra Essentials
For Dummies
978-0-470-61838-7

Microsoft Office

Excel 2010 For Dummies
978-0-470-48953-6

Office 2010 All-in-One
For Dummies
978-0-470-49748-7

Office 2011 for Mac
For Dummies
978-0-470-87869-9

Word 2010
For Dummies
978-0-470-48772-3

Music

Guitar For Dummies,
2nd Edition
978-0-7645-9904-0

Clarinet For Dummies
978-0-470-58477-4

iPod & iTunes
For Dummies,
9th Edition
978-1-118-13060-5

Pets

Cats For Dummies,
2nd Edition
978-0-7645-5275-5

Dogs All-in One
For Dummies
978-0470-52978-2

Saltwater Aquariums
For Dummies
978-0-470-06805-2

Religion & Inspiration

The Bible For Dummies
978-0-7645-5296-0

Catholicism For Dummies,
2nd Edition
978-1-118-07778-8

Spirituality For Dummies,
2nd Edition
978-0-470-19142-2

Self-Help & Relationships

Happiness For Dummies
978-0-470-28171-0

Overcoming Anxiety
For Dummies,
2nd Edition
978-0-470-57441-6

Seniors

Crosswords For Seniors
For Dummies
978-0-470-49157-7

iPad 2 For Seniors
For Dummies, 3rd Edition
978-1-118-17678-8

Laptops & Tablets
For Seniors For Dummies,
2nd Edition
978-1-118-09596-6

Smartphones & Tablets

BlackBerry For Dummies,
5th Edition
978-1-118-10035-6

Droid X2 For Dummies
978-1-118-14864-8

HTC ThunderBolt
For Dummies
978-1-118-07601-9

MOTOROLA XOOM
For Dummies
978-1-118-08835-7

Sports

Basketball For Dummies,
3rd Edition
978-1-118-07374-2

Football For Dummies,
2nd Edition
978-1-118-01261-1

Golf For Dummies,
4th Edition
978-0-470-88279-5

Test Prep

ACT For Dummies,
5th Edition
978-1-118-01259-8

ASVAB For Dummies,
3rd Edition
978-0-470-63760-9

The GRE Test For
Dummies, 7th Edition
978-0-470-00919-2

Police Officer Exam
For Dummies
978-0-470-88724-0

Series 7 Exam
For Dummies
978-0-470-09932-2

Web Development

HTML, CSS, & XHTML
For Dummies, 7th Edition
978-0-470-91659-9

Drupal For Dummies,
2nd Edition
978-1-118-08348-2

Windows 7

Windows 7
For Dummies
978-0-470-49743-2

Windows 7
For Dummies,
Book + DVD Bundle
978-0-470-52398-8

Windows 7 All-in-One
For Dummies
978-0-470-48763-1

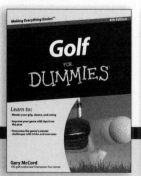

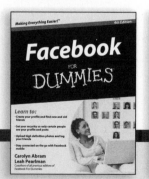

Wherever you are in life, Dummies makes it easier.

From fashion to Facebook®,
wine to Windows®,
and everything in between,
Dummies makes it easier.